Technological Revolutions
and Financial Capital

To my mother
Carlota Arenas
the artist
whose joy of work
nourished my own

Technological Revolutions and Financial Capital

The Dynamics of Bubbles and Golden Ages

Carlota Perez

Honorary Research Fellow, SPRU – Science and Technology Policy Research, University of Sussex, UK
Adjunct Senior Research Fellow, INTECH, Maastricht, The Netherlands
Visiting Scholar 2002, Cambridge University, UK
International Consultant and Lecturer on change strategies and technology policy, Eureka A.C., Caracas, Venezuela

Edward Elgar
Cheltenham, UK ∞Northampton, MA, USA.

Published by
Edward Elgar Publishing Limited
The Lypiatts
15 Lansdown Road
Cheltenham
Glos GL50 2JA
UK

Edward Elgar Publishing, Inc.
William Pratt House
9 Dewey Court
Northampton
Massachusetts 01060
USA

Paperback edition 2003
Cased edition reprinted 2008, 2015
Paperback edition reprinted 2003, 2005, 2014

A catalogue record for this book
is available from the British Library

Library of Congress Cataloguing in Publication Data
Perez, Carlota, 1939–
     Technological Revolutions and financial capital : the dynamics of bubbles and
     golden ages / Carlota Perez.
          p.   cm.
     Includes index.
     1. Technological innovations–Economic aspects. 2. Finance. I. Title

     HC79.T4 P47 2003
     338.5'42–dc21

                                                                    2002072177

ISBN   978 1 84064 922 2 (cased)
          978 1 84376 331 4 (paperback)

Printed and bound in Great Britain by T.J. International Ltd, Padstow

Contents

List of tables   *vii*
List of figures   *viii*
Preface Chris Freeman   *ix*
Acknowledgments   *xiii*

Introduction: An Interpretation   *xvii*

PART I   TECHNOLOGICAL REVOLUTIONS AS
          SUCCESSIVE GREAT SURGES OF DEVELOPMENT

1.   The Turbulent Ending of the Twentieth Century   3
2.   Technological Revolutions and Techno-Economic Paradigms 8
3.   The Social Shaping of Technological Revolutions   22
4.   The Propagation of Paradigms: Times of Installation, Times
     of Deployment   36
5.   The Four Basic Phases of Each Surge of Development   47
6.   Uneven Development and Time-Lags in Diffusion   60

PART II   TECHNOLOGICAL REVOLUTIONS AND
          THE CHANGING BEHAVIOR OF FINANCIAL CAPITAL

7.   Financial Capital and Production Capital   71
8.   Maturity: Financial Capital Planting the Seeds of Turbulence at
     the End of the Previous Surge   81
9.   Irruption: The Love Affair of Financial Capital with
     the Technological Revolution   90
10. Frenzy: Self-Sufficient Financial Capital Governing the Casino 99
11. The Turning Point: Rethinking, Regulation and Changeover 114
12. Synergy: Supporting the Expansion of the Paradigm across
     the Productive Structure   127
13. The Changing Nature of Financial and Institutional Innovations 138

PART III   THE RECURRING SEQUENCE, ITS CAUSES
            AND IMPLICATIONS

14.   The Sequence and its Driving Forces   151
15.   The Implications for Theory and Policy   159

Epilogue: The World at the Turning Point   *167*
Bibliography   *173*
Index   *183*

List of Tables

2.1   Five successive technological revolutions, 1770s to 2000s   11
2.2   The industries and infrastructures of each technological
      revolution   14
2.3   A different techno-economic paradigm for each technological
      revolution; 1770 to 2000s   18
8.1   Fluctuations in UK foreign investment (at current prices) as
      percentage of total net capital formation, 1855–1914   84
13.1 A tentative typology of financial innovations   139
13.2 The shifting behavior of financial capital from phase to phase
      of each surge   141

List of Figures

2.1   The double nature of technological revolutions   9
3.1   The life cycle of a technological revolution   30
4.1   Two different periods in each great surge   37
4.2   Steel displacing iron as the main engineering material from
      the second to the third surge   38
4.3   Decoupling of the system: the differing performance of the
      'high-tech' sector and the rest of the economy in the USA,
      1989–96   40
4.4   Oil and automobile industries replacing steel as engines of
      growth from the third to the fourth surge   45
5.1   Recurring phases of each great surge in the core countries 48
5.2   Approximate dates of the installation and deployment periods
      of each great surge of development   57
6.1   The geographic outspreading of technologies as they mature 64
7.1   The recurring sequence in the relationship between financial
      capital (FK) and production capital (PK)   74
7.2   Five successive surges, recurrent parallel periods and major
      financial crises   78
8.1   The recurrence of loan fever and default: the Latin American
      case   87
10.1 The diverging growth of the New York Stock Market and
      US GDP, 1971–99   112
11.1 The rise and fall of the NASDAQ bubble, 1971–2001   119
14.1 Development by surges: the elements of the model and their
      recurring changes   152
14.2 The dynamics of the system: three spheres of change in
      constant reciprocal action   156
15.1 Paradigm shift and political cleavage   164

Preface

Carlota Perez has made several highly original contributions to the understanding of long-term technological transformations and the way in which such changes interact with wider economic, social and political changes. This book is perhaps her most original and controversial contribution. Her intense interest in these deep processes was aroused in the 1970s when, as a young researcher, she was studying the oil industry, then and still today of critical importance for her own native country, Venezuela. In trying to explain the causes and consequences of the so-called OPEC crisis of 1973, she became convinced that the global economy had begun a long-term transition from a mass-production economy based on cheap oil to an 'information economy' based on cheap micro-electronics. The arrival of the microprocessor – a 'computer on a chip' – served as a 'big-bang' announcing this probability and she was able to develop her theory at this time through a period of postgraduate research in California – a state which was already then at the forefront of the Information Revolution.

As a result of this research and her subsequent work with government and industry, she was able to publish in 1983 a paper that became an influential landmark in this field. It was entitled 'Structural Change and the Assimilation of New Technologies in the Economic and Social System' and the title adequately reflects the content. It became influential for three main reasons. First of all, it demonstrated that very big changes in technology entailed not just the extraordinarily rapid growth of a few new industries, but also, over a more prolonged period, the rejuvenation of many 'old' industries, which found ways to use the new technology and to make changes in their organization and management, influenced by the new industries. She designated this combination of new ways of thinking about the productive system, including its organization, its techniques and its interdependencies as a change of 'techno-economic paradigm'. This concept of a paradigm change, with each major technological revolution, has become very widely accepted, particularly since Alan Greenspan began to use the expression in the 1990s to explain the upsurge in the American economy at that time.

The second major contribution which Carlota Perez made in that paper was to point out that such a 'meta-paradigm' change, affecting the entire economy entailed the very widespread use of new inputs. In each technological revolution, whether in earlier times with iron, coal, steel, or oil or with chips today, it was possible to make very great economies of scale in the production of these inputs, and frequently such a steep decline in price followed that they became very attractive for economic as well as for purely technical reasons.

Finally, she showed up some of the fallacies of what is known to historians as 'technological determinism' by her insistence that any transformation in technology could only take place through an interactive and accompanying process of social, political and managerial change. This meant that the change of paradigm affected not only management and organization at the level of the firm but it affected and was affected by the entire system of social and political regulation. This is particularly obvious in such areas as education and training, where the strong demand for new skills drives the changes, but it is also apparent in the intellectual property regime (trademarks, patents and so on) and the framework of company law, safety regulation and, even more, in international trade and competition. All this has become particularly evident with the growth of the institutions of the 'information society'. Carlota Perez made the vital point that countries and regions vary in their capacity and their desire to make such institutional changes, depending on social and political factors, the particular historical circumstances and other social and political conflicts and ideas.

In this book, she makes an even more original and seminal contribution. She examines the interaction between that part of the economy commonly known as financial capital and the upsurge of new technologies from their first beginnings to the time when they predominate in the structure and behavior of the economy. In his major work, *Business Cycles* (1939), Joseph Schumpeter, whilst interpreting the major waves of economic growth and technological transformation as 'successive industrial revolutions', insisted that these clusters of radical innovations also depended on financial capital. In fact, more space is devoted to finance in his book than to technology but, rather strangely, his followers – often known as 'neo-Schumpeterians' – neglected this aspect of his work. With characteristic boldness, Carlota Perez has attempted to fill this gap. The Internet 'bubble' has made the gap especially apparent but she began her work long before this.

Like Schumpeter, she believes that the early upsurge of a new technology is a period of explosive growth, leading to great turbulence and uncertainty in the economy. Venture capitalists, delighted at the new possibility of very high profits first demonstrated by early applications (aptly designated by Carlota Perez as the 'big-bang') rush to invest in the new activities and often in new firms. However, the uncertainty which inevitably accompanies such revolutionary developments, means that many of the early expectations will be disappointed, leading to the collapse of bubbles created by financial speculation as well as technological euphoria or 'irrational exuberance'. The explosive upsurge of the new industries and firms takes place within an environment still dominated by the 'old' institutions, so that this is inevitably a time of great contrasts, designated by many economists as a phase of 'structural adjustment'.

Carlota Perez puts the accent on the process of propagation of the new technologies and calls it the 'installation period'. She further divides it into two phases: 'Irruption' and 'Frenzy'. In the later period, financial capital spurs investment in the new industries, activities and infrastructures so intensely that they become quite strong and the need for a new regime of regulation is more clearly apparent, at least in the leading countries.

In the end, as experience of political and social changes accumulates and as many firms grow accustomed to the new technology so that it becomes everyday 'common sense', the turbulence of the installation period may give way to a period of more harmonious growth, designated by Carlota Perez as 'Deployment' and again subdivided into two phases: 'Synergy' and 'Maturity'. The deployment period can be a time of relatively stable and prosperous development based on a good match between technology and the institutional framework. Whereas structural unemployment is likely to be a feature of the installation period, high levels of employment may well be attained in many countries during 'deployment'. This factor leads people to think of deployment as a 'golden age' or '*belle époque*', even though measured GDP growth may actually have been higher in some countries during the frenzy phase of the installation period. However, in the maturity phase of the deployment period, diminishing returns set in for the (now) older and mature technologies. Arthritis may set in for some of the once vigorous new firms and activities. This phenomenon of diminishing returns has been observed by both engineers and economists and it leads to a new period of installation as attention switches to the next generation of radical innovations, which now begin to offer more exciting prospects, both for the engineers and the financiers.

The theory is certainly not intended as a straitjacket in which to force the untidy pattern of real historical events. As Goethe observed in 'Faust',

> Grey my friend is all theory,
> Green the golden tree of life.

Carlota Perez is very well aware of the complexity of the world of finance, technology and political change. Her model of four phases is not a reductionist model, it is rather a way of ordering and examining historical processes in order to illuminate some recurrent tendencies which may be present and may help us to interpret and understand better both the past and the present. A green tree is a beautiful sight in spring and summer, but deciduous trees in winter can reveal more of their structure and sources of growth by their spare and elegant fundamental features.

I strongly commend this fascinating book, not only to historians and economists but to engineers, scientists, managers, trade unionists and policy makers – indeed to all those interested in the past and future evolution of our complex social system. In one other respect, it also offers ideas which go beyond what

Schumpeter and most of his followers have discussed: it deals very effectively with the way in which new technologies spread to the 'third' world and the role of finance and of debt in this diffusion. Altogether, it is a thought-provoking and stimulating book, which should be widely read in all parts of the world economy.

Chris Freeman,
SPRU, University of Sussex
January 2002

Acknowledgments

The seeds of this book were planted years ago, in 1997, when Erik Reinert invited me to contribute a paper to a seminar in Oslo about financial and productive capital. The topic had been in my mind for a long time, and I was extremely glad to finally be able to approach it with a contract and an interested audience. Since then, both the original paper and my interest grew and grew until they resulted in the present book. My thanks go then, to Erik for the invitation and for his constant support and time for reading and commenting throughout the various versions and to his wife, Fernanda, who found time to support me, while fulfilling her fantastically efficient role as 'ground crew' for Erik and for The Other Canon project. My thanks also go to Norsk Investorforum, the Norwegian organization that generously funded my participation in two consecutive seminars on the topic.

In The Other Canon project, I was fortunate to come in contact with Wolfgang Drechsler, who patiently read the whole manuscript, gave me valuable suggestions, comments and criticisms and willingly discussed many of my doubts and even minor decisions.

Many other colleagues and friends heard presentations, read chapters or whole versions along the way. Their reactions and critical comments and advice were always welcome: Andrew Tylecote, Brian Arthur, Dafne Gil, Despina Kanellou, Francisco Louçã, Gabriel Palma, Giovanni Dosi, Giulio Santosuosso, Gustavo Núñez, Ha-Joon Chang, Howie Rush, Jan Fagerberg, Jan Toporowski, Jorge Solé, Jose Antonio Ocampo, Jürgen Backhaus, Lars Mjøset, Luc Soete, Lynn Mytelka, Mike Hobday, Morley Lipsett, Nick Von-Tunzelmann, Rafael Fuentes, Rafael Rengifo, Roger Lloyd Jones, Salvador Lluch, Simón Parisca, Slavo Radosevic and Stephanie Griffith-Jones. Those who work in similar research fields commented on the contents; those from other fields of research or endeavor, tried to help me make the book accessible to a wider range of readers. I am extremely grateful to all for their incisive questions and useful suggestions.

Very special thanks go to Benjamin Sagalovsky and Maria Elena Corrales who, with their extreme sensitivity and subtle intelligence, tried to keep me from straying into either mechanistic or voluntaristic paths. Since I didn't always heed their wisdom, they are not to blame if I did go astray. But their efforts were infinitely valuable to me.

I have left for last the deepest feeling of gratitude. Chris Freeman has certainly helped me enormously with this particular book, by reading and re-reading one version after another, by discussing with me, in person, on paper and by phone across the ocean, the many questions and difficulties involved in the model presented here. But this is only the most recent part of his support of my work, which has been untiring and constantly stimulating, ever since we met in 1983. Throughout all these years I have had the pleasure and the privilege of having him as a mentor and colleague, of working with him in joint papers, of following his work and of counting upon him to support my own. He has done this intensely, both in his approval and in his sometimes very strong criticism. The first has strengthened my self-confidence; the second has saved me from some of the worst pitfalls and forced me to strive harder and harder to improve the results.

Neither Chris nor any of the others mentioned above are at fault for the remaining errors and weaknesses.

Sometimes the size of a book can be deceptive regarding the amount of work involved. During the four years in which this particular book was nurtured and constructed, with many long periods when it was crowded out by other work and some stretches of complete concentration, I have counted upon the invaluable help of several wonderful people, research assistants, computer specialists and other support staff. Asli Gok and Federico Giammusso helped me doing research in the library while they were doing their PhD at SPRU; Lorena Araujo, in the first phase of work, made infinite versions of the figures; Susan Lees and Cynthia Little showed inexhaustible patience with the E-mail versions going back and forth from Caracas to England; my sister Maria Garford, with her experience of book writing, helped me keep out of chaos and provided constant spiritual support; my aunt Elena Pérez Arenas kept my paper files in order and gave me secretarial help; Francine O'Sullivan, Joanne Broom, Emma Meldrum and Karen McCarthy, guiding the process at Edward Elgar, and Luz Márquez and Nuncia Moccia, preparing the camera ready in Venezuela, all made sure that the manuscript would result in a beautifully printed book. Mike Bennet, over the Internet from California, generously shared with me his long experience in the difficult job of index making. Finally, Marcela Elgueda, my assistant during the last few months, accompanied every aspect of the process, with immense dedication, professional competence and care. To all of them my warmest thanks.

Caracas, June 2002

Every concept originates through our equating what is unequal.
No leaf ever wholly equals another, and the concept 'leaf' is formed
through an arbitrary abstraction from the individual differences,
through forgetting the distinctions;
and now it gives rise to the idea that in nature there might
be something besides the leaves which would be 'leaf'
– some kind of original form after which all leaves have been woven,
marked, copied, coloured, curled, and painted,
but by unskilled hands,
so that no copy turned out to be a correct, reliable,
and faithful image of the original form ...

Friedrich Nietzsche, 1873

A theory that denies that what is happening can happen,
that sees unfavorable events as the work of outside forces
(such as the oil crisis) rather than as the result
of characteristics of the economic mechanism,
may satisfy the politicians' need for a villain or scapegoat,
but such a theory offers no useful guide to the solution of a problem.

Hyman Minsky, 1986, p. 4.

Introduction: An Interpretation

The last quarter of the twentieth century witnessed the apparently boundless rise of two forces: the information revolution and financial markets. Many have chanted the virtues of the one for increasing productivity and of the other for unleashing the drive for wealth that moves the economy forward. In fact, the twenty-first century was inaugurated with claims about the advent of a 'new economy' characterized by the flourishing of both those forces and capable of relentless growth.

The collapse of the Internet bubble and the ensuing recession have shaken these beliefs and led to doubt and confusion.

This book will argue that similar productivity explosions and bursts of financial excitement leading to economic euphoria and subsequent collapses of confidence have occurred together before. They are interrelated and interdependent phenomena; they share the same root cause and are in the nature of the system and its workings. They originate in the way technologies evolve by revolutions, in the peculiar manner in which these great upsurges of wealth-creating potential are assimilated by the economic and social system and in the functional separation of financial and production capital.

The main contention is that the full fruits of the technological revolutions that occur about every half century are only widely reaped with a time-lag. Two or three decades of turbulent adaptation and assimilation elapse, from the moment when the set of new technologies, products, industries and infrastructures make their first impact to the beginning of a 'golden age' or 'era of good feeling' based on them.

For each technological revolution, that time-lag is characterized by strong divergence in the rates of growth of industries, countries and regions as well as a worsening of the trends in income distribution that had previously prevailed. Historically, those decades have brought the greatest excitement in financial markets, where brilliant successes and innovations share the stage with great manias and outrageous swindles. They have also ended with the most virulent crashes, recessions and depressions, later to give way, through the establishment of appropriate institutions, to a period of widespread prosperity, based on the potential of that particular set of technologies.

This book will develop a model to explain why this is so and why, in spite of the unquestionable uniqueness of each historical period, there is a certain sequence of events that recurs about every half century.

It will be held that the full deployment of the enormous wealth-creating potential brought forth by each technological revolution requires, each time, the establishment of an adequate socio-institutional framework. The existing framework, created to handle growth based on the previous set of technologies, is unsuited to the new one. Thus, in the first decades of installation of the new industries and infrastructures, there is an increasing mismatch between the techno-economic and the socio-institutional spheres, as well as an internal decoupling of the economic system, between the new and the old technologies. The process of re-establishing a good match and creating conditions both for recoupling and full deployment of the new potential is complex, protracted and socially painful.

Financial capital plays a crucial role all along. It first supports the development of the technological revolution, it then contributes to deepen the mismatch leading to a possible crash, it later becomes a contributing agent in the deployment process once the match is achieved and, when that revolution is spent, it helps give birth to the next.

In this respect there is a surprising lack of connection between economists studying finance on the one hand and technical change on the other. The followers of the Schumpeterian lead have neglected the financial aspects of the economic process, although they would be the first to acknowledge that the diffusion of radical innovations is inevitably a question of investment and that the role of such new technologies as engines of the economy cannot be played without the financial fuel. Yet the relationship has been consistently ignored. And this has been so, though Schumpeter himself was very clear about the two roles, that of the entrepreneur and that of the financier as the interdependent wheels turning innovation forward.[1]

On the other hand, those who have studied finance – and in particular financial crises – have seldom given attention to the real economy of the production of goods and services (or what Schumpeter called '*Güterwelt*'), nor have they dealt much with technology and its relation with investment opportunities. Using the framework to be presented here, one could suggest that this neglect stems from the fact that the biggest bubbles tend to occur when financial capital has practically decoupled from the real economy and taken off on its own. Nevertheless, an economist like Hyman Minsky, who does put innovation in financial services at the core of his explanation of crises, does not make any links between the types of financial innovation made and the specific technologies of the period in question.[2]

This book attempts to weave these two issues together within a wider interdisciplinary perspective, beyond the boundaries of economics.

---

1.   Schumpeter (1939) p. 104.
2.   Minsky (1975 and 1982).

The argument will be developed in two main parts. Part I is devoted to the discussion of great surges of technology and technological revolutions, their nature, the social process involved in their assimilation and the recurrent sequence of events which describes their diffusion, including the role of finance. This then becomes the frame of reference for examining – in Part II – the changing and also recurrent behavior of financial capital in its relation to technological revolutions. The sections in this part present a narrative of this behavior for each of the phases, illustrated with examples from the present information revolution and from the four previous ones. Part III briefly discusses the internal forces that produce the recurring sequence, summarizes the model and explores some of the implications for theory and policy.

This book is a 'think-piece,' the spelling out of an interpretation, with enough illustrations to strengthen the case and stimulate discussion. In most cases the stylized narrative is the chosen manner of presentation. This, apart from being an efficient way of transmitting a thought model, seems particularly suited to the type of explanation proposed, where a recurrent historical sequence has unique manifestations each time around.

PART ONE

Technological Revolutions
as Successive Great Surges of Development

1. The Turbulent Ending of the Twentieth Century

On a day like any other in November 1971, a small event in Santa Clara California was about to change the history of the world. Bob Noyce and Gordon Moore launched Intel's first microprocessor, the precursor of the computer on a chip. It was the big-bang of a new universe, that of all-pervasive computing and digital telecommunications. Chips were powerful, they were cheap and they opened innumerable technological and business possibilities.

At that time not many people had heard of venture capital or 'angels'. Though many common citizens in the USA had stocks and bonds, few followed the daily changes in the stock market. The word 'derivative' was generally confined to mathematics. Most middle-class people kept their money in the bank or in the savings and loan society and the self-made millionaires, although a core element of the American dream, were few and far between. In the decades to follow, all this was to change radically. Millionaires would abound and finance was to become the central concern of people with old and new wealth. By the end of the 1990s, even people with modest salaries had turned into hopeful 'investors'.

Henry Ford had been the central character in a similar event in 1908. The low-cost Model-T, with its internal combustion engine powered by cheap gasoline, was the *big-bang* opening the world of the automobile and of mass production and mass consumption.

By the mid-1920s, the New York Stock Market was perceived as the engine moving the American economy and even the world's. As was to happen later, in the 1980s and 1990s, financial geniuses appeared by the dozens and investment in stocks or real estate seemed almost guaranteed to grow and grow in an unending bull market. Great wealth for the players was the result; irrational exuberance was the mood. By the end of the 1920s even widows, small farmers and shoe-shine boys were putting their money into that glorified casino. The crash was unexpected; the following recession and depression were exceptionally deep and prolonged.

This sequence had happened three times before in a similar – though each time specific – manner. A decade after the first industrial revolution opened the world of mechanization in England and led to the rapid extension of the network of roads, bridges, ports and canals to support a growing flow of trade, there was canal mania and, later, canal panic. About 15 years after the Liverpool–

Manchester rail line inaugurated the Age of Steam and Railroads, there was an amazing investment boom in the stock of companies constructing railways, a veritable 'railway mania' which ended in panic and collapse in 1847. After Andrew Carnegie's Bessemer steel mill in 1875 gave the big-bang for the Age of Steel and heavy engineering, a huge transformation began to change the economy of the whole world, with transcontinental trade and travel, by rail and steamship, accompanied by international telegraph and electricity. The growth of the stock markets in the 1880s and 1890s was now, not only in railways but also in industry, not mainly national but more and more truly international. The crashes happened, in different forms, in the USA and Argentina, in Italy and France and in many other parts of the world.

Each technological revolution has led to the massive replacement of one set of technologies by another, either by outright substitution or through the modernization of existing equipment, processes and ways of operation. Each involved profound changes in people, organizations and skills in a sort of habit-breaking hurricane. Each led to an explosive period in the financial markets.

New actors, usually young, burst into action shaking a firmly established and complacent world. Investment in the new industries is carried out by new entrepreneurs while the young financial tycoons create a whirlpool that sucks in huge amounts of the world's wealth to reallocate it in more adventurous or reckless hands: some for speculation in real estate or in whatever is amenable at the time, some for buying existing assets and some for new investment. A part of this goes to new industries, another to expand the new infrastructure, another to modernize all the established industries, but most of it is moved about in a frenzy of money-making money, which creates asset inflation and provides a gambling atmosphere within an ever-expanding bubble. Eventually it has to collapse. But when it does, the changeover has been made. New industries have grown, a new infrastructure is in place; new millionaires have appeared; the new way of doing things with the new technologies has become 'common sense'. One crucial thing is still missing: a systematic articulation of the new regulatory framework and of the appropriate institutions, capable of steering and facilitating the functioning of the new economy in a socially and economically sustainable manner.

Each time around, what can be considered a 'new economy' takes root where the old economy had been faltering. But it is all achieved in a violent, wasteful and painful manner. The new wealth that accumulates at one end is often more than counterbalanced by the poverty that spreads at the other end. This is in fact the period when capitalism shows its ugliest and most callous face. It is the time depicted by Charles Dickens and Upton Sinclair, by Friedrich Engels and Thorstein Veblen; the time when the rich get richer with arrogance and the poor get poorer through no fault of their own; when part of the population celebrates prosperity and the other portion (generally much larger) experiences outright deterioration and decline. It is certainly a broken society, a two-faced world. But while the poor can usually see the conspicuous consumption of the ostentatious members of the new 'leisure class', to these, the poor are often hidden from view. In the globalized world of the information economy, this is all the more true, given that the cleavage between the excessively rich and the extremely poor is basically international. Were it not for satellite TV and mass illegal migrations, the invisibility could be almost total.

When the financial breakdown comes, the party is over and the time comes for analyzing what went wrong and how it can be prevented from happening again. Though the debate about the causes and the culprits can go on forever, the more practical task of setting up an adequate regulatory system and a set of effective safeguards is soon undertaken. Thanks to the crash and the recession, there is a newfound readiness to accept such rules on the part of the – until recently arrogant – financial wizards, now sobered up.

If, at this turning point, the institutional adjustment is successfully achieved, what follows may be a golden age. It can be a period of full employment and widespread productive investment, a period when *production* is at center stage, when at last the benefits of the system begin to spread down and an era of 'good feeling' sets in. The best face of capitalism can then be seen. It is the face of progress and of relative coincidence between individual and collective interests. Financial capital goes out of public sight into boardrooms and offices. It increasingly supports big production companies that are generating real wealth, and grows *with* them and at the pace they set. By this time, the main companies may already be the result of mergers and would have become what in each period would be considered *big* corporations, often operating as oligopolies.[3] This reduces the previous ferocity of competition and leads to a common interest in having comfortable profit margins and in enlarging the target markets by widening the consumer base. As the improvement in income distribution allows, consumption grows and expands. The new style of living, just established by the *nouveaux riches*, begins to diffuse down from one social stratum to another in more 'popular' versions. These are the times when capitalism is identified with progress and the idea that it can achieve social justice becomes more credible. Hope grows high. In the next phase, though, the unfulfilled expectations will lead to frustration and protests.

This book holds that the sequence *technological revolution–financial bubble–collapse–golden age–political unrest* recurs about every half century and is based on causal mechanisms that are in the nature of capitalism. These

---

3. In the first and second revolutions personal or family firms were still typical and their size, though seen as large by contemporaries, was typically small in relation to the industry as a whole. The truly giant corporations and the formation of oligopolies and cartels only became a feature of the system with the third revolution, from the end of the nineteenth century.

mechanisms stem from three features of the system, which interact with and influence one another:

1. the fact that technological change occurs by clusters of radical innovations forming successive and distinct revolutions that modernize the whole productive structure;
2. the functional separation between financial and production capital, each pursuing profits by different means; and
3. the much greater inertia and resistance to change of the socio-institutional framework in comparison with the techno-economic sphere, which is spurred by competitive pressures.

Obviously the recurring sequence is hidden under many layers of unique factors, events and circumstances. These layers happen to be some of the most important aspects in the history of any country and of the world: culture, politics, leading personalities, wars, gold discoveries, natural catastrophes and so on. In addition, because of uneven development, itself an outstanding feature of capitalism, such regularities are mainly visible in the core countries of the world system, which also change over time (as when the USA took the lead from Britain in the twentieth century).

Yet the dynamic regularities presented in this model can be identified from many angles. When A.C. Pigou, Alfred Marshall's successor in Cambridge, observed the changing views about money in the first half of the twentieth century he was precisely picking up the sequence in question:

> In the years preceding the First World War there were in common use among economists a number of metaphors ... 'Money is a wrapper in which goods come'; 'Money is the garment draped round the body of economic life'; 'money is a veil behind which the action of real economic forces is concealed'...
> During the 1920s and 1930s ... money, the passive veil, took on the appearance of an evil genius; the garment became a Nessus shirt; the wrapper a thing liable to explode. Money, in short, after being little or nothing, was now everything ...
> Then with the Second World War, the tune changed again. Manpower, equipment and organization once more came into their own. The role of money dwindled to insignificance ...[4]

However, this effort at identifying the recurrent phenomena is not aimed at simplifying history or at applying mechanistic models to its infinite complexity and unpredictability. It is mainly aimed at serving two useful purposes in relation to policy, growth and development:

---

4.   Pigou (1949) pp. 18–19.

1. To help recognize the dynamic and changing nature of capitalism in order to avoid extrapolating any particular period – be it good or bad – as 'the end of history' or as the final crisis of capitalism or as the arrival of unstoppable progress or as any 'new' and permanent nature of the system, from then on.
2. To help see ahead to the next phase of the sequence, in order to design timely actions to make the best of the impending opportunities.

According to the model that will be presented here, achieving this second purpose also requires a deep understanding of the nature of the particular technological revolution being deployed. One of the main ideas to be put forth is that each of these revolutions is accompanied by a set of 'best-practice' principles, in the form of a *techno-economic paradigm*, which breaks the existing organizational habits in technology, the economy, management and social institutions. The particular manner in which these principles are applied each time and in each case is strongly influenced by all the layers mentioned above. Therefore, the modes of growth adopted, while formally applying similar structural principles, can be profoundly different in their social content.[5]

The world is once again at a crossroads where explanations and guiding criteria are sorely needed. The twentieth century left a turbulent legacy that after chanting the advent of a 'new economy' has to cope with unraveling the meaning of the implosion of the Internet bubble and its aftermath. Comprehending some of the underlying causes of the stagflation and debt crises of the 1980s and of the financial boom of the 1990s, could be helpful for overcoming the consequences of the collapse that began in 2000. It is hoped that the model to be presented will provide a contribution to such an understanding. The possibilities open are very different: it can be a world for the few or a world for the many. Perhaps a fruitful debate about the structural causes of such changing conditions can guide positive action towards constructing the next golden age, and maximizing its social benefits in the core countries and globally.

Technological revolutions and the unfolding of their potential play a central role in the model. The following chapter is devoted to defining them and identifying the five revolutions that have shaped the last two centuries. It will also define the two associated concepts that play a major role in the model to be presented. One is *techno-economic paradigm*, which stands for the new 'common sense' guiding the diffusion of each revolution. The other is *great surge of development*, which represents the process of installation and deployment of each revolution and its paradigm in the economic and social system.

---

5. The mass-production revolution, which marked most of the institutions of the twentieth century, underlay the centralized governments and massive consumption patterns of the four great modes of growth that were set up to take advantage of those technologies: the Keynesian democracies, Nazi-fascism, Soviet socialism and State developmentalism in the so-called 'Third World,' each with very wide-ranging specificities.

2. Technological Revolutions and Techno-Economic Paradigms

A *technological revolution* can be defined as a powerful and highly visible cluster of new and dynamic technologies, products and industries, capable of bringing about an upheaval in the whole fabric of the economy and of propelling a long-term upsurge of development. It is a strongly interrelated constellation of technical innovations, generally including an important all-pervasive low-cost input,[6] often a source of energy, sometimes a crucial material, plus significant new products and processes and a new infrastructure. The latter usually changes the frontier in speed and reliability of transportation and communications, while drastically reducing their cost.

The irruption of such significant clusters of innovative industries in a short period of time would certainly be enough reason to label them as 'technological revolutions.' Yet what warrants the title for the present purposes is that each of those sets of technological breakthroughs spreads far beyond the confines of the industries and sectors where they originally developed. Each provides a set of interrelated generic technologies and organizational principles that allows and fosters a quantum jump in potential productivity for practically all economic activities. This leads each time to the modernization and regeneration of the whole productive system, so that the general level of efficiency rises to a new height every 50 years or so (see Figure 2.1).

The main vehicle of diffusion of that set of generic 'tools' – hard, soft and ideological – which together modify the best-practice frontier for all, is what the author has termed a 'techno-economic paradigm'.[7] It is 'economic' best practice because each technological transformation brings with it a major shift in the relative price structure that guides economic agents toward the intensive use of the more powerful new inputs and technologies. It is a 'paradigm,' in

---

6.   The role of the low-cost input is discussed in Perez (1983).
7.   Perez (1985), Freeman and Perez (1988). The term 'technological paradigm,' as a Kuhnian analogy in the area of technical change, was first used by Giovanni Dosi (1982) to refer to the guiding logic of the trajectory of individual technologies, products and industries. The author (Perez 1985) proposed using that concept in a more overarching 'techno-economic' – and organizational – sense, to mean a sort of *meta-paradigm*, encompassing the main principles shared by the individual trajectories of a period. Today, however, the term paradigm is very widely used in a rather loose sense to mean a 'mind set' about something. So, a revision of the terminology could eventually be wise, in order to avoid further confusion.

Figure 2.1   The double nature of technological revolutions

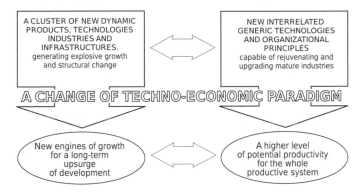

Source: Based on Perez (1998) p. 68

the Kuhnian sense,[8] because it defines the model and the territory for 'normal' innovative practice, promising success to those that follow the principles incarnate in the core industries of the revolution.

Each technological revolution, then, is an explosion of new products, industries and infrastructures that gradually gives rise to a new techno-economic paradigm, which guides entrepreneurs, managers, innovators, investors and consumers, both in their individual decisions and in their interactions, for the whole period of propagation of that set of technologies.

A.   Five Technological Revolutions in Two Hundred Years

At several moments in his thinking about development, Simon Kuznets explored the notion of *epochal innovations* as those capable of inducing significant changes in the direction of growth. In his Nobel lecture in 1971, he stated:

> The major breakthroughs in the advance of human knowledge, those that constituted the dominant sources of sustained growth over long periods and spread to a substantial part of the world, may be termed epochal innovations. And the changing course of economic history can perhaps be subdivided into economic epochs, each identified by the epochal innovation with the distinctive characteristics of growth that it generated.[9]

In that particular instance he was mainly referring to the epochs that lasted several centuries, of which capitalism since the first industrial revolution would

---

8.   Kuhn (1962).
9.   Kuznets (1971) in 1973 p. 166.

be one. However, on that same year, Kuznets suggested that it was 'difficult to conceive of a stage as static, as part of a process in which its emergence and eventual disappearance are the only relevant and major changes.' Thus, he considered 'sequences *within* each stage' as 'an indispensable part of a complete stage theory'.[10]

What is held in this book is that economic growth since the end of the eighteenth century has indeed gone through five distinct stages, associated with five successive technological revolutions. This has been captured by popular imagination when naming the relevant periods in relation to the most impressive technologies. The Industrial Revolution was the name given to the irruption of the machine and the inauguration of the Industrial Age. It was common in the mid-nineteenth century for people to refer to their time as the Age of Steam and Railways and, later on, when steel replaced iron and science transformed industry, the name was the Age of Steel and Electricity. By the 1920s it was the Age of the Automobile and Mass Production and, since the 1970s, the terms Information Age or Knowledge Society are in increasingly common usage. Table 2.1 identifies the five technological revolutions.

Each of these revolutionary clusters irrupts in a particular country, sometimes even in a particular region. Lancashire was as much the cradle and the symbol of the key industries of the first industrial revolution as Silicon Valley has been for the microelectronics revolution. In fact, each technological revolution originally develops in a core country, which acts as the world economic leader for the duration of that stage. There, it is fully deployed; from there, it propagates to other countries. The first two revolutions were led by Britain, the fourth and the present fifth by the USA. The third was characterized by a complex triple core, formed by the old – and still immensely powerful – British giant and the two dynamic challengers, Germany and the United States (see column 3, Table 2.1). This is particularly important because, although the surges of development propelled by each technological revolution are in the long run worldwide phenomena, the propagation of change occurs gradually, moving from core to periphery. This means the dating of deployment is not the same for all countries and can be delayed as much as two or three decades in some cases. (See Chapters 5, section F and 6, section B.)

Before coming together as a constellation and being recognized as such, each technological revolution goes through a gestation period that can be very long, so that many of the contributing innovations have probably been around for quite a while. This makes it difficult to find an appropriate beginning date for each revolution and a reasonable option is to indicate a broad period.[11]

---

10.   Kuznets (1973) p. 215 (original emphasis).
11.   This is what Chris Freeman and the author did in a paper in Dosi et al. (1988). It was also what Andrew Tylecote (1992) did in his book on the subject.

Table 2.1   Five successive technological revolutions, 1770s to 2000s

Technological revolution	Popular name for the period	Core country or countries	Big-bang initiating the revolution	Year
FIRST	The 'Industrial Revolution'	Britain	Arkwright's mill opens in Cromford	1771
SECOND	Age of Steam and Railways	Britain (spreading to Continent and USA)	Test of the 'Rocket' steam engine for the Liverpool–Manchester railway	1829
THIRD	Age of Steel, Electricity and Heavy Engineering	USA and Germany forging ahead and overtaking Britain	The Carnegie Bessemer steel plant opens in Pittsburgh, Pennsylvania	1875
FOURTH	Age of Oil, the Automobile and Mass Production	USA (with Germany at first vying for world leadership), later spreading to Europe	First Model-T comes out of the Ford plant in Detroit, Michigan	1908
FIFTH	Age of Information and Telecommunications	USA (spreading to Europe and Asia)	The Intel microprocessor is announced in Santa Clara, California	1971

Nevertheless, it is suggested here that for society to veer strongly in the direction of a new set of technologies, a highly visible 'attractor' needs to appear, symbolizing the whole new potential and capable of sparking the technological and business imagination of a cluster of pioneers. This attractor is not only a technical breakthrough. What makes it so powerful is that it is also cheap or that it makes it clear that business based on the associated innovations will be cost-competitive. That event is defined here as the *big-bang* of the revolution (Column 4, Table 2.1).

When Arkwright's Cromford mill opened in 1771, the future paths to cost-reducing mechanization of the cotton textile and other industries were powerfully visible. Sixty years later, in 1829, the world of railways and steam power was announced by Stephenson's 'Rocket' steam locomotive winning the contest for the Liverpool–Manchester railway. In 1875, Carnegie's highly efficient Bessemer steel plant went on stream, inaugurating the Age of Steel. Of course, it is only with hindsight that these events can be singled out, not only because at the time they are obvious only to a narrow community of entrepreneurs and technical people, but also because whether they flourish or not in a particular country will depend on a complex set of circumstances. In the case of the third revolution, for example, it was by no means clear in the 1870s that England would fall behind and that it would be the USA and Germany that would fully exploit the new wealth-generating potential to catch up and forge ahead. In fact, it could be argued that two big-bang events, one for each of the countries involved in propelling that surge, should perhaps be identified. Other choices are less controversial. Ford's Model-T is an obvious choice for the Age of Oil, the Automobile and Mass-Production. Nevertheless, the precise dating could be an issue. The truly mass-produced Model-T, from a full moving assembly line, only came out in 1913. However, even without a complete line, the first Model-T in 1908 was already the clear prototype of the standardized, identical products that were to characterize future production patterns. It also prefigured the decreasing costs that would make it accessible to the mass of the population. Finally, Intel's first microprocessor in 1971, the original and simplest 'computer on a chip', can be seen as the birth of the Information Age, based on the amazing power of low-cost microelectronics.

So, pinpointing the date of the big-bang[12] of each technological revolution is a useful device to facilitate the understanding of the chain of processes that follow. The event in question, though apparently small and relatively isolated, is experienced by the pioneers of the time as the discovery of a new territory, as a powerful announcement of what those technologies can offer far into the future and as a call for entrepreneurial action.

By contrast, any attempt at indicating an ending date for each revolution would be relatively meaningless. It is true that certain events can be felt by society as announcing the 'end of an era', such as the 1973 oil crisis and the 1971 breakdown of the Bretton Woods agreement on the dollar. Nevertheless, as will be discussed in the next chapter, each set of technologies undergoes a difficult and prolonged period of stretching when the impending exhaustion of its potential becomes increasingly visible. This phenomenon is crucial to the present interpretation. When each technological revolution irrupts, the logic and the effects of its predecessor are still fully dominant and exert powerful resistance. The generalized shift into 'the logic of the new' requires two or three turbulent decades of transition from one to the other, when the successful installation of the new superior capacities accentuates the decline of the old. By the time the process has fully taken place, the end of the previous revolution is little more than a whimper.

---

12.   Unfortunately this cosmological metaphor was also chosen to signal financial deregulation in the 1980s. In spite of the risk of confusion, it was still kept here because of its appropriateness to describe a point in time that explodes into an expanding universe of opportunities.

B.   Five Constellations of New Industries and Infrastructures

Each technological revolution results from the synergistic interdependence of a group of industries with one or more infrastructural networks. Table 2.2 identifies the constellations conforming each of the five revolutions.

The technologies and products involved are not only those where the major breakthroughs have occurred. It is often the interlinking of some of the new and some of the old that generates the revolutionary potential. In fact, many of the products and industries coming together into the new constellation had already existed for some time, either in a relatively minor economic role or as important complements for the prevailing industries. This was the case of coal and iron, which after a long history of usage during and before the Industrial Revolution, were transformed by the steam engine into the motive industries of the Age of Railways. Oil was developed for many uses since the 1880s by an extremely active industry; the same can be said about the internal combustion engine and for the automobile, which was produced as a luxury vehicle for quite some time. But it is the conjunction of all three with mass production that makes them become part of a veritable revolution. Electronics existed since the early 1900s and in some ways was crucial in the 1920s; transistors, semiconductors, computers and controls were already important technologies in the 1960s and even earlier. Yet it is only in 1971, with the microprocessor, that the vast new potential of *cheap* microelectronics is made visible; the notion of 'a computer on a chip' flares the imagination and all the related technologies of the information revolution come together into a powerful cluster.

It has often been suggested that biotechnology, bioelectronics and nanotechnology might conform the next technological revolution. Indeed, they are already developing intensely within the logic of the information society. They seem to be at a stage equivalent to the oil industry and the automobile at the end of the nineteenth century or to electronics in the 1940s and 1950s, with vacuum-TV, radar and analog control equipment and telecommunications. The key breakthrough that would make it cheap to harness the forces of life and the power hidden in the infinitely small is still unpredictable. Apart from the ethical questions that are likely to shape the rhythm and the direction of the search, that event is more likely to happen, as will be discussed in Chapter 3, when the current information revolution approaches limits to its wealth-generating potential.

So every revolution combines truly new industries and products with others that are redefined. It is when the critical technological breakthroughs articulate them into a powerful, interacting and coherent set of profitable business avenues, influencing the whole economy, that their joint impact can become truly all-pervasive.

In relation to existing infrastructures there can also be extensions in scope that make a significant qualitative difference. The *iron* railways of the second

Table 2.2 The industries and infrastructures of each technological revolution

Technological revolution	New technologies and new or redefined industries	New or redefined infrastructures
FIRST: From 1771 *The 'Industrial Revolution'*; Britain	Mechanized cotton industry Wrought iron Machinery	Canals and waterways Turnpike roads Water power (highly improved water wheels)
SECOND: From 1829 *Age of Steam and Railways* In Britain and spreading to Continent and USA	Steam engines and machinery (made in iron; fueled by coal) Iron and coal mining (now playing a central role in growth)* Railway construction Rolling stock production Steam power for many industries (including textiles)	Railways (Use of steam engine) Universal postal service Telegraph (mainly nationally along railway lines) Great ports, great depots and worldwide sailing ships City gas
THIRD: From 1875 *Age of Steel, Electricity and Heavy Engineering* USA and Germany overtaking Britain	Cheap steel (especially Bessemer) Full development of steam engine for steel ships Heavy chemistry and civil engineering Electrical equipment industry Copper and cables Canned and bottled food Paper and packaging	Worldwide shipping in rapid steel steamships (use of Suez Canal) Worldwide railways (use of cheap steel rails and bolts in standard sizes). Great bridges and tunnels Worldwide Telegraph Telephone (mainly nationally) Electrical networks (for illumination and industrial use)
FOURTH: From 1908 *Age of Oil, the Automobile and Mass Production* In USA and spreading to Europe	Mass-produced automobiles Cheap oil and oil fuels Petrochemicals (synthetics) Internal combustion engine for automobiles, transport, tractors, airplanes, war tanks and electricity Home electrical appliances Refrigerated and frozen foods	Networks of roads, highways, ports and airports Networks of oil ducts Universal electricity (industry and homes) Worldwide analog telecommunications (telephone, telex and cablegram) wire and wireless
FIFTH: From 1971 *Age of Information and Telecommunications* In USA, spreading to Europe and Asia	The information revolution: Cheap microelectronics. Computers, software Telecommunications Control instruments Computer-aided biotechnology and new materials	World digital telecommunications (cable, fiber optics, radio and satellite) Internet/ Electronic mail and other e-services Multiple source, flexible use, electricity networks High-speed physical transport links (by land, air and water)

Note: *   These traditional industries acquire a new role and a new dynamism when serving as the material and the fuel of the world of railways and machinery.

technological revolution led to *national* networks of rail transport and telegraph. The *steel* railways of the third revolution created *transcontinental* networks that, together with the steel steamships and worldwide telegraph, facilitated the functioning of truly international markets. Regarding electricity, the setting up of the basic electrical networks made the electrical equipment industry into one of the main engines of growth of the third technological revolution; whereas, during the fourth, it was its role as a 'utility', as a *universal* service encompassing every firm and every home, that made it a crucial infrastructure for the diffusion of the mass-production revolution.

Finally, it is important to note that each constellation contains several technology systems that develop at different rhythms and in a sequence that often depends on feedback loops. The information revolution begins with the explosion in chips and hardware, the growth of which leads to a flourishing in software and telecommunications equipment followed by the Internet boom and so on, each benefitting from the technical and market advances previously made by the others, while in turn favoring their further development. The same was seen in the unfolding of the potential of the third, where the impact of cheap steel is first felt in railways, ships and civil engineering and later in equipping the new chemical and electrical industries. The individual importance of some of these technology systems and their sequential visibility can make them appear as separate revolutions rather than interdependent systems under a wider umbrella.

C.   Five Techno-Economic Paradigms; Five Changes in Organizational 'Common Sense'

The irruption of a set of powerful and dynamic new industries accompanied by a facilitating infrastructure will obviously have enormous consequences both in the industrial structure and in the preferred direction of investment in that period. But, as indicated before, the old organizational models cannot cope with or take full advantage of the new potential. The new possibilities and their requirements also unleash a profound transformation in 'the way of doing things' across the whole economy and beyond. Thus each technological revolution inevitably induces a paradigm shift.

A techno-economic paradigm is, then, a best-practice model made up of a set of all-pervasive generic technological and organizational principles, which represent the most effective way of applying a particular technological revolution and of using it for modernizing and rejuvenating the whole of the economy. When generally adopted, these principles become the common-sense basis for organizing any activity and for structuring any institution.

The appearance of a new techno-economic paradigm affects behaviors related to innovation and investment in a way that could be compared to a gold rush or the discovery of a vast new territory. It is *the opening of a wide design, product and profit space*[13] that rapidly fires the imagination of engineers, entrepreneurs and investors, who in their trial and error experiments applying the new wealth-creating potential, generate the successful practices and behaviors that gradually define the new best-practice frontier.

The action of these pioneering agents blazes the trail, giving rise to increasing externalities and conditionings – including production experience and the training of consumers – that make it easier and easier for others to follow suit. Their success becomes a powerful signal in the direction of the most profitable windows of opportunity. That is how the new paradigm[14] eventually becomes the new generalized 'common sense', which gradually finds itself embedded in social practice, legislation and other components of the institutional framework, facilitating compatible innovations and hindering incompatible ones. This inclusion–exclusion mechanism is at the root of technical change by revolutions, as will be discussed in Chapter 3.

The techno-economic paradigm is a much more elusive and difficult concept to grasp than that of technological revolution. It is nonetheless as powerful, if not more, in guiding the major transformation that follows each big-bang. Its analysis and description, in each particular case, is crucial for identifying two important features of the direction of change in terms of organizational discontinuities: the first is the set of common principles behind the understanding that grows among the contemporary actors in their decisions and interactions; the second is the isomorphism in the changes occurring across the most diverse institutions, beginning with firms.

The task is demanding. A techno-economic paradigm, being a sort of mental map of best-practice options, is made up as much of an understanding of actual generic technologies with nearly all-pervasive applicability as of general common-sense principles that enter the culture of the period. The generic technologies are easy to identify, of course: mechanization, steam power, electricity, mass production, ICTs (information and telecommunications technologies) and so on. The principles and guidelines are less obvious, though at least in the present Information Era thousands of consultants have made 'before and now' tables to indicate the precise direction of change in competitive best practice. Something similar happened with the third paradigm when the societies of mechanical engineers were developing optimal practice, establishing standards and propagating them among industrialists.[15] At that

---

13.   The concept of 'design space' was proposed by Stankiewicz (2000) referring to individual wide-ranging technologies.
14.   Throughout the text the term 'paradigm' alone will sometimes be used as a short reference for techno-economic paradigm.
15.   Chandler (1977) pp. 281–3.

time they taught modified versions of Taylor's early ideas. Decades later, with the mass-production paradigm, the assembly-line version of Taylorism, called 'scientific management' (in its 'Fordist'[16] form), was taught and applied across the industrial spectrum.

The task becomes harder the further one goes into the past, because in real life the paradigm is mostly an imitative model, made up of implicit principles that soon become unconscious 'talent' and later get subsumed into 'rules of thumb'.[17] So, an explicit identification of such guidelines might not be readily found in the historical record. They can, however, be abstracted from the logic of the generic technologies of the period and from the behavior of firms, as described in contemporary accounts and in historical analyses. A good example of the latter is Chandler's[18] *Visible Hand*, an amply documented description of the changing structure and practice of enterprise, from the early personal firm to the modern managerial corporation.

The lists given in Table 2.3 are illustrative and indicative of the type of general guidelines that constitute a techno-economic paradigm and do not attempt to be exhaustive.

The reader will note that the principles listed are not strictly limited to the organization of production but stretch to involve the structure of the firms, the forms of geographic propagation, the structure of the geo-political and social space and something which approaches the 'ideals' of the period. In fact, the logic of a paradigm reaches well beyond the economic sphere to become the general and shared organizational common sense of the period. It could then be called an *organizational paradigm*. Eventually the socio-institutional framework that will accommodate and enable the full deployment of that technological revolution will follow those basic principles. Thus the mental maps for efficiency guiding both economic and non-economic activities will be congruent.

As an example, one could observe the process of organizational change brought by the information revolution. Until the 1980s, the prevalent organization was the one that served as the optimal framework for deploying the mass-production revolution: the centralized, hierarchical pyramid with functional compartments. This structure was applied in the economy by almost every corporation, but was also replicated in any other organization confronted with a large and complex task in government, in hospitals, in universities, in trade unions and political parties, in the West and in the Soviet system, in

16. The term 'Fordism' has been popularized to refer to the mass-production model of organization. However, in the sense introduced by the French 'Regulation' School, the concept goes beyond the forms of organization or norms of production, to also include the patterns (or mode) of consumption and the institutional context that enables them. See Aglietta (1976); Boyer (1988); Coriat (1978).
17. This is analogous to how Kuhn saw the establishment of the principles guiding 'normal science.' Kuhn (1962) Ch.II.
18. Chandler (1977).

Table 2.3   A different techno-economic paradigm for each technological revolution, 1770 to 2000s

Technological revolution Country of initial development	Techno-economic paradigm 'Common-sense' innovation principles
FIRST The 'Industrial Revolution' Britain	Factory production Mechanization Productivity/time keeping and time saving Fluidity of movement (as ideal for machines with water-power and for transport through canals and other waterways) Local networks
SECOND Age of Steam and Railways In Britain and spreading to Continent and USA	Economies of agglomeration/Industrial cities/National markets Power centers with national networks Scale as progress Standard parts/machine-made machines Energy where needed (steam) Interdependent movement (of machines and of means of transport)
THIRD Age of Steel, Electricity and Heavy Engineering USA and Germany overtaking Britain	Giant structures (steel) Economies of scale of plant/vertical integration Distributed power for industry (electricity) Science as a productive force Worldwide networks and empires (including cartels) Universal standardization Cost accounting for control and efficiency Great scale for world market power/'small' is successful, if local
FOURTH Age of Oil, the Automobile and Mass Production In USA and spreading to Europe	Mass production/mass markets Economies of scale (product and market volume)/ horizontal integration Standardization of products Energy intensity (oil based) Synthetic materials Functional specialization/hierarchical pyramids Centralization/metropolitan centers–suburbanization National powers, world agreements and confrontations
FIFTH Age of Information and Telecommunications In USA spreading to Europe and Asia	Information-intensity (microelectronics-based ICT) Decentralized integration/network structures Knowledge as capital/intangible value added Heterogeneity, diversity, adaptability Segmentation of markets/proliferation of niches Economies of scope and specialization combined with scale Globalization/interaction between the global and the local Inward and outward cooperation/clusters Instant contact and action/instant global communications

developed and developing countries. With the advent of computers and the Internet, large pyramids now appear rigid and clumsy. In its place, the decentralized flexible network structure, with a strategic core and a rapid communication system, has shown its capacity for accommodating much larger and more complex global organizations as well as smaller ones.[19] Its common sense or the logic that facilitates its smooth functioning, reinforced by the nature and capabilities of the available information technologies, has been diffusing gradually and will eventually encompass a very wide range of institutions, probably including those of global and local government.[20]

It is important to note that the techno-economic paradigm serves both as a propeller of diffusion and as a delaying force. It is a propeller because it provides a model that can be followed by all, but its configuration takes time – about a decade or more after the big-bang – and, given that each revolution is by definition different from the previous one, the new principles will have to be socially learned. But this learning must overcome the forces of inertia that stem from the success of the previous paradigm. Its prevalence is the main obstacle for the diffusion of the next revolution. These counteracting forces, these battles between the new and the old, are at the core of the whole interpretation presented here.

Thus, the range of transformations induced by technological revolutions goes far beyond the economy, penetrating the sphere of politics and even ideology.[21] These, in turn, will influence the direction in which the potential is deployed. This mutual influence between technology and politics does not happen by chance, but by necessity. This will be discussed in Chapter 3, which shows how the socio-institutional framework needs to change in order to accommodate the transformations that occur in the techno-economic sphere, every time a technological revolution irrupts on the scene.

---

19. Castells (Vol. 1, 1996) went deeply and widely into the multiple consequences on all spheres of life of this shift to network organizations. See also in Vol. 2 (1997) Ch. 1 and Conclusion and in Vol. 3 (1998), Ch. 5.
20. An interesting comparison of the characteristics of the British-led paradigms of the nineteenth century and those of the twentieth, led by the USA, is found in Von-Tunzelmann (1997).
21. For a complete panorama of the multiple social, cultural, economic and political implications of a change of paradigm on all areas of life, the reader can refer to the vast analysis of the present 'Information Age' carried out by Manuel Castells (1996, 1997 and 1998).

D. Revolutions, Paradigms and Great Surges of Development

The commonly held view of constant progress through linear and cumulative development is as inadequate as the idea that technological change is continuous and random. Both processes can, of course, be seen as regularly increasing by putting the accent on the long-term trends and ignoring the many minor and major variations. There are some purposes for which this is adequate. However, once the impact of successive technological revolutions is recognized, the emphasis moves toward the complex set of interrelated changes involved and a very different understanding emerges. Development is a step process that takes place by huge leaps or surges of about five or six decades, each one leading to deep structural changes within the economy and in society at large.

A *great surge of development* is defined here as the process by which a technological revolution and its paradigm propagate across the economy, leading to structural changes in production, distribution, communication and consumption as well as to profound and qualitative changes in society. The process evolves from small beginnings, in restricted sectors and geographic regions, and ends up encompassing the bulk of activities in the core country or countries and diffusing out towards further and further peripheries, depending on the capacity of the transport and communications infrastructures.

So each great surge represents another stage in the deepening of capitalism in people's lives and in its expansion across the planet. Each revolution incorporates new aspects of life and of production activities into the market mechanism; each surge widens the group of countries that conforms the advanced core of the system and each stretches the penetration of capitalism to further corners of the world, inside and across countries.

In addition, a technological revolution, through the paradigm that takes shape in its wake, sets a new higher level for the average productivity and quality that can be achieved across the board. The great surge of development, which results from the full social assimilation of this potential, ends up pulling the whole group of core economies involved onto that higher productivity plateau.

Essentially what this means is that bringing to fruition the wealth-generating forces of each new paradigm requires massive and matching changes in the patterns of investment, in the organizational models for maximum efficiency, in the mental maps of all the social actors and in the institutions that regulate and enable the economic and social processes. It also means that progress can involve significant changes in direction; that accumulation may require 'disaccumulation' from time to time; that what is installed may have to be 'uninstalled', that continued advance along certain paths could lead to dead ends, when others are already jumping onto the new bandwagons; that learning the new can require unlearning much of the old.

On the other hand, these changes in direction can be advantageous periods for newcomers. A paradigm shift opens the necessary windows of opportunity for forging ahead and catching up, while the front-runners are also learning.[22] They are also the times when excess inertia may result in falling behind. Thus the capacity for structural change in the most advantageous direction is a highly valuable societal skill in order to reach development, and then to be able to preserve and increase the gains as the context and the opportunities change.

The role of financial capital is crucial in enabling the massive shifts in investment required with each revolution. How this occurs, together with its contradictory consequences, will be discussed in Part II of the book.

---

22.   Perez and Soete (1988).

3. The Social Shaping of Technological Revolutions

If technological revolutions remained as forces of change in the economic sphere and society adapted gradually and easily to the new products and means of transport and communication the whole process could be described simply as the form taken by 'progress' and technology could be treated as an exogenous variable. Such changes, however, are far from smooth. Societies are profoundly shaken and shaped by each technological revolution and, in turn, the technological potential is shaped and steered as a result of intense social, political and ideological confrontations and compromises. It is precisely this systemic character that makes the whole question of technical change so crucial in understanding capitalist development.

A. From Technological Innovations to Institutional Revolutions

The notion of 'creative destruction', very much influenced by Nietzsche, was a significant element in the European *Zeitgeist* of the early twentieth century, as the nature of progress by innovation. Much in the same spirit as that of the Renaissance, it was seen as Mankind's noble and pleasurable duty to invent,[23] to break the forces of inertia that threatened to chain and enslave society in a cult of status quo. It was the German economist Werner Sombart, in his *Krieg und Kapitalismus*, who first used the term 'the creative spirit of destruction' in economics.[24]

Today we usually credit Schumpeter with the notion of 'creative destruction' as the way to describe the contradictory nature of technological revolutions.[25] In fact, he understood innovation, be it new products, new processes or simply new ways of doing things, as the very essence of the capitalist engine of growth. He saw capitalism as a 'process of industrial mutation ... that inces-

---

23. For a discussion of this tradition, see Reinert and Daastøl (1997).
24. Sombart (1913) p. 207.
25. Schumpeter (1942:1975) Ch. VII, p. 83.

santly revolutionizes the economic structure *from within*, incessantly destroying the old one, incessantly creating a new one.'[26]

Due to the double nature of the process of creative destruction, Schumpeter saw innovation not only as the force propelling progress but also as the cause of recurring recessions and in general of the cyclical behavior of growth rates and other economic magnitudes. Yet, in spite of his awareness of social and institutional factors, Schumpeter remained very much attached to market equilibrium forces as the determining factor and to the economy alone as the place where the transformation was absorbed. Be it the 3–5 year Kitchin cycles or the 7–11 year Juglars or the 45–60 year Kondratiev long waves,[27] they would all be related to deviations from equilibrium due to bursts of innovation. When defining the longest – 45–60-year – cycles, or long waves, he referred to each as 'the irruption of a technological revolution and the absorption of its effects'.[28]

Explaining the shorter 'inventory' and 'investment' cycles mainly in terms of economic forces may possibly be justified. However, this is certainly not warranted in the case of the longer-term phenomena usually called 'long waves', which should be understood as much more complex, society-wide processes.[29] In fact, in this book a different label has been chosen in order to definitely distance the concept and the object itself from any narrowly defined purely economic cycle. The term 'great surges of development' was introduced in the previous chapter to represent the turbulent process of diffusion of each technological revolution, lasting half a century or more. The intention is to take the accent away from the symptoms and endeavor to understand the underlying causes.[30]

These difficult long-term processes of transformation are in the nature of the capitalist system and involve intense interactions between the economy and social institutions as well as profound changes in both. Each technological revolution is received as a shock, and its diffusion encounters powerful resistance both in the established institutions and in people themselves. Hence, the full unfolding of its wealth-creating potential at first has rather chaotic and

---

26. Schumpeter (1942:1975) Ch. VII, p. 84 (original emphasis).
27. Kondratiev (1926).
28. Schumpeter (1942:1975), p. 67.
29. Perez (1983), p. 359.
30. Since 1983, and up to now, the author herself had used the term 'long waves', though attempting to mark the distance. The change of label now emphasizes the difference in concept. Kondratiev, Schumpeter and most followers measured each wave from trough to trough, which in practice meant encompassing the second half of one revolution and the first half of the next. Here they are identified – though not measured – from peak to peak, covering the complete life cycle of a single revolution. This is the reason why the present model follows the deployment of each surge and the structural transformations it induces across the economy and society, rather than examine growth statistics.

contradictory social effects, it later will demand a significant institutional recomposition. This will include changes in the regulatory framework affecting all markets and economic activities as well as the redesign of a whole range of institutions, from government, through financial regulation, to education, as well as modifications in social behaviors and ideas. It is thanks to that restructuring of the context to fit the potential of the revolution that 'golden ages' can occur.

The Victorian boom, from the mid-nineteenth century, materialized two decades after the 'Rocket' steam engine showed its power to pull the Liverpool to Manchester railway and not before a network of railroads had been installed, before and during a mania that led to a financial panic. That prosperity was brought about on the basis of a whole set of new institutions that ordered national markets and regulated the national banking and financial worlds. These facilitated the continued expansion of the railway system and the network of steam-powered factories in the growing industrial cities.

Two decades after the big-bang of the Age of Steel, profound changes had to be made again. The *'belle époque'* based on the unleashing of the full potential of the third paradigm, with its truly international markets, required worldwide regulation (from the general acceptance of the London-based Gold Standard to universal agreements on measurement, patents, insurance, transport, communications and shipping practices), while the structural changes in production, including the growth of important science-related industries had to be facilitated by deep educational reforms and social legislation.

The unleashing of the 'golden age' based on the mass-production technologies of the fourth paradigm that had been diffusing since the 1910s and 1920s demanded institutions facilitating massive consumption, by the people or by the governments. Only in such a context could full flourishing be achieved. At the time, Fascism, Socialism and Keynesian democracies were set up as very different socio-political models giving impulse to growth processes based on mass production and consumption.[31] They all tended first to homogenize consumption patterns within national markets and then to use these as a platform for international expansion.

Creating the appropriate context for cohesive growth, based on the potential of the information revolution, would seem to require a global network of institutions, involving the supranational, national and local regulatory levels.

Thus, each technological revolution brings with it, not only a full revamping of the productive structure but eventually also a transformation of the institutions of governance, of society and even of ideologies and culture, so deep that one can speak about the construction of successive and different *modes of*

---

31.   These examples point to the variety of possibilities with each paradigm and to the importance of the socio-political processes for defining the specific mode of growth.

growth in the history of capitalism.[32] The process of creative destruction occurs then, every 50 or 60 years, both in the economy and in the socio-political framework. [33]

Such changes tend to be forced by a mixture of pressures coming at first from the requirements of the rapidly changing economy and later from the consequences of the turbulent manner in which the new technology diffuses, leading to intense and sometimes violent social tensions. Ultimately, the most effective pressure for institutional change, and especially for some form of state intervention in the economy, comes from the recession following the collapse of the financial economy, which tends to occur a couple of decades after the initial big-bang.

It is in such a period that Keynes made his case for the state to implement countercyclical policies.[34] And even Schumpeter was willing to suspend his faith in the healing powers of the pure market and to recognize that 'the case for government action was incomparably stronger',[35] when it was a question of pulling the economy out of a depression.

In fact, though technological revolutions are indeed profound transformations of the economy, the working of markets cannot by itself explain the recurrence of major crashes and depressions or the appearance of long-lasting centrifugal trends, turbulence and chaos, much less to account for the return to prosperity. To explain the emergence of such wider phenomena affecting the very fabric of society the analysis must bring into the picture the tensions, resistance, obstacles and misalignments that arise from within the wider social and institutional scene.

B.   The Absorption of Technological Revolutions as Decoupling and Recoupling of the System

It is precisely the need for reforms and the inevitable social resistance to them that lies behind the deeper crises and longer-term cyclical behavior of the system. Each technological revolution, originally received as a bright new set of

---

32.   The concept is somewhat akin to that of *mode of production* proposed by Marx (Marx and Engels, 1847) for long-term historical changes. Mode of growth has a much narrower sense and refers to systemic institutional changes within capitalism.

33.   From Daniel Bell (1973), through Toffler (1980) to Castells (1996, 1997 and 1998), many voices have been hailing the present changes as leading to a different society, a 'post-industrial' one. This seems to happen with each technological revolution (the term 'revolution' is not used lightly!). For those who witness the upheaval it certainly appears each time like a fundamental discontinuity. Nevertheless, it is fair to concede that, this time, the growing share of intangibles in production and trade strengthens the case for interpreting it as a deeper break.

34.   Keynes, (1936).

35.   Schumpeter (1939) Vol. I, p. 155.

opportunities, is soon recognized as a threat to the established way of doing things in firms, institutions and society at large.

The new techno-economic paradigm gradually takes shape as a different 'common sense' for effective action in any area of endeavor. But while competitive forces, profit seeking and survival pressures help diffuse the changes in the economy, the wider social and institutional spheres where change is also needed are held back by strong inertia stemming from routine, ideology and vested interests. It is this difference in rhythm of change, between the techno-economic and the socio-institutional spheres, that would explain the turbulent period following each big-bang and therefore the lag in taking full social advantage of the new potential.

It is thus that the first 20 or 30 years of diffusion of each technological revolution lead to an increasing mismatch between the economy and the social and regulatory systems. The latter were developed to fit the requirements of the previous paradigm and cannot cope with the new conditions. In addition, the changes occurring in the techno-economic sphere imply a huge social cost in loss of jobs and skills as well as in geographic displacement of activities. The previous framework is unlikely to be prepared to absorb or counterbalance those costs. Thus, as the mismatch increases, centrifugal tensions and decoupling processes rip apart the fabric of the economy, leading to problems of governance and to questioning the legitimacy of the established institutional framework. There can be persistent social demands or violent outbreaks, which can take many different forms as was seen in the 1848 revolutions in Europe or much later in the various revolts, the *coups d'état* and the acute social tensions of the 1920s and 1930s. The demonstrations against the global free market policies of the World Trade Organization (WTO) in their Seattle meeting, in November 1999, may well have marked the beginning of growing open international political pressure to change the so-called 'Washington consensus'.

Whatever the manifestation, the political pressures calling for action finally propel the required changes. The financial collapse that usually marks the end of this period is the final and often the strongest instrument of persuasion to bring about the necessary changes. Once the new 'match' has been achieved through the articulation of an appropriate mode of growth, a process of recoupling and convergence ensues. The following 20 or 30 years witness the full deployment of the new paradigm in intensity and extension, from sector to sector and across regions and countries.

By statistical measures these 'eras of good feeling' are not necessarily the times when rhythm of growth is highest, yet they are the periods generally felt and accepted as 'golden ages', for they represent a more harmonious growth process, involving most sectors of the economy. They can also be a time of improvement in the lot of larger and larger groups of the population, especially in those countries centrally involved in the diffusion of the paradigm and where the most appropriate institutional frameworks have been set up.[36]

The sequence of 'good and bad times' would thus have its origin in the interaction between the dynamics of the economy, as such, and that of society as a whole. Further still, this very phenomenon is one of the main factors explaining why what appears as continuous technical evolution occurs inside the successive envelopes of different revolutions.

C. Why Technical Change Occurs by Revolutions

Kuznets cast doubt on Schumpeter's causal link between the clustering of innovations that form technological revolutions and the bunching of entrepreneurial abilities.[37] Indeed, this is a key question for all proponents of innovation-based economic fluctuations. It will be suggested here that these bursts of entrepreneurship actually do occur, but that they do so in response to opportunity explosions. Such bunching of opportunities occurs with the appearance of a new techno-economic paradigm, which defines a new and wide design, product and profit space that can inflame the imagination of potential innovators. In other words, the great clusters of talent come forth *after* the revolution is visible and *because* it is visible.

That raises two crucial questions. One is, if talents are always there to come forth, then why is change not continuous, why does it occur by revolutions? The other, derived from that, is the issue of the prime mover, or how do the few breakthroughs that initiate the revolution come together?

The favorable conditions for the next revolution are created when the potential of the previous one approaches exhaustion. The process involves a complex set of inclusion–exclusion mechanisms resulting from the nature of social adaptation to each paradigm. The full assimilation of a technological revolution and its techno-economic paradigm occurs when society has accepted its common sense, put in place the appropriate regulatory framework and other institutions and learned to gear the new potential to its ends. This leads to two conditions that favor compatible innovations and filter out incompatible ones.

On the one hand, the social and institutional environment has become highly conducive to the unfolding of any opportunity and possibility compatible with the paradigm. Externalities of all sorts are so overwhelmingly favorable to it that engineers, designers, managers, entrepreneurs and investors 'naturally' follow certain common principles as obvious good business. A thousand plas-

---

36. These qualitative aspects of growth are rarely included in the usual interpretations of 'long waves'.
37. Kuznets (1940) pp. 261–2.

tics followed the first breakthroughs in synthetic materials, wired houses could take on dozens of successive new electrical appliances, the agricultural revolution could combine the use of oil-driven machinery of increasing variety and specialization with any number of petrochemical pesticides and fertilizers. The same has occurred this time with computer games, with software packages, with the various generations of personal computers and then with 'dot com' services in the Internet. Once the path has been successfully signaled, growing bunches can join the bandwagon. And so it goes with each of the interrelated systems that conform a particular technological revolution and its associated 'common-sense' paradigm.

That is in fact the technological and business equivalent of what Kuhn defined as 'normal science'.[38] Once the valid trajectories for new products and processes as well as for their improvement are known, successive and successful innovations will follow. They will be compatible among themselves, they will interact smoothly, they will find the required supplies, qualified personnel and market channels and will encounter increasing social acceptance based on learning with the previous products.

On the other hand, these favorable conditions become a powerful *exclusion* mechanism for all possible innovations that are *incompatible* or not well geared to the existing framework. Attempts to introduce such innovations could be rejected by investors or customers or, as often turns out to be the case, could be successfully adapted in a minor way to the prevailing paradigm. Such adaptations can nevertheless lead to the growth of important industries that will become central in a future paradigm. For the moment, they grow restricted to whatever uses fit well in the existing fabric of the economy before their most important uses are even surmised. Railways were first developed to help get coal out of the mines; their real significance as the main means of transport of people and goods was difficult to even imagine in a world of canals, turnpikes and horses. Oil refining and the internal combustion engine developed within the steam-engine world of the third revolution, being used mainly for luxury automobiles. Semiconductors, in the form of transistors, served to stretch the market for radios and other basic appliances of the mass-production paradigm by making them portable, before anyone could possibly conceive of a microcomputer.

The most conspicuous exception to the exclusion mechanism is war-related expenditure. The application of political and military criteria, rather than economic logic, opens avenues of research, technology and production that could lead far from the reigning techno-economic paradigm, usually involving extravagant costs that could not be normally recovered in the market. When the war takes place in the maturity phase of the paradigm, these voluntaristic ex-

---

38.   Kuhn (1962:1970) pp. 10 and 24.

cursions into new technological territory could become a seedbed for the next technological revolution. The 1960s Space and Arms Race is, of course, the most notorious example of such expenditures.

Whatever their origin, the real possibilities of a radical innovation can be so difficult to envisage, before the appropriate paradigm is there, that even those who carry them out may grossly underestimate their potential. Edison thought the phonograph he invented in the 1870s would be useful for recording dying people's wills; in the 1950s the boss of IBM still thought a few computers would cover the world's total demand, and so on.[39] Those innovators who do see far into the future can have great difficulty in being understood by others, as happened to Alexander Graham Bell, with his still primitive telephone in a world of efficient telegraph.[40]

By contrast, when an innovation is within the natural trajectory[41] of the prevailing paradigm, then everybody – from engineers through investors to consumers – understands what the product is good for and can probably suggest what to improve. Even such minor and doubtfully useful products as the electric can-opener or the electric carving knife are thought worth designing, producing, buying and using in a world that is already accustomed to dozens of electrical appliances in the kitchen. The same happens with the successive applications of the general principles of the prevailing paradigm. In the case of continuous mass production, for example, after manufacturing had fully developed all its principles and refined its organizational practices, the task of applying the model to any other activity became straightforward. Mass tourism, of the 'assembly-line' type, moving people from airplane to bus, from bus to hotel and from hotel to bus, was obvious to conceive, easy to put into practice and readily accepted by consumers at the time.

Yet, trajectories are not eternal. The potential of a paradigm, no matter how powerful, will eventually be exhausted. Technological revolutions and paradigms have a life cycle of about half a century, which more or less follows the type of logistic curve characteristic of any innovation.

As shown in Figure 3.1, in phase one, after the big-bang, there comes a period of explosive growth and rapid innovation in the new industries. New products follow one another revealing the principles that define their further trajectory. Thus the paradigm is configured and its 'common sense' can guide the propagation of the revolution.

Phase two is one of fast diffusion, seeing the flourishing of the new industries, technology systems and infrastructures with intensive investment and

39. There are of course cases of foresight such as Diebold (1952), who from very early on wrote about the future potential of computers.
40. Mackay (1997).
41. Nelson and Winter (1977, pp. 36–76) used the expression 'natural trajectory' to refer to the path which appears to be naturally followed by successive innovations to a technology.

Figure 3.1   The life cycle of a technological revolution

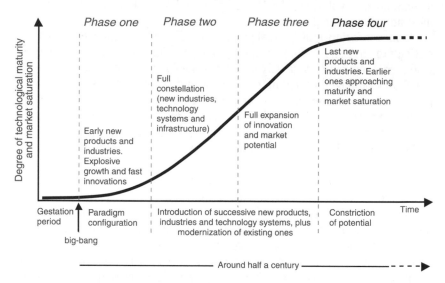

market growth. Fast growth continues in phase three with the full deployment of the paradigm across the productive structure.

Phase four is the encroachment of maturity. At a certain point, the potential of the revolution begins to confront limits. There are still new products being introduced, new industries being born and even whole technology systems, though they are fewer and less important. But the core industries that had served as the engines of growth begin to encounter market saturation and decreasing returns to technological innovation. This announces the approaching maturity of those industries and the gradual exhaustion of the dynamism of that whole revolution. [42]

When the potential of a paradigm begins to reach limits, when the space opened by a paradigm becomes constricted, productivity, growth and profits are seriously threatened. Thus the need and the effective demand appear for new solutions, for radical innovations, for stepping out of the well-trodden paths.[43] Yet, by this time, after decades of successful development under the established paradigm, the environment has over-adapted. Not only firms but

---

42.   The phenomenon is similar to Wolf's (1912) Law of diminishing returns to investment in incremental innovations to individual products and processes. It is also akin to the product life-cycle theory developed by Hirsch (1965 and 1967), Vernon (1966) and others.

43.   Kuznets (1953, p. 113) had already suggested something of this sort, when trying to understand Schumpeter's point about clustering: 'we may say that electricity did not become available sooner because it had to wait until the potentialities of steam power were exhausted by the economic system'.

also people and society as a whole have accepted and adopted the logic of the established paradigm as *the* 'common-sense' criterion. Yet the way forward along that route is now barred by impending exhaustion.

The core industries of the technological revolution, now maturing, are reaping the last benefits of economies of scale and are probably tied up with huge fixed investment.[44] They are also likely to be in a very strong position (oligopoly or near-monopoly), which gives them the means to seek effective solutions to break out of the trap. These probably include mergers, migration and some unorthodox practices that will be discussed in Chapter 8 in relation to financial capital. For the present purpose, however, the significant processes are those that lead to the next technological revolution. Of these, one of the most important is the willingness to try out truly radical innovations as improvements that will stretch the life cycle of established technologies or reduce the cost of peripheral activities.

Crude versions of the high pressure engine were tried in the early 1800s to increase the productivity of textile machinery; 'scientific management' of work organization, which is the core of mass production, was first developed by Taylor at the turn of the century to increase the productivity of moving steel products in the steel yards; automation was given trial runs by the automobile industry in the early 1960s, control instruments in their pre-digital forms went far in development in the process industries from early on, numerical control machine tools were introduced in shoe manufacturing and aerospace in the 1960s and 1970s. So, the introduction of some truly new technologies can be tied to revitalizing mature industries in trouble.

There can also be a readiness to introduce radical innovations that widen the range of technologies already in the market, as was the case with transistors in audio products that, by allowing portability, opened huge new markets from the late 1950s.

The more sectors and firms confront maturity and saturation, the more intense the various trial and error activities become. As in Kuhn's model of 'revolutionary science', breaking the trend and searching in new directions is fostered and facilitated by the confrontation of limits and crises in the established paradigm.[45] The specific obstacles encountered by each techno-economic paradigm as it is developed to its ultimate consequences, will serve as powerful guidelines in the search for the new set of technologies.[46] Yet, in order for a technological revolution to emerge, radical new paths have to be opened and crucial breakthroughs have to be made.

---

44. Soete (1985) made this point in support of the possibility of catching up for newcomers who are not bogged down by heavy investment in the old technologies. It was taken up again in Perez and Soete (1988).
45. Kuhn (1962) Ch. VII–VIII.
46. Freeman and Perez (1988), Table 3.1 Column 7, pp. 50–53.

Radical innovations can occur at any time, though their gestation period can be long. Due to the relative autonomy of the production of science and technology, there are always potential innovations in various fields waiting in the wings. At any point in time, therefore, the spaces of the scientifically conceivable and the technologically possible are much wider than those of the economically viable or the socially acceptable. Hence, many major technologies at various stages of development can already be in the economy, in minor or narrow uses. The real potential of some will become fully visible once they converge to form a revolution (others may have to wait many more decades or never be fully exploited). So, given the appropriate conditions of pressure and demand, a new constellation of radical technologies can gradually come together from already available developments.[47]

Thus, technology evolves by revolutions because the prevalence of a specific paradigm, with its vast interrelated opportunities, induces deep social adaptation to its characteristics. This creates powerful inclusion–exclusion mechanisms, which avoid radical departures from the prevailing paradigm until the huge potential of that revolution has been spent and approaches exhaustion.[48] It is then that entrepreneurial abilities of the sort that nurture radical innovations are more likely to be in demand. However, just as there is a high likelihood that the successful candidates to become the new paradigm in a particular science might be found by practitioners from another science, so the radical new departures in technology are likely to come from 'outsiders', from technologists or entrepreneurs who were not imbued with the previous paradigm, who may well be young and outside the powerful established firms like Carnegie or Alexander Graham Bell, Edison or Ford, Noyce, Steve Jobs or Bill Gates.

In order to understand how the gates break open so the excluded can enter in a throng, the role of financial capital needs to be examined.

---

47. Gerhard Mensch (1979) advanced a very similar hypothesis, suggesting that a 'stalemate in technology' was at the origin of recessions (such as the stagflation which began around the early 1970s). Unfortunately his method of proving this was counting and comparing the radical innovations made at various periods to identify clusters coinciding with recessions. So he took the actual date of first introduction as the full birth of an innovation. This made him open to criticism from Freeman et al. (1982) who showed that radical innovations can be scattered widely in time and that what really matters for significant growth impact is diffusion of combinations of innovations.

48. The identification of such an exclusion mechanism was one of the conditions demanded of long-wave proponents by Rosenberg and Frischtak (1984).

D.   The Role of Financial Capital in the Emergence of New Paradigms

In contrast with the scientific world, commercial innovation is made with profit in mind. Whether the innovator works in the laboratory of a big firm or in his/her garage, someone will have to see it as a possible source of huge profit and be willing to put up the required investment money to test the process, launch the product or expand production. It is here that, as Schumpeter says, the institution of credit, in one form or another, plays a crucial role.[49]

Someone's money has to be available to break the routine trajectories and make radical changes. The big established firms, as they face paradigm constriction, will probably put forward money to try stretching solutions to their own products and processes, which could involve, as they often do, minor uses of radical new technologies. They might also try to widen the range of known technologies and do research in new directions. All these activities can lead to completely new products and technologies (as was the case of Bell labs with the transistor, for example). Yet, they are not likely to fund true 'outsiders'.

It is here that the separation between financial and production capital has its most fruitful consequences. It is because there is available money looking for profit in the hands of non-producers that the new entrepreneurs can bring their ideas into commercial reality. It is here that the possibility of operating with borrowed money becomes a truly dynamic force. Financial capital will back the new entrepreneurs and it will be more likely to do so, in spite of the high risks, the more exhausted the possibilities are for investing in the accustomed directions.[50]

As the low-risk investment opportunities in the established paradigm begin to diminish, either in innovation or in market expansion, there is a growing mass of idle capital looking for profitable uses and willing to venture in new directions. Thus, the exhaustion of a paradigm brings with it *both* the need for radical entrepreneurship *and* the idle capital to take the high risks of trial and error.

Under these conditions several strands of innovation come together, some from the big firms overcoming obstacles, others from novel entrepreneurs with new ideas and others associated with the many underutilized or marginalized innovations that had been introduced before. These are likely to incorporate part of the vast pool of applicable knowledge waiting in the wings or to bring

---

49.   Schumpeter (1939:1982) Vol. 2, Ch. III, pp. 109–18.
50.   This was one of the main points made by Mensch (1979). His formulation came quite early in the debate, just as venture capital was being made available to Silicon Valley and other innovators.

forth new knowledge. Eventually, the necessary breakthroughs are made – or recognized – and brought together with other new or redefined technologies to conform the next technological revolution. From then on, financial capital is even more widely available for entrepreneurs to innovate exploiting the novel trajectories of the new paradigm. As will be discussed later (Chapters 9 and 13), new financial instruments are developed at this time to accommodate the peculiarities of the new products and their diffusion.

There is probably no easy way of testing whether during other times there are as many would-be entrepreneurs trying to get their innovations funded as there are at the end of the life cycle of a paradigm. What one can say with little risk of erring is that, once the design, product and profit space of a new paradigm is made visible, the imagination of a vast number of potential engineers, designers and entrepreneurs is fired to innovate within the new general trajectories. As available finance makes their projects possible and as their astounding successes makes the paradigm even more visible and attractive to a greater number of people, the ranks of those that feel the calling will invariably swell.[51]

So, the signs of exhaustion of the prevailing paradigm create the demand for profitable new innovation trajectories, pent-up supply of technological options begins to flourish, idle financial capital provides the fertilizer, the ensuing articulation of new technologies eventually leads to crucial breakthroughs, the new paradigm multiplies the supply of innovative entrepreneurs, their successes bring forth more financial capital and more entrepreneurs and so on.

Thus, there is certainly variability in entrepreneurship as Schumpeter held, but the origin of this variability is in the changing conditions and opportunities surrounding it. This is not to be understood as claiming that only 'outsiders' are real innovators. On the contrary, if it were mainly a question of numbers, over time one would probably find that the great majority of innovations are made inside existing firms, not only the minor and major modifications of technologies in use but also the introduction of many new products and processes. Even some of the crucial breakthroughs (such as the precursor of the integrated circuit in Bell Labs, already mentioned) can occur inside established firms or are acquired and introduced by them.

Nevertheless, long-standing firms are the main carriers of the prevailing paradigm. As discussed before, the paradigm is such a powerful guiding model that it becomes an inclusion–exclusion mechanism, strongly reinforced by social adaptation and gradual overadaptation. Therefore, in technological terms, one could say that the most powerful firms at the time of the exhaustion of a particular paradigm are likely to become the most conservative forces. Although some intelligent firms may make major innovations, their heavy investment in some of the now mature technologies makes them prefer to avoid

---

51.   Schumpeter's (1942) bandwagon effect.

truly revolutionary change, which might make their equipment and practices obsolete. Yet, ironically, since their productivity, market and profit growth rates are probably stagnating, their main hope for revitalization lies in radical change.

Thus, existing large firms are likely to be both agents and victims of paradigm closure. Breaking out of it is bound to demand the participation of outsiders. When they appear, idle financial capital allows them to manifest themselves fully and fructify.[52]

---

52. One could wonder if the reason why Soviet socialism was unable to make the innovations that would have helped it overcome paradigm constriction since the 1970s was not in part the lack of an institution capable of providing equivalent flexibility to facilitate change. See Gomulka (1990).

4. The Propagation of Paradigms: Times of Installation, Times of Deployment

In real life, the trajectory of a technological revolution is not as smooth and continuous as the stylized curve presented in Figure 3.1. The process of installation of each new techno-economic paradigm in society begins with a battle against the power of the old, which is ingrained in the established production structure and embedded in the socio-cultural environment and in the institutional framework. Only when that battle has been practically won can the paradigm really diffuse across the whole economy of the core nations and later across the world. As defined in Chapter 2, the complex processes of propagation of technological revolutions and techno-economic paradigms through the economy and society are the great surges that make development discontinuous.

In very broad terms, each surge goes through two periods of a very different nature, each lasting about three decades. As shown in Figure 4.1, the first half can be termed the *installation period*. It is the time when the new technologies irrupt in a maturing economy and advance like a bulldozer disrupting the established fabric and articulating new industrial networks, setting up new infrastructures and spreading new and superior ways of doing things. At the beginning of that period, the revolution is a small fact and a big promise; at the end, the new paradigm is a significant force, having overcome the resistance of the old paradigm and being ready to serve as propeller of widespread growth.

The second half is the *deployment period*, when the fabric of the whole economy is rewoven and reshaped by the modernizing power of the triumphant paradigm, which then becomes normal best practice, enabling the full unfolding of its wealth generating potential.

The *turning point* from Installation to Deployment is a crucial crossroads, usually a serious recession, involving a recomposition of the whole system, in particular of the regulatory context that enables the resumption of growth and the full fructification of the technological revolution. As will be discussed in Chapters 10 and 11, towards the end of the installation period, there is a phase of frantic investment in the new industries and the infrastructure, stimulated by a stock market boom that usually becomes a bubble that inevitably collapses in one way or another. As represented in Figure 4.1, this frenzy involves an untenable acceleration of the diffusion of the paradigm. The recession creates the conditions for institutional restructuring and for re-routing growth onto a sustainable path.

Figure 4.1   Two different periods in each great surge

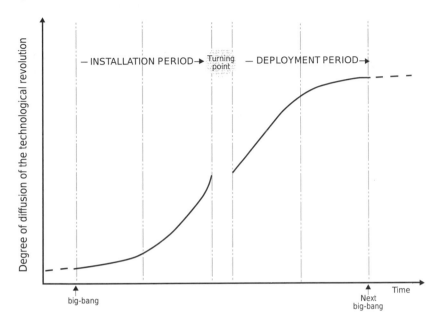

This chapter takes a broad look at the interrelated technological, economic and institutional changes involved in the process.

A.   Creative Destruction and Social Polarization

Schumpeter's notion of 'creative destruction' aptly portrays the effects of radical innovations. When the core products of a technological revolution start coming together, they inevitably clash with the established environment and the ingrained ways of doing things. Arkwright's water frame was a clear threat to hand spinners both in England and in India. The Liverpool–Manchester railway announced the demise of the horse-drawn carriage for long-distance passenger travel, affecting various occupations from innkeepers to veterinarians.[53] The Suez Canal practically eliminated sailing ships from the route to India, while, by cutting travel time from three months to one, it made obsolete the network of huge cargo depots in England, threatening the power of the big

---

53.   Contrary to what one would have expected, the *number* of horses actually *increased* for more than 50 years because of the need for horse transport *from* railway stations to ships, houses, inns and so on. This is similar to the unfulfilled expectations of a paperless office in the wake of the ICT revolution.

trading companies and opening opportunities for smaller ones.[54] Cheap Bessemer steel was a clear menace to wrought iron producers (see Figure 4.2). The
fast, powerful steel steamships with refrigerated cargo opened the world meat
and produce markets of the North to competition from the countries of the
southern hemisphere. The mass-produced automobile was a clear foreboding
of the displacement of steam-powered trains and horse-drawn carriages as the
main means of passenger travel.

Figure 4.2   *Steel displacing iron as the main engineering material from the*
             second to the third surge

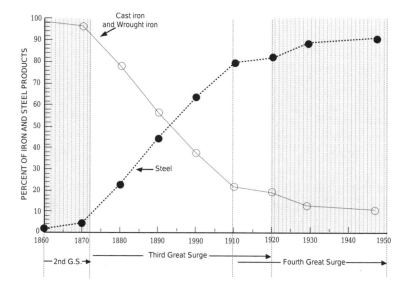

Source: Ayres (1989). Surge indications by the author.

Of course, these threats take time to become a reality and resistance from
those affected may prolong the transition. But the fact is that once a truly
superior technology is available, with higher productivity and clear growth
potential, the outcome in the medium term is practically inevitable. This is all
the more so, given that, as suggested above, these revolutionary developments
generally occur when the profitable investment opportunities attached to the
previous paradigm are nearly exhausted.

What these big-bangs inaugurate is a new direction and a powerful attractor
for investment. Successful radical innovations receive and promise extraordinary profits in a sluggish mature industrial landscape. The new products and

---

54.   Wells (1889:1893) p. 32.

infrastructures experience amazing rates of growth. Soon, the new generic technologies and the organizational innovations that accompany them allow other products and industries to join the bandwagon through modernization. This new lease of life is particularly welcome by the still powerful firms in the core industries of the previous revolution, which are likely to be facing serious paradigm constriction by this time. Railways changed to steel rails and improved steel engines as soon as they were able in the 1870s and 1880s. The maturing automobile industry in the 1970s and 1980s incorporated electronic chips in vehicles, computer-controlled production equipment and the flexible organization model, first developed by the Japanese. In general, it was the mature giant corporations in the 1960s and 1970s that tried to increase administrative control and white-collar productivity by trying out the early computers and minicomputers.

Thus, the irruption of the technological revolution also signals a cleavage in the fabric of the economy along several lines of tension:

- between the new industries and the mature ones;
- between the modern firms – whether new or upgraded by the new methods – and the firms that stay attached to the old ways;
- regionally, between the strongholds of the now old industries and the new spaces occupied or favored by the new industries;
- in capabilities, between those that are trained to participate in the new technologies and those whose skills become increasingly obsolete;
- in the working population, between those that work in the modern firms or live in the dynamic regions and those that remain in the stagnant ones and are threatened with unemployment or uncertain incomes;
- structurally, between the thriving new industries and the old regulatory system, and
- internationally, between the fortunes of those countries that ride the wave of the new technologies and those that are left behind.

These polarizing trends worsen as the firms wedded to the previous paradigm increasingly confront exhaustion, in the form of depleted innovative trajectories, diminishing profits and stagnation of productivity and markets, while the new ones display extraordinary profits, growing productivity and rapid market penetration. Depending on the institutional and macroeconomic framework of the particular period, the declining industries face either deflation or inflation in their constricted markets.[55] The regions where they predominate

---

55. Those economists who believe the economic sphere to be self-contained will probably cringe at the thought that the same fundamental cause can lead to deflation in a period of unrestrained markets, such as the 1870s and 1880s, and to inflation in economies shaped by oligopolies and state intervention such as those of the twentieth century.

will decline; their labor force will face growing unemployment. The contrast between the dynamism of modern firms and the sluggishness and deterioration of the laggards ends up translated into a polarized income distribution. Worse still, when changes are made that suit the flourishing of the new technologies, the situation for those not modernized becomes even more difficult. Figure 4.3 shows how *Business Week* saw the US economy gradually decoupling from the late 1980s to the mid-1990s, differentiating the 'high-tech' sector, belonging to the so-called information economy, from the rest.

Figure 4.3   Decoupling of the system: the differing performance of the 'high-tech' sector and the rest of the economy in the USA, 1989–96

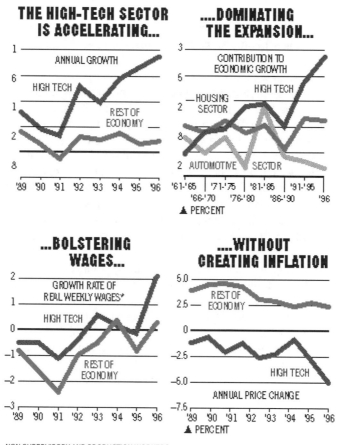

NON SUPERVISORY AND PRODUCTION WORKERS
DATA BUREAU OF ECONOMIC ANALYSIS, BUREAU OF LABOR STATISTICS BUSINESS WEEK ©BW

Source: Mandel (1997) Reprinted from the March 31, 1997 issue of *Business Week*, Latin American Edition, by special permission, copyright © 1997 by McGraw-Hill.

These diverging fortunes are reflected in the stock market where, as will be discussed in Part II, a bubble tends to develop around the new technology firms and their associated new infrastructure.

Gradually, as the rich and the successful get richer and more successful, while the poor or weak get poorer and weaker, the legitimacy of the established political regimes comes increasingly under question and pressures for reversing the centrifugal trends become stronger and clearer. Hence, the first two or three decades of creative destruction after the big-bang are increasingly turbulent and the benefits of growth are very unevenly distributed. As mentioned above, the protests that are likely to develop can take highly different specific forms, from the explosive social revolts of 1848 in the early days of industrialization in Europe to the transnationally organized demonstrations against globalization in Seattle, Genoa and elsewhere. The political responses also vary enormously, depending on the particular historical context. Similarly desperate social conditions facilitated Hitler's rise to power in Germany and inspired Roosevelt's New Deal in the United States in the 1930s.

B. Installation and Deployment Periods: Decoupling and Recoupling of the Economy and Institutions

To accommodate each technological revolution, then, many changes need to occur at different levels. In the first place, the new technologies will require the establishment of a whole network of interconnected services such as the specific infrastructure and the specialized suppliers, distribution channels, maintenance capabilities and others that provide the territorial externalities to facilitate diffusion. Without roads, gasoline stations and mechanics, people cannot use automobiles, yet only enough automobiles on the road will make it profitable to run a station or a garage. So diffusion occurs through intricate feedback loops.

Then, there is the cultural adaptation to the logic of the technologies involved. A vast learning process must take place among engineers, managers, sales and service people and obviously consumers, about the production and use of the new products. This not only supposes learning to drive a car, use a radio or a washing machine, but also an understanding of the direction of innovation, so that novelties can easily be adopted and accepted. The progression from desktop to laptop to palm top is gradually understood as the 'normal' sequence of change both in production and in consumption. Adaptation also involves acquiring the organizational notions embodied in the corresponding paradigm. These begin transforming the enterprise and gradually spread out to more and more non-economic activities.

Finally there is the wider set of institutional enablers, involving rules and regulations, specialized training and education, standards, supervisory bodies, financial innovations and so on. The traffic code and consumer credit for monthly payment of automobiles and electrical appliances were equally necessary for the growth of the respective markets of the fourth surge.

Of course this adaptation is not passive. The specific ways in which a society transforms the context to assimilate a technological potential will, in turn, shape the direction the technologies will take and the intensity of their diffusion. An extreme case of these variations was seen with the Western democracies and the Soviet system, which both adopted mass production, the automobile, Taylorism, mass electrification, synthetics and most of the other technologies associated with the fourth technological revolution, but the resulting lifestyles and production profiles were very different.

However similar or varied, the process of social assimilation of a technological revolution shapes and adapts the environment and the economy so that, when it is done, there is near complete coherence between all spheres of society. It becomes the reign of a particular paradigm to the point where it is believed to be universal common sense and becomes unconscious and invisible.

At this point, it is important to note that this process of deep adoption of a paradigm, though tending to inhibit truly revolutionary change outside the scope of the particular technological revolution being deployed, facilitates the full diffusion of each surge. By this inclusion–exclusion mechanism, the system permits reaping the full fruits of the vast investment made in infrastructure, equipment, technological development, training, experience and social learning associated with that paradigm. All this economic and social effort becomes a set of externalities for further investment and wealth creation based on market expansion and compatible innovations. Thus there is a virtuous cycle of self-reinforcement for the widest possible use and diffusion of the available potential. It is when signs of exhaustion appear that the terrain is ready for its replacement.

When the economy is shaken again by a powerful set of new opportunities with the emergence of the next technological revolution, society is still strongly wedded to the old paradigm and its institutional framework. The world of computers, flexible production and the Internet has a different logic and different requirements from those that facilitated the spread of the automobile, synthetic materials, mass production and the highway network. Suddenly, in relation to the new technologies, the old habits and regulations become obstacles, the old services and infrastructures are found wanting, the old organizations and institutions are inadequate. A new context must be created; a new 'common sense' must emerge and propagate.

This means that a painful and difficult process of learning and adaptation must take place, involving creative destruction across all spheres. It also explains why the fruits of that new growth potential cannot be fully reaped in the first decades, when the accommodation and mutual shaping of society and the new economy occur, pushed by the profit motive in spite of institutional inertia and human resistance.

Hence, increasing polarization and decoupling both inside the economy and between the new economy and the old social framework characterize the initial diffusion of a technological revolution. So, the installation period is one of tense coexistence of two paradigms, one declining and the other occupying more and more space on the ground, in the market and in the minds of people. These diverging processes are bound to shake, challenge and change the institutional environment. These spells of turbulent structural transformation have historically lasted from 20 to 30 years, beginning with the big-bang of the revolution and usually coming to an abrupt end with a crash or a panic. As will be discussed in Part II, the advent of a technological revolution attracts financial capital by enormously raising profit expectations, which eventually lead to asset inflation and a financial bubble that ends in collapse.

This financial frenzy is a powerful force in propagating the technological revolution, in particular its infrastructure, and enhancing – even exaggerating – the superiority of the new products, industries and generic technologies. The ostentation of success pushes the logic of the new paradigm to the fore and makes it into the contemporary ideal of vitality and dynamism. It also contributes to institutional change, at least concerning the 'destruction' half of creative destruction.

At the same time, as mentioned before, all this excitement divides society, widening the gap between rich and poor and making it less and less tenable in social terms. The economy also becomes unsustainable, due to the appearance of two growing imbalances. One is the mismatch between the profile of demand and that of potential supply. The very process by which intense investment was made possible by concentrating income at the upper end of the spectrum becomes an obstacle for the expansion of production of any particular product and for the attainment of full economies of scale. The other is the rift between paper values and real values. So the system is structurally unstable and cannot grow indefinitely along that path.

With the collapse comes recession – sometimes depression – bringing financial capital back to reality. This, together with mounting social pressure, creates the conditions for institutional restructuring. In this atmosphere of urgency many of the social innovations, which gradually emerged during the period of installation, are likely to be brought together with new regulation in the financial and other spheres, to create a favorable context for recoupling and full unfolding of the growth potential. This crucial recomposition happens at the *turning point* which leaves behind the turbulent times of installation and paradigm transition to enter the 'golden age' that can follow, depending on the institutional and social choices made.

The following two or three decades, characterized by the generalization of the now triumphant new paradigm, constitute the *deployment period*. When it arrives, the surge of development, based on the full diffusion of the higher levels of productivity, becomes clearly visible across the whole economy. The new common sense embraces all activities, from business, through regulation and education, to government. As a result, an era of general 'good feeling' sets in, characterized by increasing coherence within the economy. The institutional set-up that enables full deployment includes means of expanding demand to accommodate the enormous potential of increase in production, already installed. This can occur in many ways and has tended to involve the spreading of the benefits of growth to successive layers of the population.

By this time the original industries of the technological revolution have become the engines of growth for the whole economy and the country where they developed stands at the core of the world system. Together, these industries represent a significant portion of the national product of that core and the main firms have usually by then become the largest in that country and probably in the world. Figure 4.4 uses Chandler's data on the ten largest US corporations by asset size,[56] from 1917 to 1948, to illustrate the shift of power from the third to the fourth surge. Steel continues to be extremely important for the automobile and other products of the fourth technological revolution but the real investment boom is in the latter and they soon far outpace the steel companies and crowd them out from the top.

Furthermore, during the period of deployment, a process of internal catching up takes place within the economy. The dynamic pioneers of the revolution slow down, from sheer size, while those now joining the paradigm bandwagon accelerate. It is a question of relative weights and rates. The new industries that had developed explosively in the installation period are now giants growing at a 'normal' rhythm, whereas later industries, products and systems within the revolution – or those modernized or induced by it – may be reaching the same or faster rates of productivity increase and market growth. So employment rises steadily and, depending on the institutional framework set up, there can be a shared feeling of pending improvement in the general quality of life, very different from the centrifugal fortunes of the installation period.

Nevertheless, as these times of prosperity wear on, the potential of the technological revolution is gradually depleted. Technological maturity and saturation of markets begin to restrain the growth of productivity and production in the core industries, while widespread market and production experience shorten

---

56.   No attempt is made to turn current values to constant ones for two reasons. First, the object is to see relative proportions at each point in time and this can be done well in current values. Second, the period spanned is one of great economic turbulence including also the depression and a major war at each end, so all attempts at standardizing would be both heroic and doubtful.

Figure 4.4   *Oil and automobile industries replacing steel as engines of growth from the third to the fourth surge*

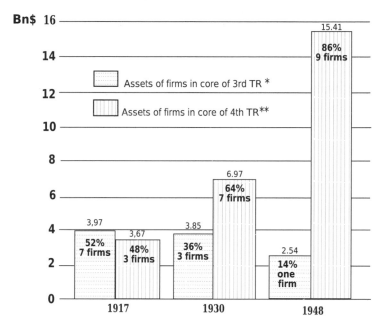

The top 10 US firms by asset size in 1917, 1930 and 1948, grouped by technological revolution (TR)

Notes: * Steel and meatpacking.

      ** Oil, automobiles, agricultural machinery, organic chemicals and electrical appliances.

Source: Our classification of data in Chandler (1990) pp. 639–57

the life cycles of the later products. This increasing constriction reduces the capacity of the system to fulfill its promises of constant progress, though the signs of an affluent society are still strong and visible. This, in turn, leads to labor and political unrest. Historically, some of the major strike waves have taken place towards the end of the deployment period.

A historian of the British Trade Union Movement refers to such final periods of the second and third surges thus:

> The late 1860s and early 1870s were, indeed, exciting years for the trade unions. The Trades Union Congress was effectively formed ... in 1868. The Amalgamated Society of Engineers[57] struck for the nine-hour day ... and the Yorkshire miners

---

57.   At that time the term 'Engineers' referred to qualified engine drivers, mainly in railways.

became particularly aggressive in their demand for wage increases ...[58]

Industrial conflict began to increase dramatically on the eve of the First World War ... Improved economic conditions encouraged trade unions to attempt to win back the wage reductions they had suffered in the previous decade ...[59]

So what begins promising a golden age ends up in economic trouble and intense political confrontation. Both will contribute to the coming together of the next technological revolution and the cycle will begin all over again in another unique and specific manner.

---

58.   Laybourn (1991) p. 53.
59.   Laybourn (1991) p.104. As Hobsbawm remarks, the *'belle époque'* in most of Europe incorporated the middle classes into prosperity but did not reach the working classes Hobsbawm (1987:1989) p. 55. This is consistent with the observation made in section 5F above that the whole of the third surge in Britain had some features of a maturity phase.

5. The Four Basic Phases of Each Surge of Development

This chapter will take a closer look at the installation and deployment periods, distinguishing two different phases in each. As shown in Figure 5.1, the period of installation of each techno-economic paradigm goes through an early *irruption phase*, just after the big-bang, when the new products and technologies, backed by financial capital, are showing their future potential and making powerful inroads in a world still basically shaped by the previous paradigm. The second half is the *frenzy phase*, when financial capital drives the intense build-up of the new infrastructure and the new technologies, so, in the end, the potential of the new paradigm is strongly installed in the economy and ready for full deployment. But this phase develops growing structural tensions in the system, which make it unsustainable. Thus, full deployment cannot be unleashed without overcoming such tensions. There is then a *turning point*, usually in the recession that follows the collapse of the financial bubble, when the required regulatory changes are made to facilitate and shape the period of deployment. This period begins with a *synergy phase*, when all conditions are favorable to production and to the full flourishing of the new paradigm, now clearly predominant. It ends with a *maturity phase*, when the last industries, products, technologies and improvements are introduced while signs of dwindling investment opportunities and stagnating markets appear in the main industries of the revolution.

The sequence being described involves profound changes that upset people's lives and views of the world, and motivate some to get deeply involved in taking advantage of the opportunities while others, who feel negatively affected, will strongly resist the changes. This will condition the political tone of each phase and define a climate or a 'feeling' of the times. The character of each of the phases is presented below in a stylized narrative, including such features. The narrative will concentrate on the core country or countries where the technological revolution originally develops (Britain in the first two, the USA in the last two and a mixed triple core in the third). In the next chapter, there will be a brief discussion of what happens in the peripheries and how it contributes to blur the regularities being depicted here.

Figure 5.1   Recurring phases of each great surge in the core countries

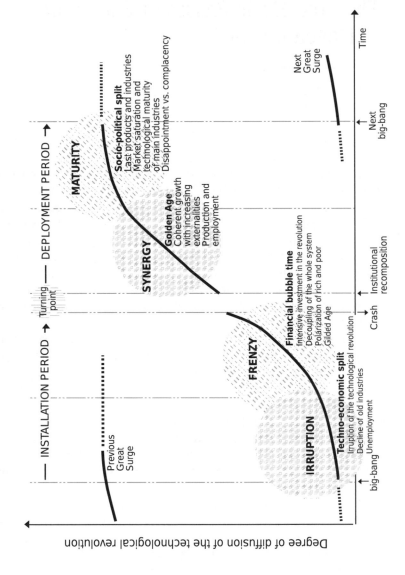

Before going on, it should be clear that what is being constructed is a heuristic device, not a straitjacket to force upon history. In spite of the regularities and the isomorphism the model claims to be identifying, there is full awareness that the subject matter rebels and refuses. It is full of exceptions and of huge independent events that constantly twist and break the proposed regularity. Wars, droughts and gold discoveries, are not included in the 'clean' model, nor are many other significant social and political occurrences. The sequence has been stripped of all those events not causally related to the absorption of technologies, which leads inevitably to streamlined simplifications that hardly ever occur as such. Nevertheless, this risky attempt at gleaning the strains of causal order underlying chaos, at structuring the unwieldy mass of historical events into a meaningful sequence, is still worthwhile. After this job is done – if it ever can be – the infinite enrichment of real life can be brought back in, but this time with the benefit of an organizing background, which highlights even more all the unique unexplained events.

With those caveats in mind, the reader can approach the stylized description that follows. The historical illustrations included are meant to bring forth images that can facilitate the transmission of the model to the reader. In the final section of this chapter, the approximate dates of the phases of each surge will be indicated (Figure 5.2) with a brief discussion of the differences, specificities and uniqueness involved in real history.

A.   The Irruption Phase: A Time for Technology

The irruption phase inaugurates the surge. It begins with the big-bang of the technological revolution amidst a world threatened with stagnation, as in Britain in the 1830s and 1870s or the USA in the 1970s. The new design, product and profit universe of possibilities inflames the imagination of young entrepreneurs, while the industries of the old paradigm are technologically mature, facing saturated markets and looking for solutions.

There is a mass of potential investment money in the market, still being generated by the firms of the old paradigm. These are looking for opportunities and migrating further and further away, together with industry or alone. Soon the amazing growth and productivity feats of the new industries attract investors and the new products, ever better and ever cheaper, begin massively to attract consumers and new competing entrepreneurs. The very intense activity of the new paradigm carriers contrasts more and more with the decline of the old industries. A techno-economic split takes place from then on, threatening the survival of the obsolete and creating the conditions that will force modernization.

The period is marked by increasing unemployment stemming from various sources, ranging from economic stagnation, through rationalization efforts, to technological replacement. The bulk of the old economy also exhibits perverse price behavior, either persistent deflation as in the 1870s and 1880s or runaway inflation as in the 1970s and 1980s, depending on the institutional framework conditioning the economy of the period.

Despair and impotence affect those losing out, be they workers who lost their jobs, industries with declining profits and markets or decision-makers in government whose policies no longer work. For those wedded to the old model and especially to the ideas and ideals of the established paradigm these are times of bewilderment. The world seems to be falling apart and the old behaviors and policies are impotent to save it. Meanwhile, the new entrepreneurs are gradually articulating the new ideas and successful behaviors into a new best-practice frontier that serves as the guiding model or techno-economic paradigm.

Divergence between the new and the old characterizes this phase. Inside political parties, both left and right, a cleavage takes place between the modernizers and the nostalgic, sometimes leading to divisions, recompositions or completely new movements. There is also a marked revival of the stock market, first in relation to the new industries and soon with new instruments and various forms of speculation.

B.   The Frenzy Phase: A Time for Finance

Frenzy is the later phase of the installation period. It is a time of new millionaires at one end and growing exclusion at the other, as in the 1880s to 1890s, the 1920s and the 1990s. In this phase, financial capital takes over; its immediate interests overrule the operation of the whole system. The paper economy decouples from the real economy, finance decouples from production while there is a growing rift between the forces in the economy and the regulatory framework, turned impotent.

It is the time of Veblen's scathing portrait of the 'leisure class',[60] a phase characterized by very strong centrifugal trends in society at large. A small but growing portion at the top is rich and getting richer while there is deterioration and growing outright poverty at the bottom. It is what Engels[61] depicted with pain and outrage in the 1840s. The same happens with regions within countries and across the world between nations. Some flourish, others wane. Massive migrations move with great hopes from the poor to the rich areas, sometimes welcome on arrival, at other times ruthlessly rejected.

---

60.   Veblen (1899).
61.   Engels (1845).

It is also a time of speculation, corruption and unashamed (even widely celebrated) love of wealth. Perhaps 'The Gilded Age' is the most appropriate label for this period, with its appearance of shining prosperity and its socially insensitive inside of base metal. The term is used by American historians to distinguish the period from the end of the Civil War to the turn of the century (which in the present model would roughly correspond to the installation period). It was taken from the 1873 novel of that title by Mark Twain and C.D. Warner[62] portraying what they saw as the corrupt money-mad alliance between financiers and politicians of their time.

Yet the frenzy phase is also one of intense exploration of all the possibilities opened up by the technological revolution. Through bold and diversified trial and error investment, the potential of the diffusing paradigm for creating new markets and for rejuvenating old industries is fully discovered and firmly installed in the economy and in the mental maps of investors. Hence the productivity explosion reaches more and more activities, inducing a process of restructuring in the productive sphere where the new or renewed prosper and the old wilt or die. The process is intensified by the availability of the new infrastructure, which at this time achieves enough coverage to provide clear externalities and promise more.

This is a phase of fierce 'free' competition, perhaps the closest to what the textbooks say, though gradually leading in the end, and depending on the general degree of concentration of the epoch, to oligopolies or cartels by industry.[63]

Individualism flourishes both in business and in political thinking, sometimes confronted by anti-technology or anti-system ideas or groups. But the turbulent nature of this period emerges from its fundamental tensions. The wealth that has grown and concentrated in relatively few hands is greater than can be absorbed by real investment. Much of this excess money is poured into furthering the technological revolution, especially its infrastructure (canal mania, railway mania, Internet mania), often leading to overinvestment that might not fulfill expectations. So at this time there tends to be a sort of gambling economy with asset inflation in the stock market,[64] looking like a miraculous multiplication of wealth. Confidence in the brilliance of financial geniuses grows and attempts at regulation are seen as hindering the way to a successful society.[65] This new capacity of money to make money attracts more

---

62. Twain and Warner (1873).
63. Here the accent is on what happens within the leading country or countries and on what they try to impose on others. Those countries that feel threatened by free competition in their effort to catch up or forge ahead often take strong protectionist measures at this time. Such was the case in the USA in the transition periods of the second and third surges, and also the case of many European countries, particularly Germany, in that of the third, when trying to develop in the face of British competition.
64. Toporowski (2000).
65. Galbraith (1990).

and more people to get a piece of the action; so late Frenzy is financial bubble time.

C.   The Turning Point: Rethinking and Rerouting Development

The notion of a 'turning point' is a conceptual device to represent the fundamental changes required to move the economy from a Frenzy mode, shaped by financial criteria, to a Synergy mode, solidly based on growing production capabilities. The turning point then is neither an event nor a phase; it is a process of contextual change. It can take any amount of time, from a few months to several years, it can be marked by clear-cut events such as the Bretton Woods meetings, enabling the orderly international Deployment of the fourth surge, or the repeal of the Corn Laws in Britain, facilitating the Synergy of the second. It could also be happening in the background with a series of changes that seem to come together as deployment begins.

The turning point has to do with the balance between individual and social interests within capitalism. It is the swing of the pendulum from the extreme individualism of Frenzy to giving greater attention to collective well being, usually through the regulatory intervention of the state and the active participation of other forms of civil society. What is held here is that this switch does not occur for ideological or voluntaristic reasons but as the result of the way in which the installation of a new paradigm takes place. The unsustainable structural tensions that build up in the economy and society, especially during Frenzy, must be overcome by a recomposition of the conditions for growth and development.

Such tensions are behind the bursting of the financial bubble that marks the end of Frenzy, of the serious recession that is likely to follow and of the political unrest and violent protests that erupt at these times.

The turning point is then a space for social rethinking and reconsidering. It is an important crossroads for socio-institutional decision making. It is the time when the leading actors in the economy, society and government recognize the excesses as well as the unsustainability of recent practices and trends, however wonderful they may have seemed until then. The imbalances between the profile of potential production and that of existing demand lead to premature market saturation and become an increasing obstacle to growth. The social unrest and the indignation at injustice that had begun to manifest themselves during Frenzy hang over decision makers. The hard conditions that were already present for the poor worsen considerably after the collapse and can turn to desperation and anger.

Conditions are ripe for regulation to be conceived, implemented and accepted, both to put order in financial markets and to move towards full market expansion and greater social cohesion. But nothing guarantees that decision makers will take this route. This is, in fact, a time of indetermination, when the particular *mode of growth* that will shape the world of the next two or three decades is defined. Its characteristics will be within the range made viable by the potential of the paradigm, but the choice within that wide range will depend on the interests, lucidity, relative power and effectiveness of the social forces participating in the process.

The resulting framework can enable a 'golden age' or only a modified, but still unstable version of the 'gilded age'.[66] It can establish institutions for increasing social cohesiveness, improving income distribution and general well-being or it can try to reinstate the 'selfish prosperity' of the frenzy phase, though more closely connected with real production and finding some means to expand demand.

This rerouting of the system is rarely clearly conceived as such. The structural tensions tend to be interpreted as temporary setbacks and it is when the usual recipes to confront them fail, that intuition finds new paths and alternative proposals are considered and applied. So, the mode of growth adopted will often be incomplete and far from perfect. Reform and further enrichment and consolidation of the institutional structure are likely to continue well into the deployment period. This is especially so if the recomposition has not been deep enough to overcome social tensions and structural instability.

D.   The Synergy Phase: A Time for Production

Synergy is the early half of the deployment period. This phase can be the true 'golden age'. It is likely to be the closest the system ever comes to convergence within the economy of the core countries of the system. It can be an era of good feeling and of pride in the structure of society, as in Victorian England after the Great Exhibition and America after the Second World War.

The basic externalities for the build-out of the revolution – especially the infrastructure – were installed during the frenzy phase, as well as the basic investment in the industries that serve as engines of growth. So conditions are there for dynamic expansion and economies of scale. Given the appropriate framework, growth will tend to be steady and harmonious while not necessar-

---

66.   After the panic of 1893, the power of the robber barons and the great financiers in the USA was so overwhelming that they practically took control of the economy. Even regulation set up to constrain them was either not applied or deviated in practice (Sobel 1965). So, the 'gilded age' practices continued at least until 1907. Nevertheless, American historians have labeled the period the 'Progressive Era', putting the accent on the political changes and on the many attempts at controlling the trusts and establishing greater social justice, as opposed to the preceding callousness.

ily as exuberant as in Frenzy. It can be felt across society and proceed at a healthy rhythm. Full employment – or the nearest thing to it, depending on the period – may become a realized possibility.

When a mode of growth based on social cohesiveness is established, moral principles are in force, ideas of confidence flourish and business is satisfied about its positive social role. It is a time of advance in labor laws and other measures for social protection of the weak, a time for income redistribution in one form or another, leading to enlarged consumption markets. It is above all the reign of the 'middle class'. Fast and easy millionaires are rare, though investment and work lead to persistent accumulation of wealth. *Production* is the key word in this phase.

The renovating power of the paradigm and the advantages of its new infra-structure – by now very much in place and rapidly achieving full coverage – are such that they naturally favor the spreading of the new higher levels of productivity and quality across all sectors of the economy, even the most tradi-tional. Therefore, even if the mode of growth continues to be shaped by the interests of financial capital, it is now more directly tied to production than in the frenzy phase and a certain amount of prosperity will trickle down to the various layers of society through diverse channels.[67]

The new paradigm now governs supreme; its logic permeates every activ-ity, from business to government and education. Technology is seen as a posi-tive force and, in the best of cases, so is finance, which now becomes the true support of production capital. It is a time of promise, work and hope. For many, the future looks bright.

E.   The Maturity Phase: A Time for Questioning Complacency

This is the twilight of the golden age, though it shines with false splendor. It is the drive to maturity of the paradigm and to the gradual saturation of markets. The last technology systems and the last products in each of them have very short life cycles, since accumulated experience leads to very rapid learning and saturation curves. Gradually the paradigm is taken to its ultimate conse-quences until it shows up its limitations (Jevons[68] worries about the exhaus-tion of cheap coal sources in the 1860s; the Meadows Report on the *Limits to*

---

67.   Sobel (1965) remarks that, in the first years of the twentieth century, there was significant industrial and agricultural prosperity in the USA, spurred by extraordinary crops, the de-mands of the Russo-Japanese war, increased gold production *and* rising wages 'so the worker had his share of the general prosperity and his purchases could keep the factories humming' (p. 186).

68.   In his book *The Coal Question*, Jevons (1866) warned about the end of low cost coal and the danger it could pose to economic growth.

Growth,[69] published in 1972, reinforces the environmental concerns voiced in the 1960s, with data about depletion of natural resources).

Yet, all the signs of prosperity and success are still around. Those who reaped the full benefits of the 'golden age' (or of the gilded one) continue to hold on to their belief in the virtues of the system and to proclaim eternal and unstoppable progress, in a complacent blindness, which could be called the 'Great Society syndrome'. But the unfulfilled promises had been piling up, while most people nurtured the expectation of personal and social advance. The result is an increasing socio-political split.

The acts of machine breaking (Luddism) of the 1810s or the protests against the Corn Laws and demands for universal suffrage that led to the 'Peterloo' massacre in Britain in 1819 are widely separated historically and ideologically from the violent protests of May 1968 in the main countries of continental Europe.[70] However, the dissatisfaction and frustration driving them both is of a fundamentally similar origin: capitalism had been making too many promises about social progress and not delivering enough, showing too much capacity for wealth creation and not distributing enough. The workers' protests seeking salary increases and greater security or participation, are sometimes echoed and magnified by those of others who may also feel defrauded by the system such as women, immigrants and any others who feel marginalized from the wealth of what some claim is a 'great society'. The young, who open their adult eyes to a world that proclaims it is all right, while to them it appears 'all wrong', stage their rebellions and romantic protests, together with artists and other non-conformists. The most recent case of the romanticism that tends to emerge in this phase is the 'hippie' movement in the USA and some aspects of May 1968 in Europe.

So this is a time when deep questions about the system are being asked in many quarters; the climate is favorable for politics and ideological confrontations to come to the fore. The social ferment can become intense and is sometimes quelled with social reforms.

Meanwhile, in the world of big business, markets are saturating and technologies maturing, therefore profits begin to feel the productivity constriction. Ways are being sought for propping them up, which often involve concentration through mergers or acquisitions, as well as export drives and migration of activities to less-saturated markets abroad. Their relative success makes firms amass even more money without profitable investment outlets. The search for

---

69. Meadows et al. (1972).
70. Historically major strike waves have concentrated in two periods: in the Installation Period, when they can be interpreted as anger about unemployment and extreme inequality; and in the maturity phase, when the source may be frustration of expectations (while feeling that there is enough wealth to fulfill promises). For statistics, dates and discussion of this issue, see Freeman and Louçã (2001) pp. 355–63.

technological solutions lifts the implicit ban on truly new technologies outside
the logic of the now exhausted paradigm. The stage is set for the decline of the
whole mode of growth and for the next technological revolution.

F.   Recurring Sequence; Parallel Phases

The preceding narrative is the stylized presentation of the model, where the
illustrations serve to make the basic connection with history. In this section the
sequence described will be located in real time. Beginning with the original
'Industrial Revolution', Figure 5.2 places the five great surges of development
in parallel strips, beginning with the big-bang of each. The tentative dates for
the phases are also indicated. The continuation of each of the strips, beyond
what seems like the 'end' of the surge, is a reminder that each revolution continues until its final exhaustion, while the next one is being installed.

As should be expected when models try to slice up living history, the pic-
tures fit some periods better than others and there are significant differences in
the length of the surges and of each of the phases. These vary from about eight
to fifteen or more years and there is no inherent reason for them – or for the
surges – to be of the same duration. The processes of diffusion and assimilation are taking place in different circumstances, with multiple unique intervening factors. The passages from one phase to another are more likely to be
continuous and invisible to contemporaries. With the exception of such events
as big crashes or great wars that mark significant changes in conditions, phases
naturally overlap. In fact, the choice of a particular year as the beginning or
end of a phase is a question of judgment and, in this case, is meant more as an
aid to clarify the concepts.

The places where overlaps have been pointed out in the figure are those that
do matter for the model, which are the ones that occur between successive
surges. For instance, the tentative dating of the third and fourth surges shows
that between 1908 and 1918, the maturity phase of the third surge and the
irruption phase of the fourth coincide. Something similar happens between
1971 and 1974 between the fourth and fifth surges. And, in the case of the
second and third surges, there is a gap between 1873 and 1875. This is to be
expected. As soon as there are signs of maturity of a technological revolution,
by a reduction of investment opportunities, conditions become favorable for
the next big-bang to emerge. That still leaves a very high element of random-
ness, and the presence of many other determinants, regarding the moment of
occurrence of the necessary breakthrough. Whether earlier or later, the overlap and coexistence of two technological revolutions – one rising, one declining – is what normally happens in the irruption phase, leading to the characteristic decoupling of the installation period.

Figure 5.2   Approximate dates of the installation and deployment periods of each great surge of development

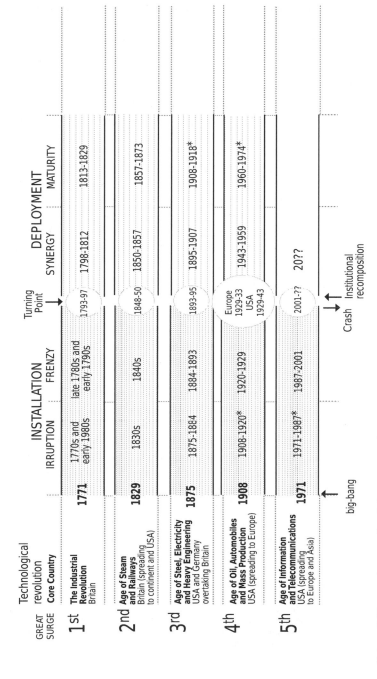

Note: * Observe phase overlaps between successive surges.

Yet, the particular case of the third surge merits special attention. As mentioned before, this is the surge during which Britain loses its leadership to the USA and Germany, which are forging ahead. The 30 years from the end of the American Civil War and the Franco-Prussian War to the *belle époque* synergy, around 1900, constitute a very special type of installation period, with an undeclared triple battle for the core. Britain, whose immense imperial power was underpinned by its control of the Gold Standard, of world finance and of transcontinental trade routes, did not consider investment in the new steel, electrical and chemical technologies a priority for wealth generation. She was the queen of the seas and the City was the financial center to the empire and to most other countries. So British financial capital installed the transcontinental infrastructures – rails, ships and telegraph – and supported the development of mining and agriculture across the world, while neglecting her own build-up of the key industries of the technological revolution. Meanwhile her two challengers – each recently unified – were becoming technologically and economically stronger and decidedly forging ahead. By the turn of the century, both the USA and Germany had overtaken Britain in steel production and were clearly ahead in the electrical industry. By 1907, Wall Street was in a position to challenge Lombard Street as the financial center of the world[71] and Germany felt strong enough to defy Britain's naval leadership.

Thus, the whole of the third surge in Britain had some of the flavor and the features of a maturity phase; whereas in the USA there were features of the implantation period throughout, including in the synergy phase.[72]

Some similarities can be found between the forging-ahead countries in the third surge and the recent experience of Japan in the fifth. This country made an early leap to the front ranks, going through a production-centered phase that had features of Synergy, while the USA as core of the system, was going through the maturity and irruption phases. After that, Japan had an earlier and extreme frenzy phase followed from 1990 by a protracted collapse and a long recession, while Frenzy in the core was only beginning. A subtle parallel can also be made between the sources of the decline of British technological leadership in the third surge and what happened to France in the second. French financial capital in the 1840s founded the gas companies of several European and African countries and Paris operated as the second financial center in the world, while its own potential for industrial power fell irreversibly behind.[73] All this suggests that, though the model emphasizes the sequence in the countries that act as the core of the revolution, there is wide scope for enriching it,

---

71.   Sobel (1965) p. 202.
72.   For the German case, see Berghahn (1994) pp. 1–42; for Britain, Cain and Hopkins (1993); for the USA, Wiebe (1967).
73.   Hobsbawm (1962) pp. 212–14.

through exploring the possible regularities in the cases of catching up, forging ahead and falling behind.[74] In Chapters 6 and 11 below, some additional elements will be brought into the picture.

Naturally, the fit of the impressionistic periodization proposed becomes fuzzier the further one goes back in time, because development of capitalist institutions and behaviors has only gradually encompassed whole countries, and even more slowly the whole world system. The 'Industrial Revolution', for instance, took place only in some parts of Britain and within a fundamentally pre-capitalist world. Besides, the synergy phase occurred during the Napoleonic Wars, while Maturity was the difficult aftermath. Financial capital in the first surge was rather a disconnected set of commercial and banking agents plus wealthy individuals willing to invest, quite different from the institutionalized financial world of the third surge and onwards. So, depth of development and penetration of the system have to be taken into account, together with outstanding conditioning events and factors, when assessing the operation of regularities.

In general, the model makes abstraction of the long-term trends that have brought the small capitalist world, concentrated in some corners of Britain and Europe at the end of the eighteenth century, to the gigantic global capitalist economy of the twenty-first century. The sheer change in dimensions produces qualitative differences that obviously cannot be ignored when doing the analysis of a concrete period. The claim is that there are basic causal chains that operate in any scale and that the long-term changes are achieved through discontinuous leaps of creative destruction, with processes of propagation of about half a century.

Hence, this effort at isomorphism and selective categorization is indeed a 'strong' stylization and purposely so. What are being identified are causal mechanisms that are in the nature of the system. This will become clearer when the above sequence is used as a framework in Part II, for analyzing the changing relationship between financial and production capital and the consequences that stem from it.

Before going into that, two important points will be briefly addressed. One is the difference between the present model and that of most 'long-wave' proponents. The other, connected with the first, has to do with the unequal spread and the uneven rhythm of propagation of each surge across the world. This will help understand why such recurrent sequences are not easy to identify in the economic data series. In fact if things were really as simple and straightforward as the previous narrative could be seen to imply, the process would be obvious to everyone and the debate about long waves, of one form or another, would have been solved in favor of them long ago.

---

74. The terms and the distinctions were introduced by Abramovitz (1986).

6. Uneven Development and Time-Lags in Diffusion

Since the end of the nineteenth century, there have been several attempts at recognizing and explaining the occurrence of 50–60-year cycles or long waves in economic growth, generally associated with the name of Nicolai Kondratiev, who in the 1920s made an attempt at systematically measuring the phenomenon.[75] The debates have continued ever since, both about their very existence and about their possible causes.[76] On the whole, long-wave interpretations have been bogged down by three conceptual shortcomings involving expectations that cannot be fulfilled:

1. the attempt to confine the analysis of the long wave within a narrowly defined economic system and to search for endogenous causes;
2. the insistence on finding regular up and downswings in GNP and other aggregate variables; and
3. the conviction that such cycles must be simultaneous worldwide phenomena.

The model being presented here avoids these three ideas considering them misleading directions of research.

The first point has already been addressed by suggesting that long waves are not economic cycles but a much wider systemic phenomenon where social and institutional factors play a key role by first resisting and then facilitating the unfolding of the potential of each technological revolution. This difference led to proposing the term 'great surges' to shift the focus from economic measurement to the qualitative understanding of the complex tensions and forces involved in the process of assimilating change.[77] Moreover, the very occurrence of those big revolutionary leaps in technology has been explained here

---

75. Kondratiev (1926).
76. For a discussion of the various positions in the long-wave debate and a reassessment of the data and the dating, see Van Duijn (1983). For collections of the main papers, with introductions about the different approaches, see Freeman (ed.) (1996) and Louçã and Reijnders (eds) (1999).
77. Freeman and Louçã (2001) also express dissatisfaction with the long-wave metaphor but continue to use the expression because it has become the established framework for the discussion of long-term structural change.

by a combination of economic pressures and s*ocial* 'overadaptation'. The other two points will be addressed below.

A.   Uneven and Differentiated Growth Patterns Rather than Long Swings in the Aggregate

In the present model there is no expectation of neat upswings and downswings in GNP or in any other economic aggregate. This coincides with Schumpeter's own view that aggregate figures conceal more than they reveal.[78] In fact, it is not even likely that the turbulent process by which new paradigms are assimilated should lead to regular up and down trends in the economy as a whole.

The phenomenon being analyzed can only express itself in the inner workings of the economy, where increasing differentiation takes place. Some new branches will be growing at astonishingly high rates while many others will be declining, stagnating or growing slowly. So the expectation would be of an internal loss of synchrony between new and old branches as a feature of the two or three decades of the installation period and of resynchronizing and synergy as the mark of the deployment period (especially in the early phase). After the irruption of the technological revolution, a divergence in trends would be observed between the modern or modernized activities and those that have become old and traditional. This divergence would slowly decrease during Frenzy, as more and more firms adopt the paradigm. Whether the sum of these differing trends comes out as a 'downswing' or not depends on the changing relative weights and relative growth rates.[79]

A further complication arises from the fact that most of the measuring attempts use money values (sometimes with constructed 'constant' values). This is not valid for a simple reason: the quantum jump in productivity brought about by a technological revolution leads during the period of installation to the coexistence of 'two moneys' operating under the guise of one. The change in the relative price structure is radical and centrifugal. Money buying electronics and telecommunications today does not have the same value as money buying furniture or automobiles, and the difference has been growing since the early 1970s. The price of steel, in the installation period of the third surge, came down because of immense increases in productivity, while that of iron was forced down by competition in the market.[80]

Rates of inflation or deflation during installation periods are chaotic and all

---

78.   Schumpeter (1939) Vol.1, pp. 43–4.
79.   Chris Freeman has often remarked that ignoring the weight–rate relationship is behind many of the arguments about whether technological revolutions or long waves really occur and whether they can be measured in the statistics.
80.   Wells (1889:1893) p. 43.

statistical efforts to construct constant money series, in spite of their sophistication, are doubtful to say the least. Volume, which is the usual way of attempting constancy, is an elusive measure in many cases. How do you compare one computer in the 1960s with one in the 1970s, in the 1980s and now? How do you measure the volume of communications? In the nineteenth century, was money paying for transport by railway comparable to that by horses? Was telegraph or telephone to India comparable to mail by ship? When costs are violently decreasing and qualities increasing and changing, comparability is quite impossible and aggregates are disparate. People living through the period of paradigm transition experience great uncertainty as to the 'right' price of things (including that of stocks, of course). It is only when the productivity levels become comparable across the economy, during the deployment period, that the single money economy returns, the relations between components of the relative cost structure become stable again and constant money indexes can be safely constructed (at least for a while).

It would in fact be justified to assert that long-term aggregate series, truly long-term ones, attempting to span two or three paradigms in terms of money, are senseless. Thus, the efforts at testing the long-wave hypothesis through manipulating such series are in a trap. Yet, the sort of disaggregated statistics that would be appropriate are rarely available.

Nevertheless, the present interpretation *does* expect a set of increasingly coherent trends in the synergy phase, with a certain level of stability of the relative productivities of groups of branches (some consistently higher, some consistently lower; most growing), which could appear as an 'upswing' in the aggregate.

But such clean figures do not last long in the unstable scene of the capitalist economy. By the maturity phase, there is a mixture of dynamic growth in the latecomer branches and sluggish growth in the now 'traditional' core industries of the paradigm (although this difference might not be obvious in profit terms, due to oligopolistic price behavior and market manipulation on the part of the larger firms). So, even what might look like peak overall growth already contains contradictory trends.

B.   Delayed Sequences in the Spread of Technologies Across the World

The third misleading direction of some long-wave proponents is to expect the phenomenon to coincide in time worldwide. Kondratiev himself tended to believe in this near synchronicity. After asserting that the long waves he had established, 'relative to the series most important in economic life, are international; and the timing of these cycles corresponds fairly well for European capitalist countries', he added that, though the USA may have peculiarities, 'we can venture ... that the same timing holds also for the United States'.[81]

What is held in this book is that, though major crises tend to be nearly simultaneous across industries and the world, because of instant transmission of the violent contraction of markets, most diffusion processes are sequential and lagged, taking the form of wider and wider ripples of propagation. As paradigms mature in the core countries, investment opportunities move further and further out, seeking comparative advantages, different conditions and possibilities for outstretching saturated markets.

It would seem that each paradigm spreads in ripple-like fashion,[82] both from sector to sector across the industrial structure and geographically inside each country and across the world.

In terms of its sectoral impact, each technological revolution begins with a group of core industries, usually involving some energy source or another all-pervasive input, a new infrastructure and a few main products and processes.[83] From there it spreads to the most closely connected industries forming a strongly interactive constellation with very high synergy and intensive feedback effects. This helps the generic elements of the paradigm become clear and well tested, facilitating their adoption by a wider circle of industries and activities. This, in turn, strengthens the externalities and lowers the cost of adoption for an ever-wider circle and, as institutional conditions become favorable, the whole fabric of the economy tends to adopt the paradigm following its general innovative trajectories until they are seen as the 'natural way' of doing things effectively, efficiently and profitably.

Geographically the process has been rather similar. The revolution has generally irrupted in the core country of the previously prevailing paradigm, and spreads there first and then propagates to the periphery. The third surge, however, is an example of how the processes of either forging ahead and vying for pre-eminence or catching up from behind, which are more likely to happen when riding the new technologies from the beginning, can modify the expected sequences. From the 1870s the technological revolution diffused much faster and went much deeper in the USA and Germany than in Britain, which was still the financial, commercial, political and military world leader. This created an uneasy triple core for several decades. Whichever the core, the installation period is very much marked by the polarization between the front-running

---

81.   Kondratiev (1926:1979) p. 535.
82.   There are problems with metaphors such as waves and ripples because they suggest an underlying steady state. For a discussion, see Freeman and Louçã (2001) Ch. 4.
83.   The actual process of gestation of each technological revolution goes far back before its big-bang, though for the present purposes the visible crystallization is the most important. For the complete sequence of the life cycle, see Freeman and Louçã (2001) p. 146.

country or countries, where the new industries are being deployed, and those areas of the world that are left out and falling behind.

During Synergy, investment concentrates in the core countries, where the whole economy is flourishing and opportunities across the complete industrial spectrum now abound. It is a time of aggressive exports from the core countries and the growth that occurs in the far peripheries is generally tied to the production of inputs for the requirements of that paradigm (cotton, metals, grain, meat, oil and so on).

When Maturity arrives, though, as technologies gradually lose dynamism and markets begin to stagnate, the surge of growth moves to the near periphery and later even to the farther peripheries that had had little chance of industrializing until then.

The process is akin to what Wells depicted in his diagram (Figure 6.1) in relation to single products in the USA economy (and referring to observations made in the years before 1972, which are those of Maturity).

Figure 6.1 The geographic outspreading of technologies as they mature

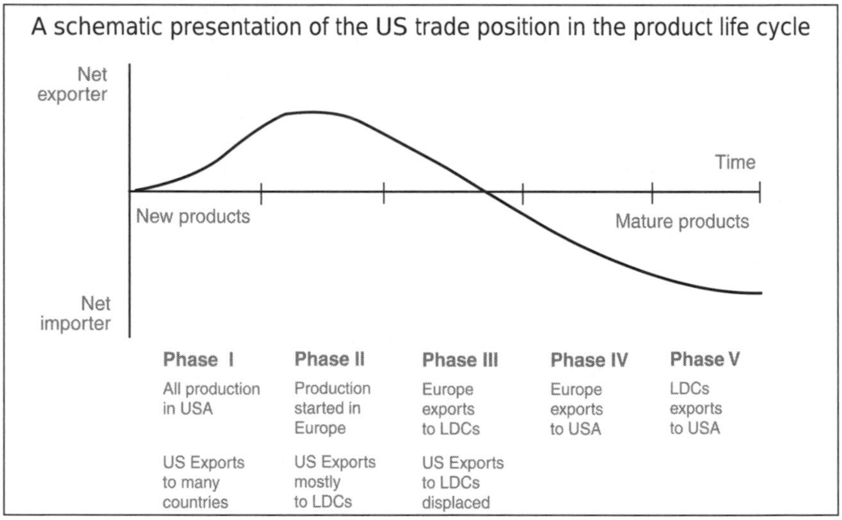
A schematic presentation of the US trade position in the product life cycle
Net exporter
Time
New products
Mature products
Net importer
Phase I
All production in USA
US Exports to many countries
Phase II
Production started in Europe
US Exports mostly to LDCs
Phase III
Europe exports to LDCs
US Exports to LDCs displaced
Phase IV
Europe exports to USA
Phase V
LDCs exports to USA

Source: Wells (ed.) (1972), p.15. Reprinted by permission of the publisher Copyright © 1972 by the President and Fellows of Harvard College.

This means that the 'miracles' of synergy, intensive growth and prosperity fueled by each technological revolution, move out to further and further rings, from the areas of maximum development towards the least developed. This could be considered as the last manifestations of widespread world convergence with the final stage of diffusion of that particular paradigm. Though divergence is, by then, beginning to differentiate the core, where the next technological revolution has irrupted, and its elements are being installed. This is soon to annul some of the advances achieved in the periphery.

The earlier manifestations of the phenomenon can be gleaned from the data relating to the first surge, based on the mechanization of cotton in Britain. During the installation period at the end of the eighteenth century, the bulk of cotton production was for home consumption. By 1805, during Synergy, a third of British cotton textiles went to export markets. By 1814 the proportion was approaching a half. As exports continued growing, they went further and further away. In 1820, in the maturity phase of the first surge, 61 per cent of British textiles went to Europe and the USA, and 39 per cent to Spanish America, China, the East Indies, Africa and others. By 1840, when British production had tripled, 71 per cent was already being sold to the periphery.[84] In the meantime, in Europe and the USA great efforts were being made to increase their manufacturing capacity by copying and developing British technology, often with the help of skilled immigrants.[85]

Yet, in the earlier surges, deployment to the periphery, from Maturity onwards, took two main forms: exports and communications. What spread to the periphery were some aspects of the consumption patterns and the infrastructures, such as canals, ports, railways, telegraph, telephone and other modernizing investments that, apart from their own profitability, increased markets for the mature industries of the core, by making medium- or long-distance commerce easier, faster and less costly. They also unwittingly prepared the territory for industrialization.

It is not the object of the present book to analyze what happens in the periphery with each successive technological revolution. For this reason, the discussion has concentrated on the phases of diffusion in the core countries. Great surges, however, are better described as consisting of six, rather than four phases. The first one would be gestation, or the time of preparation for irruption, which is of indefinite duration. Then would come the four being discussed here, which characterize diffusion in the core countries. Finally, the last phase would be the time of stretching and spreading to successive peripheries. In that final period, the last possibilities offered by the prevailing paradigm serve to propagate capitalism across the world. But those two later phases take place in parallel with the first two of the next technological revolution. So each great surge rolls out to the periphery supporting development with the last wealth-producing capacities of its mature technologies, meeting at the end its final defeat (or transformation) by the new paradigm.

The mass-production paradigm is the most recent example. The 1950s was a period of expansion in the USA, which served to pull the front-running

---

84.   Hobsbawm (1962) pp. 53 and 373.
85.   Landes (1969) Ch. 3.

European countries. By the 1960s the main dynamism moved towards Europe and Asia, producing the so-called 'miracles' in Germany, Italy and Japan. In the 1970s, it was Brazil, Taiwan and Korea that had taken over the baton. After the mid-1970s, some of the oil countries were able to attempt growth using the mature energy-intensive technologies in aluminum, petrochemicals and so on. But by then, the information revolution was already taking force in the USA and other core countries and the organizational revolution was catapulting Japan to the front ranks[86] while the stagflation of the irruption phase was entering the scene of the old advanced countries.[87] Soon globalization was defining international market survival. This meant that, in the developing countries, the mature technologies had to be modernized with the new paradigm. By the 1990s, in the casino prosperity of the frenzy phase in the North, joining global firms was made possible by the modernization of mature technologies.[88] This has very much been the case of the North of Mexico, further spurred by the North American Free Trade Association (NAFTA) between the United States, Canada and Mexico, which attracted competitive investment from Japan and Europe to take advantage of Mexican conditions plus easy access to the US market.[89]

Another phenomenon worth analyzing in this respect is the case of peripheral countries leaping ahead and catching up in development during the period of installation in the core, such as Argentina in the 1880s and the 'Asian Tigers' in the 1980s and 1990s. These instances will be discussed in Chapter 10, in relation to the behavior of financial capital in the frenzy phase.

It is important to note, however, that the current surge is likely to be world-wide in character in every phase. Since a key feature of the current Information Age is the establishment of a globalized economy, the spreading of both production and trade networks across core and peripheral countries began from

---

86.   The fact that the main organizational concepts (such as networks, enriched tasks, flexibility, adaptability and so on), which came together with information technology to conform the presently diffusing paradigm, were developed by the Japanese within the old mass-production technologies is an interesting phenomenon to analyze. A possible explanation lies in the peculiar factor endowment of Japan when catching up using a materials-intensive paradigm (no raw materials, plenty of cheap labor, long-distance to export markets), which stimulated innovation to overcome the limits and use the advantages in a different direction from the USA. See Womack et al. (1990).

87.   No such process of relocation and rejuvenation to overcome internal decline and decay was part of the functioning of the overcentralized Soviet system and this lack may have been an important part of the causal chain that led to its collapse.

88.   Perez (2001).

89.   It is worth noting that outspreading to the periphery will not happen automatically or evenly. Much will depend upon intelligent policies for attracting the technologies and for absorbing them. Whether success in this will actually lead to a leap in development is likely to depend upon the ability of each particular country to use each advance as a platform to innovate and to take advantage of successive windows of opportunity. See Perez (2001).

the early installation period. This feature is likely to distinguish this surge from all previous ones in terms of rhythm of propagation to non-core areas.

So again, and not surprisingly, nothing in the capitalist system is clear and simple. What the model suggests is that the overlapping surges will make the analysis of each period very fuzzy, with some countries experiencing late miracles of synergy with one paradigm while others are already going through the turbulence and tensions provoked by the next technological revolution.

PART II

Technological Revolutions
and the Changing Behavior
of Financial Capital

7. Financial Capital and Production Capital

A. Different Functions; Different Criteria

The time has come to make explicit the definitions of finance and production capital, which have been implicit in the previous discussion. Neither refers to the actual capital (which is both paper and real at the same time), but rather to the agents and their purposes. In both cases, the term 'capital' is used here to embody the *motives and criteria* that lead certain people to perform – or hire others to perform – a particular function in the process of wealth creation within the capitalist system.[90]

Thus, *financial capital* represents the criteria and behavior of those agents who possess wealth in the form of money or other paper assets. In that condition, they will perform those actions that, in their understanding, are most likely to increase that wealth. In the process, they may acquire deposits, stocks, bonds, oil futures, derivatives, diamonds or whatever. They may receive interest, dividends or capital gains, but in the end, by whatever means, their purpose remains tied to *having wealth in the form of money ('liquid' or quasi-liquid) and making it grow*. To achieve this purpose, they use the services of banks, brokers and other intermediaries who provide information, perform the contracts and in general embody the drive to make paper wealth grow. It is the behavior of these intermediaries *while fulfilling the function of making money from money* that can be observed and analyzed as the behavior of financial capital. In essence, financial capital serves as the agent for reallocating and redistributing wealth.

By contrast, the term 'production capital' embodies the motives and behaviors of those agents who generate *new* wealth by producing goods or performing services (including transport, trade and other enabling activities). By ana-

---

90.   This is somewhat akin to Schumpeter's distinction of the financial and the entrepreneurial function (1939, Vol. 1, Ch. III). In this case, however, the routine functions of production are being encompassed together with the innovative ones in the concept of production capital (approaching the more conventional distinction between money economy and real economy). Although recognizing the enormous importance of Schumpeter's distinction when referring to innovation and extraordinary profits, in this case, all agents of direct production, innovative or routinized, will be considered as production capital. The present distinction is therefore more in line with Veblen's (1904) view of the difference – and even opposition – between the 'captains of finance' and the 'engineers.'

lytical definition, these agents do this with borrowed money from financial capital and then share the generated wealth. If they are using their own money, they are then performing both functions. Their purpose as production capital is to produce in order to be able to produce more. They are essentially builders. Their objective is *to accumulate greater and greater profit-making capacity*, by growing through investment in innovation and expansion. They can be owner managers or employed managers and directors. Their power stems from the power of the specific firm and their personal wealth will depend on the success of their actions as producers.

The object here is to clearly distinguish between the actual process of wealth creation and the enabling mechanisms, such as finance, which influence its possibility and shape the ultimate distribution of its results. This functional distinction is essential to the nature of the capitalist system.[91]

Schumpeter defined capitalism as 'that form of private property economy in which innovations are carried out by means of borrowed money'.[92] So, the separation between the agents and their roles leads to complementary though very different behaviors.

Financial capital is mobile by nature while production capital is basically tied to concrete products, both by installed equipment with specific operational capabilities and by linkages in networks of suppliers, customers or distributors in particular geographic locations. Financial capital can successfully invest in a firm or a project without much knowledge of what it does or how it does it. Its main question is potential profitability (sometimes even just the *perception* others may have about it). For production capital, *knowledge* about product, process and markets is the very foundation of potential success. The knowledge can be scientific and technical expertise or managerial experience, it can be innovative talent or entrepreneurial drive, but it will always be about specific areas and only partly mobile. Both financial capital and production capital face risks that vary with circumstances from great to minimal. Yet, while financial capital can choose widely how to invest its money, avoiding or withdrawing from risks which it deems too high for the likely returns, most agents of production capital are in path-dependent situations and must find alternative actions within a limited range, often needing to lure financial capital or face failure. As far as truly new ventures are concerned, innovators may

---

91. Nevertheless, the distinction being made here, between financial and production capital, serves the purposes of the specific model being presented. Hilferding's (1910:1981) notion of finance capital, as the fusion of industrial and financial capital, is a category in a different theoretical framework. Another level of discourse, which is not attempted here, is the distinction between the changing forms of capital in the process of wealth creation and accumulation, especially of the role of money as motivation and instrument in its different forms and transformations. For such an in-depth analysis, see Wolfgang Drechsler (2002).
92. Schumpeter (1939) p. 223.

have brilliant ideas for which they are willing to take huge risks, devoting their whole lives to bringing their projects to reality, but if finance is not forthcoming they can do nothing.

All these distinctions lead to a fundamental difference in level of commitment. Financial capital is footloose by nature; production capital has roots in an area of competence and even in a geographic region. Financial capital will flee danger; production capital has to face every storm by holding fast, ducking down or innovating its way forward or sideways. Yet, though the notion of progress and innovation is associated with production capital – and rightly so – ironically when it comes to radical change, incumbent production capital can become conservative and then it is the role of financial capital (whether from family, banks or 'angels') to enable the rise of the new entrepreneurs.

B. The Changing Relationship Between Financial and Production Capital

According to the present interpretation, continuous technical change takes place within discontinuous surges, diffusing successive technological revolutions. The types and amounts of profit-making opportunities vary significantly along the life cycle of each technological revolution. Now is the time to analyze how the relationship between financial and production capital changes along the phases of each surge.

The same sequence that was described in Chapters 4 and 5, from the standpoint of technological change and its assimilation by the economic and social system, will now be viewed concentrating on the behavior of financial capital. Figure 7.1 summarizes the sequence.

The love affair of the irruption phase

In the period immediately following the big-bang that announces a technological revolution, financial capital begins a passionate relationship with the emerging production capital. The new revolutionary entrepreneurs soon outstrip the profit-making potential of all the established production sectors and there is a rush of financial capital towards them, readily developing new appropriate instruments whenever necessary. The agents of financial capital (brokers, banks and other financial institutions) are quick to adopt whatever innovations facilitate and widen their range of operations, in particular those associated with communications and transport.

Thus, the role financial capital plays in this period is to help spread the revolution. As discussed in Chapter 3, the functional separation between production and financial capital facilitates the movement of investment money

Figure 7.1   The recurring sequence in the relationship between financial capital (FK) and production capital (PK)

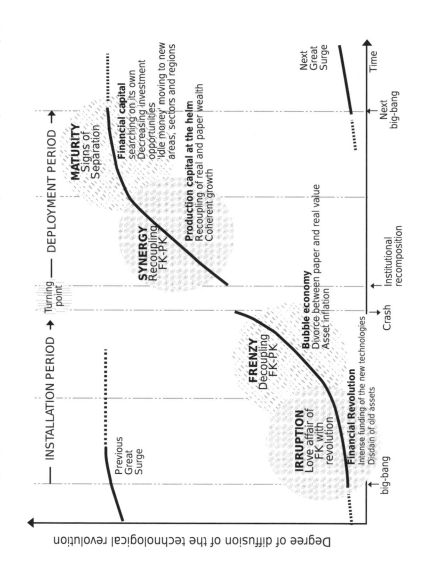

towards a new breed of technological entrepreneurs, who might not have had any financial connections before. This movement is all the more likely at this time, given that the revolution crystallizes partly because the opportunities for profitable investment with the now old paradigm have been approaching exhaustion. So there is 'idle money' in search of profitable use.

Old production capital is facing diminishing returns to innovation as well as market saturation. By comparison with the new sectors, its profits become uninteresting and financial capital tends to flee from them. This deepening techno-economic split was behind the 'stagflation' experienced by the advanced countries in the 1980s. Soon, however, it becomes clear to financial capital that no matter how high the rate of growth of the new sectors they are still only a small fraction of the economy. Yet the habit of obtaining high yields has caught on and become the normal level of expectations. In order to achieve the same high yield from all investments as from the successful new sectors, financial capital becomes highly 'innovative'. Imagination moves from real estate to paintings, from loans in far away countries to pyramid schemes, from hostile takeovers to derivatives or whatever.

Decoupling in the frenzy phase

After the growing confidence acquired in the previous phase, financial capital becomes convinced it can live and thrive on its own. Brilliant successes in a sort of gambling world make it believe itself capable of generating wealth by its own actions, almost like having invented magic rules for a new sort of economy. Production capital, including the revolutionary industries, becomes one more object of manipulation and speculation; the decoupling between financial and production capital is almost complete.

Nevertheless, this is a time of innovation for production capital; the new paradigm opens vast opportunities for new products, processes and services as well as for rejuvenating the old. It is also – and especially – the time of fast development of the infrastructure of the new paradigm, which facilitates a host of other related innovations. So during this period, financial capital generates a powerful magnet to attract investment into the new areas, hence accelerating the hold of the paradigm on what becomes the 'new economy'. Financial capital then acts as the agent of massive creative destruction.

The entrepreneurs of new firms as much as the management of the old (whether modernizing or not) are forced to do whatever is necessary to attract the players in the casino and then worry as much – or more – about the performance of their stock valuations as about their actual profits. Financial capital reigns arrogant and production capital has no alternative but to adapt to the new rules; some agents with glee, others with horror.

In a world of capital gains, real estate bubbles and foreign adventures with money, all notion of the real value of anything is lost. Uncontrollable asset inflation sets in while debt mounts at a reckless rhythm; much of it to enter the casino. Thus grows the vast disproportion between paper wealth and real wealth, between real profits or dividends and capital gains. But the illusion cannot last forever and these tensions are bound to end in collapse. This can happen in a series of partial crises in one market after another, in one huge crash or a combination of both; however it happens, the bubble needs to burst.

Collapse and recession: The turning point

The painful processes of implosion that mark the end of the frenzy phase bring paper values in line with real values and, through their consequences, are likely to bring reluctant financial capital back to reality. What follows can be a time of reckoning and acceptance, when regulation of various sorts is put in place or generalized, in particular that which puts order in the behavior of financial capital and tends to re-establish the proper connections with production capital. An adequate institutional readjustment is needed, all the more urgently given the difficult recessive situation that usually follows. The basic task of institutional recomposition involves creating the conditions for expanding markets and putting production capital in control. The length of the recession will depend on the social and political capacity to establish and channel the institutional changes that will restore confidence and will put the accent on real wealth creation.

The happy marriage of the synergy phase

Once the appropriate conditions have been created, the period of deployment begins. In this early phase, the recoupling of financial and production capital can lead to a happy and harmonious marriage, where production capital, based on the by now prevailing paradigm, is clearly recognized as the wealth-creating agent and financial capital as the facilitator. When this is effectively achieved, innovation and growth can take place across the whole productive spectrum and financial wealth may take its share in the profits in what is clearly a positive sum game. Less harmonious frameworks (as suggested before, rather than a golden age, a gilded age), still under the *aegis* of financial capital, can occur, maintaining some of the previous tensions. But the ferocious competition of the frenzy phase has by this time led production capital to form oligopolies and to begin favoring the expansion of markets. So whatever the institutional set-up, the renewed link between financial capital and actual production will increasingly involve real growth and real dividends.

Hence, the role of financial capital when the period of deployment begins is to strengthen production capital across the economy and to give support to the real growth process. This is the time when the theoretical notion of financial capital as an intermediary comes closer to being realized in practice.

Trouble again in maturity

In the late phase of deployment comes disappointment. Some of the erstwhile fastest-growing and highly profitable sectors of production capital begin to reach limits to growth in both productivity and markets. Technological outstretching and geographic migration are some of the routes followed by production capital, still supported by financial capital. The profits that continue to flow from this ailing part of the economy and from the still dynamic firms and sectors, find a decreasing spectrum of outlets for fruitful investment and become 'idle money'. Thus financial capital is under pressure from eager money growing faster than good opportunities and begins to look around for other profitable or exciting things. These include loans to distant places and radically new technologies. The first will later lead to debt crises; the second, to the next technological revolution.

C. Recurrent Phases and Financial Crises

The framework so far presented does not claim that all financial collapses are of the same nature or that they all follow a strict causal sequence connected with the diffusion of technological revolutions. What is suggested is that among the many mechanisms at play in any particular crisis, there are causal chains that have their origin in the role of technological life cycles in providing changing amounts and qualities of investment and profit opportunities. They may thus act as background causes for what appears to be happening merely in the financial sphere.

There is one type of collapse, though, which is directly connected with technological revolutions. It is the crash – or series of mini-crashes – that tends to close the casino bubble at the end of the frenzy phase, when the decoupling between financial and production capital is extreme, when paper values are mainly related to the asset inflation game and break loose from the expected dividends or other measures of actual performance. This is the crisis that most directly enters the causal links being discussed here and it is both its occurrence and its outcome – or even its possible absence – that can play a determining role in shaping the institutions of the world to come after it. At the same time, the specific way in which this crisis is overcome will strongly influence the directions taken by the potential of the paradigm during the ensuing deployment period.

Figure 7.2 locates the main financial crises of the two centuries being analyzed in the corresponding phases of each technological wave. The purpose is to help the reader identify the isomorphs, locate the approximate dates of the parallel phases being discussed, as well as to open the record for the analysis of the various crises.

Figure 7.2   Five successive surges, recurrent parallel periods and major financial crises

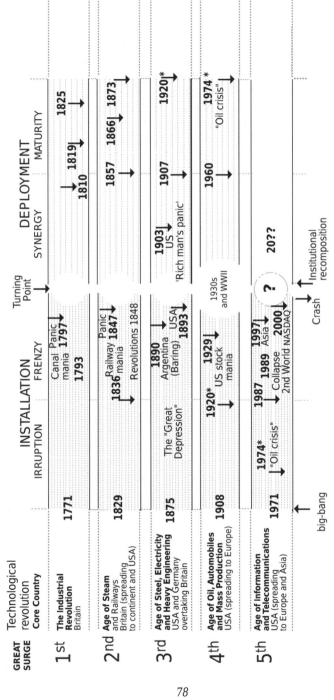

Note: * Phase overlaps between successive surges.

Source: Dates of crises are from Kindleberger (1978:1996), Appendix B.

The figure shows the truly major collapses located about two or three decades after the big-bang of each revolution. Apart from the relatively regular timing, it is interesting to note that these particular bubbles have tended to bear the name of the infrastructure of the corresponding revolution: canal mania, railway mania and now the Internet bubble, so that in these cases the 'main objects of speculation,' as defined in the Kindleberger model,[93] happen to be of a technological nature.

Other regularities are worth noting:

- collapses are less likely during Irruption and Synergy,[94] though frequent at the passage from the installation to the deployment period and vice versa;
- there is a bunching of crises in the turbulent economy of the frenzy phase and in the decelerating economy of the maturity phase; and
- the passage from the early to the late phase of each period is sometimes marked by a financial crisis.

There is a certain amount of circularity in all these observations, because the phases have been dated taking the occurrence of crises into account. It is in the nature of the model being presented that these features should roughly hold.

* * *

Having briefly defined the characteristics of the recurring sequence, the next chapters enter into a detailed analysis of the behavior of financial capital in each of the phases of propagation of the technological revolution. This will be done following the discussion about changing investment opportunities put forward in Part I. As up to now, a stylized narrative will be used.

The narrative will not begin in the irruption phase, with the big-bang of the technological revolution. Instead, it goes back a decade or so to begin with the description of the maturity phase, which is the time when the previous paradigm begins to confront the limits to its potential. This choice is fundamental because the model requires starting from the period of gestation of the next technological revolution. That is the time when the conditions are created for financial capital to play a role in sowing the seeds for its emergence. From then on, the narrative follows the changing performance of financial capital

---

93. Kindleberger (1978) pp. 6 and 38–41. Following Minsky, Kindleberger identifies the elements that combine for each of the big mania-type panics: an exogenous shock that sets off the mania, a specific object of speculation (commodities, real estate, bonds, stocks and so on) and a particular source of monetary expansion.
94. The crisis of 1903 only lasted about four months. It was called 'rich man's panic' because it hit mainly the biggest investors. Sobel (1965) pp. 981–2.

with each phase of diffusion of the paradigm. As far as possible, the arguments will be illustrated with examples from parallel phases of different surges.

8. Maturity: Financial Capital Planting the Seeds of Turbulence at the End of the Previous Surge

The preparation for the big-bang of each technological revolution occurs in the very contradictory context of the previous maturity phase, though some of the contributing technologies could have a long previous history.

Maturity is the end of the deployment period. As discussed before, it is a phase that combines signs of exhaustion in many of the original core industries of the prevailing paradigm, with very high growth rates in the last few new industries within that same paradigm. While the older industries find it difficult to increase productivity or markets, the success of the newer ones is marred by the rapidity with which they reach maturity and saturation. The accumulated experience and the already well-developed infrastructure and business practices create very favorable conditions for the fast diffusion of the last products and industries exploiting the established externalities. They are also routinized enough to make it relatively easy to begin spreading out geographically, reaching for peripheral markets or for lower-cost production.

Financial capital, which after the successful experience of the synergy phase had re-established the habit of profitable cooperation with production capital, is behind the swift flourishing of the last sectors and the last regions. It also accompanies the most powerful firms in their attempt to prop up their threatened profits. These firms have by now become huge and are facing increasing difficulty in finding fruitful investment for their mass of profit. This pushes them into buying up smaller competitors to increase market share, trying untested technologies for stretching their trajectories and venturing into distant markets or production locations.[95] Paradoxically, the more successful they are

---

95. There is a long-standing discussion among some of the long-wave proponents (see, for example, Mandel 1975, Shaikh 1992) about whether a decrease in profit rates is behind the onset of recessions. Proving or disproving this hypothesis would involve distinguishing between the total profits received, by whatever means, and those that come from 'real' productivity and market growth. It would also have to look at profit distribution between sectors and among firms. This is an extremely difficult task. According to the present interpretation, to detect a profit squeeze, one should look at the industries that had been serving as the engines of growth to detect signs of decreasing productivity growth, market stagnation and diminishing investment. Other telling signs would be the appearance of

in these attempts, the more profits accumulate and become idle capital desperately looking for alternative investment. So, financial capital begins to overflow and to search for other outlets. The behavior it exhibits at this time plants the seed of both the future debt crises and the emergence of the next technological revolution. What follows is a brief overview of the typical practices of financial capital during the maturity phase of each paradigm.

A.   'Power-Seeking' Behavior

After years of prosperous and successful synergy, financial capital continues supporting the strategies of production capital, especially that of the 'blue chip' sort. Its behavior in this period continues to be closely attached to that of its strongest production clients (often partners), who are likely to be among the first to reach the limits of the paradigm.

One of the early solutions that the most powerful firms find to confront the signs of exhaustion is increasing market control. This is achieved by various means: through mergers, as were the railroad 'amalgamations' of the 1860s in Britain,[96] by squeezing out of the market or buying up smaller competitors to create closed oligopolies or by acquiring firms in other sectors to build diversified giants, as with the conglomerate wave in the USA in the 1960s.[97]

This type of drive for monopoly power is a response to dwindling market growth. It should be distinguished from the concentration trends that will happen later, towards the end of the frenzy phase of the next paradigm. In that period, markets will be growing strongly in ferocious competition, so mergers and acquisitions seek, among other things, to reduce both the number of competitors and the intensity of price competition. By contrast, in the maturity phase being discussed now, economies of scale are sought to capture a larger share of saturated and diminishing markets.

Yet, the financial concentration of production capital within and across sectors and countries, which occurs in the twilight of the paradigm, turns out to be only a band-aid solution to the crunch, because it cannot overcome the productivity and profitability problems brought about by paradigm constriction.

It should be noted that the massive war expenditures of the First World War came to the rescue of investment opportunities and profits in the maturity phase of the third surge in the main advanced countries. Later, the Vietnam war, plus

---

new behaviors that indicate that the firms are seeking unorthodox ways to search for benefits. This would apply to the maturity phase but not to the mid-surge recessions after the major financial bubbles. Their signs and meaning will be discussed below, in Chapter 11.

96.   Dyos and Aldcroft (1969) p. 205.
97.   Blair (1972) Ch. 11.

the intensification of the Cold War and the Space Race, had a similar effect for the US economy during Maturity in the fourth surge. By contrast, the Napoleonic wars actually ended as the maturity phase was setting in, so they boosted growth during Synergy in the first surge in Britain and their end aggravated the market constriction of Maturity. In that case (as in many others), war also served to spread technology among the adversaries and thus create future peacetime competitors.[98] So, although wars have been explicitly excluded from the causal chains discussed in the model, their major impact on the economy and the different roles they can play, depending on the phase, have to be taken into account when analyzing specific historical periods.

B.   Redeployment: Investing Away from the Core Countries and Sectors

The mixture of market saturation, technological exhaustion and political unrest in their traditional strongholds, drives firms in mature industries to attempt to spread out from the established areas of investment, sectoral and geographic. Financial capital starts to support investment in marginalized sectors, sales to new distant clients, and the moving of production to cheaper locations. Among the early investment opportunities abroad are those related to the transport and telecommunications infrastructure that will accompany the market expansion push of the mature industries towards the periphery.

These explorations further and further away have the backing of all the learning and experience accumulated in the maturing process so they can usually be done relatively quickly, in comparison with the original diffusion. So, this too is only a temporary stretching of business possibilities rather than a permanent solution. Nevertheless, this outspreading of infrastructures and mature processes has been one of the forces diffusing capitalism throughout the world and widening its potential markets, at the same time as it is one of the mechanisms fueling the catching-up efforts of lagging countries. Additionally, successful redeployment also creates the conditions for financial capital to invest in other activities in the destination territories, by reducing the risks and increasing the knowledge about possible distant investment. So, both productive and financial capital tend to arrive in peripheral countries at the time when the diffusing revolution is in the last phase of its life cycle, moving the dynamics of the system outwards from its 'home bases'.

In the 1860s, in the maturity phase of the second surge, abundant and idle British capital poured into the USA as loans for the reconstruction after the

---

98.   Crouzet (1964).

civil war and especially for railways. During the decade before the First World War, towards the end of the third great surge, the core countries, by then including the USA and Germany next to Britain, staged a huge wave of worldwide investment, direct and indirect.

A sort of pulsating movement inward and outward between core and peripheral countries seems to characterize the availability of investment capital in the periphery. It is during Maturity and Frenzy, as will be seen later, that idle capital goes out searching for opportunities. In the other two phases it has plenty of profitable opportunities at home in the core countries: in Irruption with the burgeoning technological revolution; in Synergy staging the full deployment of the paradigm.

Table 8.1 represents the pulsating movements for the case of Britain between the second and the third surges. During the synergy and irruption phases, investment concentrates 'at home'. More than 70 per cent of capital formation during the Victorian Synergy in the 1850s and the *belle époque* at the turn of the century was done within the United Kingdom. The same happens in the irruption phase of the 1870s with investment in the industries of the technological revolution. By contrast, Maturity and Frenzy are times of capital migration. In the case of the UK, capital formation abroad reaches between 40 and nearly 53 per cent in those periods. Again, the character of these outflows is different. In Maturity it is tied to production, the search for markets and the outstretching of the mature paradigm; during Frenzy it is much more speculative and more strictly 'financial'.

Table 8.1   *Fluctuations in UK foreign investment (at current prices) as percentage of total net capital formation, 1855–1914*

Years	%	Phase and surge*
1855–1864	29.1	(Since 1851) Synergy second great surge
1865–1874	*40.1*	*Maturity second great surge*
1875–1884	28.9	Irruption third great surge
1885–1894	*51.2*	*Frenzy third great surge*
1895–1904	20.7	Synergy third great surge
1905–1914	*52.9*	*(After 1907) Maturity third great surge***

Notes: * Periods roughly classified by phases in the corresponding surges.
         ** In the USA, this is also the beginning of the irruption phase of the fourth surge, which makes it a powerful magnet for idle British financial capital.

Source: Data constructed by Landes (1969) p. 331, from Imlah and Deane (the emphases and the classification of phases are the author's).

The figures for the London Stock Exchange show similar trends. The proportion of foreign securities quoted in the City went from 32.8 per cent in 1840 at the end of Frenzy, down to 8 per cent in 1853 and up again to 37 per cent by 1873, at the end of the maturity phase of the second great surge. In the equivalent periods for the third great surge, the proportions were 54 per cent for 1893, 49 per cent for 1903 and 53 per cent for 1913.[99]

These overflows of investment to the peripheries can give the last push to catching-up processes in countries that are ready for it. In the cases of forging forward, self-propelled processes are more likely to be the rule. Such seems to have been the case of the British with the 'Industrial Revolution', of Germany in the third surge towards the end of the nineteenth century and of Japan in the 1960s and 1970s with the fifth paradigm. The case of the United States is more mixed. British capital was certainly crucial in helping the USA to catch up in the 1830s as well as in the 1860s and 1870s. Yet the impulse was doubtlessly self-fueled from the 1880s, when the real leap ahead took place. Nevertheless, if not from financial help, most cases of truly significant advances do benefit from knowledge and technology flows, which in one way or another come from the leading countries at the time.[100]

C.   Idle Money Leads to Bad Loans

Idle money does not stop growing in the maturity phase.[101] There is an inertial wealth-accumulating potential at the end of the technological revolution. It is made up of the monopoly power of the big established firms and the ease with which the last technologies and products can enter the market and expand. Yet these last investment opportunities are not enough to absorb available financial capital, mainly because their life cycles are intense and swift. Those last 'young' industries quickly catch up with the old ones, encountering together what Grübler has called the 'Kondratiev barrier'[102] of maturity and saturation.

---

99.   Michie (1987) Ch. 2, pp. 36–7 and 52. The figures represent declared paid-up capital but not real value. Many of the foreign securities included in the 1840 figures had already defaulted in the 1920s and 1930s and were of little value by then (ibid.). This could also be the case for the 1893 figures.

100. The classic argument in favor of such flows was put forward by List (1841) when the German states were trying to imitate the British industrial success.

101. Baran and Sweezy (1966) Ch. 3, identified what they called 'the tendency of surplus to rise,' which they interpreted at the time as an immanent law of the new monopoly capitalism. Yet, this phenomenon of masses of money looking for opportunities was already there much earlier in capitalism. It is estimated that in the 1830s and 1840s Lancashire, the land of the then mature cotton industry being modernized by the steam engine, provided a dominant share of the funds invested in the main early railways throughout Britain. See Dyos and Aldcroft (1969) p. 201.

102. Grübler (1990) p. 280.

So, as the maturity phase wears on, worthy borrowers with good projects dwindle and financial capital becomes less and less demanding when it comes to lending. Loans are granted to weaker and weaker creditors, perhaps with higher and higher risk premiums. In particular, lending to governments becomes popular among investors through various financial instruments. It is these periods of Maturity that witness the creation of *great volumes of sovereign debt* as well as agricultural, national government, consumer and other credit in inordinate proportions. It is in this phase that the future debt crises with their inevitable defaults are nurtured.

The funds that Britain lent to individual states of the USA in the 1820s to 1830s for building canals and turnpikes defaulted in the crash of 1837; those lent in the late 1860s and early 1870s, to the same or other states, for building railways defaulted in the crash of 1873.[103]

The debt crisis of the 1980s, which at the turn of the century was still weighing heavily upon the Third World, began growing with the development loans received since the 1960s and intensified with the petrodollar plethora of the late 1970s. Of course, the hunger for funds experienced in the poorer periphery makes it relatively easy for idle capital to find willing borrowers. Still, financiers can be pushy and government officials more than obliging (all the more so if there are juicy commissions involved). According to Kindleberger, several years before the rise in oil prices, 'multinational banks swollen with dollars ... tumbled over one another to uncover new foreign borrowers and practically forced money on the less developed countries'.[104]

The case of the Latin American countries is a striking illustration of the recurring cycle of loan fever at the end of a paradigm in the maturity phase, and of default during the process of paradigm shift in the installation period. Figure 8.1 organizes the data presented by Carlos Marichal[105] in his history of debt in the subcontinent, locating it in the framework being presented here.

As the figure indicates, the loans came regularly to Latin America in the maturity phase of each surge. Every 50 to 60 years, from the independence period through the 1960s and 1970s, plentiful credit poured into the periphery, as soon as opportunities in the core countries began to wane. The defaults came in the installation period, some sooner and some later depending on the unique circumstances. The most rapid were the defaults on the independence loans, which occurred almost immediately and led to a moratorium that in many cases lasted more than two or even three decades. The longest delay took place between the two world wars. The loan fever began around 1904 and continued to come to many countries after the First World War, during the

---

103. Galbraith (1990) pp. 61–6.
104. Kindleberger (1978) p. 19.
105. Marichal (1988).

Figure 8.1   The recurrence of loan fever and default: the Latin American case

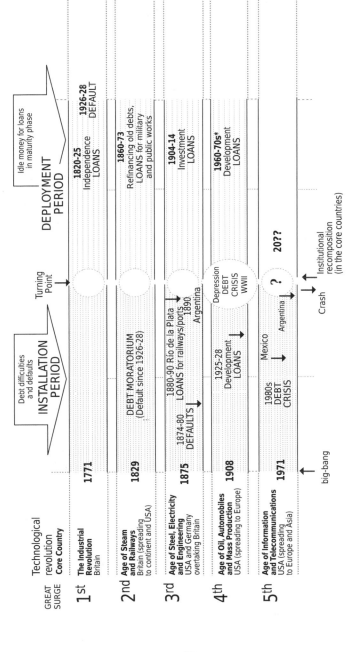

Note: * Observe phase overlaps between successive surges.

Source: Based on data from Marichal (1988).

euphoria of the frenzy phase in the 1920s only to go through a serious debt crisis during the great depression of the 1930s.

The case of the Rio de la Plata stocks and loans splurge, associated with the catching up of many countries in the southern hemisphere during the third great surge, was different. In that occasion, as with that of the Four Asian Tigers in the 1990s, the collapse came later, not as defaults, but as a financial crash.

D.   Other Questionable Practices

During the maturity phase, especially towards the end, as handlers of financial capital learn new ways to scramble for profits whenever and wherever they can get them, not only do they lower their standards when lending, they also indulge in unorthodox practices. In the 1960s there were damaging leads and lags in international payments as well as playing with currency exchange variations. In fact, there were several national currency 'collapses' influenced by such action (for example, Canada 1962, Italy 1963, Britain 1964, France 1968, USA 1973 and so on).[106] Tax avoidance by various means also plays a significant role. In the 1960s and 1970s there was a flurry of 'tax havens' set up abroad, which 30 years later were still hurting national budgets.

E.   Discovering the New Technologies

Yet there is one very important phenomenon which, together with the impulse given to the catching-up processes, is the positive result of the dispersion of financial capital in search of profitable opportunities in this twilight of the established paradigm. This phase harbors the embryonic development of the next technological revolution. Financial capital becomes ready to take risks in it, precisely because the previous trajectories had approached exhaustion.

As discussed before, the process is most likely to begin as stretching solutions to the limits of the paradigm inside the main industrial firms looking for new ways of increasing productivity in maturing products or processes. The forces helping this exploratory process are crucial for the emergence of the next technological revolution and for the articulation of a new paradigm. This is especially so given that the overadaptation of the environment to the established paradigm has been systematically excluding, underestimating or marginalizing the innovations that fall outside the established trajectories.

---

106.   Kindleberger (1978) p. 210.

When the signs of exhaustion appear in the space opened by the reigning paradigm as the 'normally' profitable innovation possibilities, financial capital becomes more and more willing and ready to take risks exploring the emerging new attractions. It thus lifts one of the limits for radical innovations outside the well-trodden paths and opens opportunities in the truly new technologies, some of which are likely to come together into the next technological revolution.

After the opening of the Suez Canal in 1869 there was wide availability of investment money for the rapid development of the steamship, of international telegraph lines and everything that contributed to swifter world trade. After Ford's first assembly line, there were funds available for further applications of mass-production methods in and out of the automobile industry as well as for the expansion of oil refining, roads and urban development and so on. From the mid-1960s, it became easier to find funding for developing electronics and computers.

So, this last phase in the life cycle of each paradigm is when the forces gather both for the impending pain of decline of the long-established industries, with all its social hardship, and for the emergence of another great surge of development.

9. Irruption: The Love Affair of Financial Capital with the Technological Revolution

A. Coexistence of Two Paradigms; Coexistence of Two Behaviors

The beginning of each great surge has been identified here with the irruption of a technological revolution and, for practical purposes, the birth has been dated at a single symbolic event which represents the big-bang of that potential universe of opportunities. But obviously such discontinuities can only be really identified with hindsight. The initial events occur in restricted spaces. As seen by most contemporaries, even if they often make front-page news, their multiple implications are visible mainly to an entrepreneurial minority. Elsewhere there is continuity, with perhaps an inkling of threat. So, in the present scheme the final phase of the life cycle of a paradigm is being treated separately from the initial phase of the next. This is only an analytical device. It cannot be overemphasized that, in real life, *everything that was described for the maturity phase continues in the background, sometimes even in an exacerbated manner, for practically the whole duration of the phase that will be discussed now.*[107] This is why, in the irruption phase, aggregate measures can be particularly deceptive. Trends in many economic variables, such as growth, productivity, employment, investment and profits are internally divergent.

This long period of coexistence of two paradigms is a bifurcation in the production structure, dividing the dynamic new from the obsolescent old. It is also a period of bifurcation in that the core countries begin experiencing real trouble, both economically and socially, while perhaps some of the catching-up countries are reaching their maximum splendor. The technological revolution in the core countries – for all its glitter – commands a very small minority share of the economy, which in its bulk is creaking from maturity and beginning to face unemployment and uncontrollable price behavior. In the new-comer countries, there is still ample space for using the mature paradigm and

---

107. As mentioned before, for the case of 1908–18, the two phases actually coincide.

there is no burden of old investment stopping those that are forging ahead from entering the new.[108]

Financial capital is still intensely engaged in the outspreading process of the old, but the appearance of the new territory is very quickly realized. There is suddenly a completely new situation in certain pockets of the economic landscape. Huge successes, incredible rates of growth and even more incredible profit margins become potent magnets for the still looming quantities of idle capital. What ensues can best be described as an infatuation, as a passionate love affair of financial capital with the technological revolution. Idle money rapidly engages in the enthusiastic backing of the new industries and their entrepreneurs; the financial and banking worlds jump to the quick adoption of modernizing innovations for their own operations.

B.　New 'Risk Capital' Instruments

By definition a technological revolution implies risk. Products are new, processes are being tested, markets are unknown, consumers are unaccustomed, and supplies are not guaranteed. Although radical breakthroughs often require relatively small amounts of capital, especially compared with the huge amounts required by most technologies reaching maturity and economies of scale, there are nonetheless many new entrepreneurs and many successive and parallel innovations all vying for success and looking for money. There is also the added risk of winners against losers, a risk that by the time a paradigm matures, about 40 or 50 years later, becomes infinitely lower due to the power which by then is accumulated in the hands of producers and the experience accumulated among the users.

So, the most salient characteristic of these times of revolutionary breakthroughs and multiple trial and error applications is also an innovative attitude in the creation of risk capital instruments on the part of financial capital.

It is well known that many of the initiating innovations of the microelectronics revolution were made in garages with personal funds and with the help of family and friends. The same happened in the Industrial Revolution in England. The first of the pioneers often have to break the new ground on their own. However, the expansion, the continuing momentum and the long series of radical innovations that follow do usually require and receive substantial support from the financial system (in whatever form it takes at the time).

The role of outside finance is often determined by the nature of the specific innovations involved. Discussing the conditions for the Industrial Revolution

---

108.　Soete (1985).

in Britain, Landes[109] has pointed out that the mechanization of the cotton industry did not require huge outlays of fixed capital. For this reason it was possible for family finance and previous accumulation in foreign trade (the famous 'nabobs') to fund the process. By contrast, the development of railways in the installation period of the second surge did need great quantities of investment from the beginning that were rarely available to a single firm. At that time the development of joint-stock companies concentrated capital, spread the risks and made the diffusion of that important innovation possible. Nevertheless, the stock market and the other elements of the financial system were still underdeveloped, so it was individual promoters who usually did the underwriting.[110]

It was during the third surge that investment banking and institutionalized financial capital became a powerful and indispensable part of the industrial system. Yet, the process took some time to develop. Carnegie's new Bessemer steel plant, the big-bang of that surge, was still funded by fellow capitalists as independent investors.[111] Three years later, in 1878, Edison was already getting financial backing for his early projects from young Morgan's bank. But what would become the driving power of the financial system in relation to industry was originally built upon railway stocks, government and foreign bonds, the agricultural processing business and the spread of trade, infrastructures and the exploitation of natural resources in the empire.[112] Only when industry became heavy (with electricity, chemistry and the like) and as capital hungry as infrastructure did financial capital really organize to fund it. By the end of the nineteenth century, in Germany and the USA, it was even taking control of it. As Harold Faulkner put it,

> The shift of power from the industrial to the finance capitalist came when the expansion of industry reached a size beyond the resources of individual entrepreneurs or banks, and when the movement for consolidation reached a stage where the services of a central investment house became necessary to handle the finance involved'.[113]

More recently, in the microelectronics, computers and software explosion, once the opportunities were made visible since the 1970s, the emergence of a plentiful supply of risk and venture capital in small quantities, for the intro-

---

109. Landes (1969) pp. 64–6 and 74–5.
110. Dyos and Aldcroft (1969) pp. 202–3.
111. In fact, the crash of 1873 hits it and the company doesn't go bankrupt because Carnegie had amassed so much personal wealth in steel and railways that he was able to buy out the partners and wait for better times, while many of his competitors disappeared. Carnegie (1920) pp. 189–92.
112. Sobel (1965) p. 127 and Kindleberger (1984) p. 205.
113. Faulkner (1951) p. 37.

duction of successive series of products and services, became a well-known feature of the period.

What this availability does is to allow the emergence of new entrepreneurs, a few of whom might later become the giants of their industry. It also opens a window of opportunity for catching-up countries and regions. As mentioned before, the outspreading of capital to distant places from the maturity phase incorporates them into the range of action of financial capital and makes various ventures possible, including those related to the new industries and products.

Yet not only private capital is conducive to the development of the revolutionary industries in the early days. The recent examples of state involvement in Japan in the 1960s and 1970s are fresh in everyone's memory,[114] and looking further back one finds that government provided capital for industrial catching up in Belgium in the 1840s and in Germany from the 1870s to the 1890s[115] while in the United States as much as 40 per cent of the funding for the railways was put up by the state governments.[116] In fact the catching-up periods of most European countries and the USA had strong backing from the state in various areas, particularly in acquisition of technology (modern machinery for reverse engineering), immigration of skilled personnel and technical education and training,[117] but also in decidedly protectionist policies.[118]

In studying latecomer catch-up, Gerschenkron[119] put financial innovations and their promotion by the state at the center of his theory and Jang-Sup Shin,[120] Ha-Joon Chang,[121] Peter Evans[122] and others provided further evidence from various countries, especially from the recent example of Korea.

C. Facilitating Production, Trade and Purchase of New Goods

Technological revolutions involve vast changes in the established patterns of production, transport, trade and consumption. Often the existing practices in each of those areas can be clumsy or inadequate for the flow of the new goods

---

114. Johnson (1982).
115. See Landes (1969) p. 157 and Trebilcock (1981) pp. 55–61.
116. Sobel (1965), p. 87.
117. Landes (1969), Chs. 3 and 4.
118. See Dore's (2000) analysis in his book *Stock Market Capitalism: Welfare Capitalism. Japan and Germany versus the Anglo-Saxons.*
119. Gerschenkron (1962).
120. Shin (1992).
121. Chang (1994 and 2002).
122. Evans (1995) proposes the notion of the 'developmental State', based on the experiences of Brazil, India and Korea.

or services. The rhythm of growth of the cotton industry and trade in the early days of the Industrial Revolution was aided by the provision of 90-day revolving and open credit.[123] In the beginning of the third surge, the swiftness of ocean travel with faster steamships and the Suez Canal made it possible for small entrepreneurs to trade in small quantities of goods for which much smaller, shorter-term, credit instruments were made available,[124] as happened some time later in that same surge when the German producers of small electric motors needed adequate – medium-sized, medium-term – export funding.

For consumers also, appropriate credit instruments are often needed. After the First World War, when the fourth technological revolution was diffusing with increasing force, hire-purchase credit systems were developed so that masses of home durable equipment, such as refrigerators, vacuum cleaners and automobiles could be paid for from monthly salaries. With the information revolution, since the early 1970s there has been an explosion of international plastic money, which is gradually becoming even more 'virtual' through Internet trade. This will be discussed further in Chapter 13.

So the development and diffusion of each technological revolution tends to stimulate innovations in finance and then to benefit from the impulse they provide.

D.   Funding the Rejuvenation of Old Core Branches

Some of the 'idle' money is in the hands of production capital in the – still powerful but declining – core branches of the previous revolution. The firms involved are by this time much fewer, after having gone through mergers and acquisitions, often acting as oligopolies. Their markets are still large but saturated and their production processes have generally hit a ceiling in terms of improvements and 'rationalization'. This puts them in the position of wounded giants looking for a cure to their ills, ready to experiment even with 'witchcraft', if necessary, and with the financial strength to pay for it.

The fact that each revolution provides generic technologies and new organizational principles capable of rejuvenating most of the existing industries fits the bill well. Even if in some cases those technologies and principles are in their primitive early versions, only partially tested and often very doubtful and costly, the old core firms are willing to take the risk and give them a chance in the hope of recovering the old dynamism. So, a growing part of the funds that

---

123. Landes (1969) p. 75. Later, 'by the 1820's and 1830's ... when the problem of disposing of the products of British factories had become more difficult that that of financing technological change, bank credit was a pillar of the industrial edifice' (ibid.).
124. Wells (1889:1893) p. 32.

might have been used for geographic redeployment or other forms of escape from declining sales and profit rates, are reinvested in the modernization of the home firms.

In the 1870s and 1880s, in the irruption phase of the third surge, business was slow for traditional industries and prices were falling. Steel proved technically superior to iron and it was cheaper. So transport companies moved to modernize. The railways swiftly shifted to steel and the merchant fleet was revitalized with ever more powerful innovations in steel ships and marine engines.[125]

The more recent case of the automobile industry is also noteworthy. As early as the late 1950s the US auto industry felt the productivity pinch and began touting 'automation' as the saving innovation. But by 1971 it was still facing serious problems in terms of cost pressure worsened by market saturation. This was compounded with growing environmental concerns and, after 1974, with the oil price rise. The answer to all of these was a combination of the Japanese production organization (just-in-time, total quality, redesign, structured networks of suppliers and so on), the incorporation of microelectronics, both in the cars themselves and in computer-controlled equipment for design and manufacture and, finally, globalization, supported by the early digital telecommunications.[126] These profound, difficult and costly transformations brought the industry away from the threat of commoditization of its product and to a complete revitalization in just over a decade.

One could also mention the case of the oil, energy and petrochemical industries, very hard hit by the oil price hike and environmental pressures. The introduction of digital control systems for optimizing production processes, saving energy and avoiding toxic emissions and waste was their initial answer.[127] In the case of chemicals, moving away from mass-produced commodities to computer-aided development of specialty chemicals was the following strategy.

All these rejuvenating investment projects could be funded either from their own accumulated profits without further profitable uses (one form of idle capital) or with the help of willing outside finance.

Thus the old core firms, because they need it and are able to afford it, become important test beds for many of the innovations of the technological revolution, in particular, those that are generic and can help modernize the rest of existing activities. They then unwittingly become agents in the construction, diffusion and installation of the new techno-economic paradigm.

---

125. Wells (1889:1893) p. 30.
126. Altshuler et al. (1984).
127. Walker (1986).

E.   Adoption of New Technologies by the Financial World

But the most demanding test bed of the technological revolution is the financial world itself, always ready to increase the speed of transactions and to expand their range. By becoming one of the most willing and daring clients for its products and services, financial capital propels each technological revolution in an indirect but extremely important way.

Among the technological, infrastructural and organizational innovations of each paradigm, there are those that accelerate the transport and transmission of goods and information. These can usually serve in turn as a source of innovation in money, banking and the financial sector itself. Perhaps because of the close links and early contact of financial agents with the new entrepreneurs, there is very rapid take-up of any form of communication that will facilitate the flow and /or increase the fluidity, speed or security of money, banking, credit, finance and so on.

Whether it was gold ingots or information that they had to relay, banks were among the early clients of the penny post, the railways and the telegraph on the national level in the early days of the second surge, as well as of international railways, telegraph and steamships, together with telephone, typewriter and calculator from the beginning of the third revolution. International stock markets were quickly set up as soon as they were made possible at that time.[128] The pace of adoption of information and telecommunications technologies by the banking and financial systems was equally breathtaking since the mid-1970s.[129] In each case, there has also been very rapid application of the advances in printing technologies and all security-enhancing innovations.

This early adoption accelerates the formation of larger and larger networks of banks and financial nets. Branch banks developed into national networks in England as soon as the railway and telegraph lines made it possible; the same occurred later worldwide when long-distance telegraph permitted British national bank networks to connect with international branches. Since the 1970s and 1980s, instant global money and finance movements as well as universal credit cards began giving shape to world-scale financial service super-markets and other globalized networks.[130] These organizational models appear earlier and prefigure what will gradually become the scale and the structure of the largest production and commercial enterprises under each new paradigm.

---

128. Michie (1987).
129. Strange (1998) pp. 23–9 reviews the range of such innovations since the 1970s. See also Barras (1986 and 1990).
130. German economist Karl Bücher had already commented towards the end of the nineteenth century that the financial system is the first of all activities to break through new geographical barriers and that the inevitable global economy would be led by the financial sector. Discussed in Reinert (2000).

F.   Expecting All Investment to be as Profitable

Towards the end of this phase, the intense love affair with the technological revolution leads the financial system astray. Experiencing the amazing growth and profit rates of the new industries and infrastructures, financial capital forgets its previous difficulties with idle money, becomes inebriated with these higher levels of profit and expects to get them from all investments.

It is true that the new industries and infrastructures continue to gather momentum in this period and are growing and diffusing at an amazing pace. But, the technological revolution, with all it mobilizes around it, is still a small – though rapidly growing – fraction of the existing economy. It obviously cannot absorb all the available investment money that more and more looks to it as its most secure source of good profits. Indeed, the more the new products develop and gain market acceptance, the less risky they appear and the more favorable all conditions become for the complete transformation of the relevant production and consumption patterns.

In the meantime, the exhaustion of the potential of the previous revolution is becoming clear. The swift take-up of the last products and the rapid diffusion of the old paradigm to the last corners of the productive structure and of the territory is, by now, making traditional activities less and less profitable and – ironically – increasingly risky for creditors. Moreover, the diffusion of the new paradigm in its technical and organizational dimensions to further and further branches is raising the expected levels of productivity in one activity after the other. It is also making much of the established equipment obsolete and often valueless.

This is a time of intensifying clash between the two paradigms. A time when whole industries can be wiped out. Figure 4.1 showed the rapid replacement of iron by steel. In the installation period of that same surge, chemical substitutes put many producers of natural materials out of business.

> Previous to 1872, nearly all the calicoes of the world were dyed or printed with a coloring principle extracted from the root known as madder; the cultivation and preparation of which involved the use of thousands of acres of land in Holland, Belgium, eastern France, Italy, and the Levant, and the employment of many hundreds of men, women, and children, and of large amounts of capital ... Today [1889], two or three chemical establishments in Germany and England, employing but few men and a comparatively small capital, manufacture from coal-tar, at a greatly reduced price, the same coloring principle; and the former great business of growing and preparing madder – with land, labor, and capital involved – is gradually becoming extinct ...[131]

---

131.   Wells (1889) pp. 54–5.

By the end of Irruption, the technological revolution is hugely successful, but there is not enough of it; the old industries that are not disappearing show disappointing profits and modernization can be a difficult and often protracted process with relatively high risks. The clearly favorable externalities and institutions that will propel the diffusion of the new paradigm are not yet there.

So, once again, the amount of money available to financial capital has grown larger than the set it recognizes as good opportunities. Since it has come to consider normal the huge gains from the successful new industries, it expects to get them from each and every investment and will not be satisfied with less. So rather than go back to funding unsophisticated production, it develops sophisticated instruments to make money out of money. The decoupling of financial capital from production capital has begun. The 'love affair' with the technological revolution makes the bulk of the real economy look boring and leads to divorce.

Halfway into the installation period, the tensions from this decoupling can lead to a crisis that may take the form of a stock market crash (see Figure 7.2 above), as in England in 1836 or France in 1882 or in the USA and most advanced world markets in 1920 and again in 1987.[132] Such an event can be understood as the first violent manifestation of the divergences between the growth of paper wealth and real wealth and the tensions between financial and production capital, which characterize this period. As such, it can serve to mark the passage from the early to the late phase of the installation period, that is, from Irruption to Frenzy.

But, with or without an intervening crisis, Frenzy arrives as the triumph of financial capital, which from then on will call the tune in the economy. It will obviously continue to back the strong growth of the new industries but it will now set its own conditions, impose its own criteria to production capital, new and old, and act as an autonomous force through its own strictly financial logic. The seeds of chaos will now be sown in the wind; the whirlwinds will come sooner or later.

---

132. For an in-depth analysis of 1987 as an event in a continuing process of asset inflation, see Toporowski (1993).

10. Frenzy: Self-Sufficient Financial Capital Governing the Casino[133]

A. Decoupling and Widening Social Gaps

Frenzy is the tumultuous period when financial capital takes off on its own. It is at the same time – and partly for the same reason – a time of extremely unbalanced prosperity and of polarization on all fronts. The bifurcation between the new and the old which begins with the irruption of the technological revolution now becomes more and more of a chasm dividing the successful firms, industries and countries from the lagging ones; the mismatch between the changing economy and the inertial social practices and institutions becomes increasingly tense. The decoupling of financial capital from production capital aggravates both phenomena. New and old producing firms must, from then on, bend their decisions to provide the high short-term gains required by the stock market. The general behavior of the economy is increasingly geared to favoring the multiplication of financial capital, which moves further and further away from its role as supporter of real wealth creation. Its outstanding successes become ironic harbingers of the chaos to come.

As may be recalled, this is also the time when two contradictory phenomena are taking place. On the one hand, there is the full flowering of the technological revolution itself, the installation of its infrastructure together with the clear establishment of the new paradigm as the set of technologies and organizational principles for modernizing all other activities. So there are parts of the economy in an increasing number of countries that are experiencing rapid growth and displaying their enormous potential for transformation and wealth creation, through applying the new paradigm, still with the support of financial capital. Though confronting regulatory and institutional obstacles and voids, the new industries and their largest firms, wherever they may be located, are already replacing the previous engines of growth (see Figure 4.4). This is the

---

133. The term 'Casino Capitalism' was the title given by Susan Strange (1986), following Keynes, to her book about financial behavior in the 1970s and 1980s, which in the present model would be the irruption phase. When the frenzy phase arrived, things got so much worse that she then used the title 'Mad Money' (Strange 1998). A more neutral term 'eras of finance' was proposed by Toporowski (2000).

prosperous side of the fence, the reason for singing the 'new economy' as the arrival of uninterrupted growth. All those benefitting from this flourishing of opportunities believe the world is going through a marvelous time.

On the other hand, the industries, countries, regions and firms that have not taken – or cannot take – the modernization path, are clearly deteriorating and entering a vicious spiral of low growth and lack of funds. That is the other side of the fence, where the grass is no longer growing and where the majority live. For them, these are terrible times; the world is falling apart and does not make any sense any more.

Frenzy is thus a time when the rich get richer and the poor get poorer. Financial capital enters this polarized stage as an accelerator of the centrifugal forces.

Ironically, the unappeased hunger for funds of the poor happens in the midst of excess capital, because idle money looking for profitable uses also grows in the frenzy phase, though for different reasons than in Maturity. The very success of the successful generates enormous wealth and concentrates it in a small proportion of the economic agents, who in turn want to multiply their wealth at the same vertiginous rate at which they made it. So, at these times of Frenzy, there is even more idle capital around and probably more pressure to make it profitable, because it is in the hands of the *nouveaux riches* in contrast with the maturity phase, when the excess money pursuing opportunities is in the coffers of the – by then – long-time powerful.

B.   Speculating with Old Wealth: Asset Inflation

Financial capital, after having introduced many innovations in support and application of the technological revolution, has learned to create new instruments and to overcome the old mental blocks.[134] So, when the imagination of financiers, the young and the veterans, is put to the task of making money from money, a whole range of purely financial, speculative instruments are invented – or reinvented – and applied to make more wealth out of existing wealth. Most means are legal, though not always legitimate; some are even illegal.

One area of new activity is still indirectly tied to production. It relates to taking control over operating firms, sometimes with very little capital and usually by building 'inverted pyramids' where a small base captures several layers of holdings. The leveraged buy-outs of the late 1980s and 1990s and some

---

134. For a review of the main financial innovations of the 1980s and 1990s and their consequences, see Strange (1998) pp. 29–41.

forms of mutual and hedge funds are the reinvention of age-old practices that resurface each time in periods such as this.[135]

According to *Newsweek*, the Long-Term Capital Fund, an exclusive hedge fund in the USA reserved only for the largest investors, which had to be rescued in 1998, 'started the year with about $4.7 billion of investors' capital, and it borrowed as much as $120 billion ... That's a mighty thin cushion if things go bad – which they did'.[136]

Derivatives, 'junk bonds' and other instruments serve as rakes to bring in capital for a wider than usual range of investment in productive assets and to make 'everybody into an investor', which is part of how the financial agents and the larger players increase their margins.

The other route for imagination is diverting finance from wealth creation and simply finding whatever objects of speculation are at hand. Investment in real estate, gold and other precious metals (varying in different historical periods), futures markets, art, 'pyramids' of loans, hedge funds and many other instruments of financial manipulation can serve the purposes of using the money that cannot find profitable use in productive activities.

Real estate is one of the preferred targets for speculation. In Tokyo, in the 1980s, real estate climbed to such absurd heights that the grounds of the Imperial Palace had the same nominal value as all the land in the state of California (or in all of Canada).[137] In the Chicago of the late 1880s it was clear that prices had reached equally impossible levels, however the *Chicago Tribune* of the time explained the phenomenon saying that 'people bought property at prices they knew perfectly well were fictitious ... [being sure] that some still greater fool could be depended on to take the property off their hands and leave them with a profit'.[138]

As the various assets go up in price, confidence grows that they will continue to do so. Gradually the notion of 'fundamentals', so dear to the financiers at other times, is set aside and price/earnings ratios augment out of all proportions. Ironically, this creates a favorable climate to bring back all sorts of firms to the stock market. New and old, revolutionary and mature, local and distant, solid and shaky, real and even imaginary firms and activities can now come to the gambling house, without fulfilling strict profitability criteria, as long as they can play the capital gains game. Naturally, the required practices had to become more sophisticated in the 1990s, compared to the outright fraudulent practices possible in the uninformed and unregulated world of the 1840s, 1880s or even 1920s. But the 'growth' of the market and the increase in vol-

135. Galbraith (1990) Ch. 2.
136. Sloan (1998).
137. Chancellor (1999) p. 302.
138. Reported in Kindleberger (1978:1996) p. 102.

ume of transactions and in number of actors involved attract even more money and more actors into the game.

Thus, with growing amounts of money available, the increases in nominal value are self-reinforcing, and the result is generalized 'asset inflation'. [139]

C.   Crises in the Weaker Nodes of the World Economy

The increasing stagnation in the lagging sectors and in what has now become the traditional economy, tied to the waning paradigm, increases the risk of default of those fragile debtors, especially the weaker countries that received the idle money in the previous Maturity and Irruption. (The reader may recall the Latin American case presented in Figure 8.1.)

As the instability increases so does the probability of bankruptcies and crises in the weaker banks or financial institutions. The problems can already appear in the late irruption phase. The 1980s provided examples of this in the Third World debt crisis and in the US Savings and Loan collapse.

As regards debtors in peripheral countries, many of the loans taken one or two decades earlier were meant for redeployment of the established paradigm. In other words, they propelled the last thin splash of the previous surge. Those were investments in mature technologies serving stagnant markets or in old infrastructures, probably still needed, but no longer very profitable. The economic benefits from these activities are insufficient to amortize debt and their levels of efficiency soon become inadequate to operate in markets increasingly governed by the superior productivity of the new technological revolution.

Several American states defaulted during the frenzy phases of the second and third surges in the nineteenth century. In the first case, in the 1830s they had built canals and turnpikes when Britain was already about to enter the first railway boom; in the second case, in the 1860s they built the railways with the old iron technologies when Bessemer steel ones were about to replace them. Gabriel Palma has amply documented the rise and fall of the Chilean mechanical engineering industries in the last quarter of the nineteenth century. The great advances related to manufacturing iron-based railways almost literally vanished, in spite of government efforts to protect them from imports. [140] In the 1930s depression, there were massive defaults of several countries on bonds and loans for building railways and ports or for mining and agricultural ex-

---

139. Toporowski (2000) provides a thorough analysis of the asset inflation phenomenon. For the present period, he suggests that the replenishment of the process by pension funds might make this phenomenon a more enduring feature of the system.
140. Palma (1978).

ports, when already the industries manufacturing mass-consumption products had become the new dynamic sectors.[141] As regards the present fifth surge, the debt crisis – which exploded in the 1980s and is far from overcome in the new century – is the tail end of the loans taken to set up mature mass-production industries or, worse still, to massively finance imports for luxury consumption without investing.[142] As a result, the economies of most debtor countries are stretched to their limits in a situation that makes the debts structurally unpayable in most cases.

As this reality hits home, debt–equity swaps, 'Brady' Bonds, privatizations and other 'takeover' innovations are reinvented each time.[143] That is how the US-owned United Fruit Co. was 'born' in Central America.[144] In the current surge, control over Latin American firms – both public and private – experienced a massive changeover. This apparent solution, by leading to increasing foreign control over the already battered wealth-generating capability of these economies, weakens them even further in their debt-paying capacity.

D. Windows of Opportunity for Catching Up

But not all peripheral investment remains as a failed development process. In periods of paradigm shift there is a window of opportunity for real catching up as well as for forging ahead,[145] Belgium, France and the USA caught up in the installation period of the second surge; Germany and the USA forged ahead in that of the third. Most of Europe, Japan and the Soviet Union, caught up in the fourth (though the latter fell dramatically behind with the fifth). The forging forward of Japan in the fifth, overtaking several more advanced countries, was clear until the collapse of its early casino bubble plunged it into a recession that lasted through the 1990s. Whether it will set up an appropriate socio-institutional framework to stay in the front ranks in the next decades is still to be seen.

There is, however, a particular type of catching up where the behavior of financial capital, from the maturity phase through the installation period, plays a particularly important part. There are areas of the world that happen to be in a position, for national, international, historical and geographic reasons, to make a catching-up leap with the new paradigm. Examples of this are Argen-

---

141. See Marichal (1988) for the Latin American countries and Latham (1981) for an overview of the developing world.
142. This is the point made by Palma and Marcel (1989) when analyzing the sources of the Latin American debt crises.
143. Galbraith (1990:1993) pp. 19–21.
144. Marichal (1988).
145. Perez and Soete (1988).

tina with the third great surge in the last quarter of the nineteenth century and the Asian Tigers a hundred years later, in the installation period of the fifth.

In the case of the Asian Tigers, paradigm constriction plus the geopolitical forces of the Cold War came together from the 1960s to facilitate a wave of foreign investment in the area, which happened to have the mass-production electronics industry as one of the most active. Both factors also opened the US markets to manufactured exports from those countries.[146] The success of Japan in forging ahead and in riding a high wave in the 1980s, when the Western economies were riddled with stagflation, created a sort of oasis for the neighboring countries to attempt catching up from behind. Financial capital, Japanese and Western, was more than willing to contribute to their emergence. And after the first successful period, when the glut of idle money, coming also from the Asian boom itself, began to pile up wanting high profits, foreign finance became available in that area for any purpose, from production, construction and exports to real estate and jewels. Whatever the immediate reasons for the bursting of the bubble in 1997, this overprovision of funds backed more by the booming atmosphere than by the credit-worthiness of the specific borrower had to come to a head.[147]

Something similar happened to Argentina before the Baring crisis in 1890. Steam-powered and refrigerated shipping technology made it possible for her to become a supplier of meat and wheat for Britain and the northern hemisphere. The investment boom that brought the English and the Germans to build railways and ports and to develop the huge expanses of 'pampas' created a situation very comparable to the recent Asian boom. The international stock market was awash with stocks and bonds to profit from the South American success story. The City of London even thought Argentina would be the next USA.[148] After the crash, it took the Argentinians nearly a decade to half get back on their feet, though the British Central Bank had bailed the Baring Brothers out right away.[149]

Though it is more complex, an argument could be made to interpret the case of the USA in the 1820s and 1830s as a phenomenon of the same kind. As in the other two cases, the United States, then a peripheral country, also had a booming economy with internal dynamics and intense foreign investment coming from Britain during the installation period of the second great surge. The crash of 1837 'engulfed the entire nation in a depression which would con-

---

146. South Korea took more advantage of the market opening than of foreign investment. Its state-led industrial policy favored Korean firms and excluded foreign investment from the dynamic sectors and from finance. See Chang (1996), Wade (1990) and Amsden (1990).
147. For in-depth analyses of the 1998 Asian collapse, see Wade (1998), McKinnon and Pill (1997) and Chang et al. (2001).
148. Sobel (1965) p. 132.
149. Kindleberger (1978) pp. 138–40, Marichal (1988) Ch. 6.

tinue for seven years,' while the British investors withdrew both credit and capital.[150]

In any case, Argentina in the 1890s was not alone in collapsing. It was accompanied, earlier or later, by Australia, South Africa, California, the West Indies, Egypt and the Ottoman Empire. Asia in the 1990s shared the stage with Mexico, the Russian meltdown, the Brazilian tremors and the Argentinian crisis at the turn of the century.

Latecomer economies are naturally more fragile than the already developed economies and thus probably more vulnerable to a sudden retrieval of funds. They can also be severely affected by the shrinking of markets. The polarization of the world economy also creates a widening gap between the rates of growth of luxury goods and staple goods markets. So, producers in the non-luxury segments, even in the new industries, can see their demand grow too slowly or be reduced. Thus, the weaker members of the successful few can be badly crushed when they get hit.[151]

E.   Over-Funding the Revolutionary Industries: Manias and Frantic Competition

The collapse of some of those adventures abroad sends financial capital back home scathed and ready to make another attempt at making high profits from the local hyperactive revolutionary industries and infrastructures. In the frenzied and confusing atmosphere of the casino economy, the core industries of the revolution are still the safest and most exciting game. They exercise a violent, magnetic attraction on financiers and on anyone who has any money to spare. There is enormous excitement and a feeling of prosperity at the top that captures the emotions and the confidence of the leaders and gradually of the general public.

The whole of the installation period could in a sense be understood as an exploratory time, when the engineers, the entrepreneurs, the consumers and the financiers test the various directions of development of the technological revolution, both in production and in the market. It is a huge trial and error process eventually to affect the whole of society. This is one of the sources of the general turbulence in the economies of this period. Markets experience irregular chaotic growth and intense investment can lead to overcapacity problems.

---

150. Sobel (1965) pp. 47–50.
151. Ernst (2001) has argued, for instance, that the 1997 crisis in the Asian Tigers had structural roots in the focusing on mass-production commodities and in the overcapacity in production facilities for standard chips.

In particular, towards the end of Frenzy, the financiers (and the investors who trust their money to them) seem to be convinced they have discovered the most profitable vein. They then indulge in the intense repetition of the same successful recipe, be it canals from any river to any river, as in the first revolution, or more and more dot.coms and telecommunications, as in the current fifth. This leads to an increase in momentum until the process turns into delirium, into irrational exuberance. It is to those years of late-Frenzy that the expression mania or bubble is properly applied in the present model.[152]

The canal mania leading to the panic of 1798, the railway mania panic of 1847 and the real estate[153] and stock market mania before the crash of 1929 were all such types of phenomena. 'Internet mania' was a name often given to the madness of the 1990s.

In relation to the canal mania of the 1790s, Mathias points out the general disorder and lack of coordination that prevailed in investment decisions. Canals were built 'with different widths and depths and much inefficient routing', while, with the railways, 50 years later, 'this was to be duplicated on an even larger scale, including the liability of over-investment when capital was cheap and the expectations of potential shareholders uncritically optimistic'.[154]

As Ransom comments, 'railway promotion [in the 1840s] was originally a matter for routes where the need was evident and the engineering practicable', then it spread to 'routes where demand was doubtful and the engineering full of problems'. Finally, 'with the public clamoring for railway shares, companies were being formed so that promoters might in due course unload their shares at a premium'.[155]

Dan Roberts in *The Financial Times* described telecommunications investment in the late 1990s as a 'trillion dollar scrap-heap'. According to his data, in 2001 it was estimated that only 1 to 2 per cent of the fiber optic cable buried under Europe and the United States had so far been turned on (or 'lit'). Court-appointed receivers of bankrupted telecommunications companies were recovering an average of less than 10 per cent of the original cost of building the networks when they tried to sell the assets.[156] The cemetery of 'dot.coms' after the NASDAQ collapse is another witness to the madness of late-Frenzy.

---

152. Neither the Tulip mania of the 1630s nor the South Sea Bubble of 1720 qualifies in this particular sense. In fact there are many collective psychology phenomena associated with speculative behavior, but not related to the assimilation of technological revolutions in a capitalist context. There are also many other financial crises in capitalism, following particular episodes of speculation, which have more immediate explanatory factors.
153. The advent of the automobile liberated the value of real estate from the constraints of urban centers and railway tracks. Any piece of territory could be connected by roads and made highly valuable.
154. Mathias (1969/1983) p. 105, quoted in Freeman and Louçã (2001) pp. 193–4.
155. Ransom (1990) p. 86, quoted in Freeman and Louçã (2001) p. 197.
156. Roberts (2001) p. 12.

Since the profits to be had are amazing, everybody – including widows and orphans – eventually becomes aware of the incredible possibilities. They gradually dare to enter what used to be alien territory, trying to get a piece of the action. What Bruce Nussbaum says in *Business Week* about the late 1990s could just as well have applied to the late 1920s:

> Confidence was exceptionally high, and Americans were comfortable taking more chances in the stock market. Academics told them that the risk premium for stocks long term was no higher than bonds. So investors accepted sky-high p-e's [price-earnings ratios], puffed-up bottom lines, and some strange business plans – because who really knew what was possible? It was a time of opportunity, a time to place bets. And they paid off ...[157]

That is the stuff 'manias' are made of. In the United States, as 1929 was approaching, ordinary people were so eager to invest in industry that it was they who were taking out the loans in order to buy the shares, while firms switched massively from taking loans from banks to issuing securities.[158] The result is the overcrowding of the bandwagon.

Such manias tend to attract not only local funds but also funds from abroad. In the 1790s, much wealth from France took refuge in Britain from the French Revolution and ended up as investment in the English canals.[159] The present surge has witnessed the siphoning out of the majority of the available capital of the rich in the poorer nations into the whirlpool of the stock market in the core countries. The process was enormously facilitated by digital telecommunications. Obviously this has increased the net outflow of funds from these countries – already heavy with debt payments – and has worsened economic decline and global income polarization.

This intense concentration of capital, local and international, furthering the infrastructure of the new economy can be seen as another of the dynamic roles played by financial capital in furthering technological advance. It is unwittingly an effective way to attract enough funds to make the significant investment necessary to install the basic infrastructure and put it in operation. It is wasteful and likely to overshoot; it can be painful for many, but it does the job of creating the fundamental externalities and facilitating intense social learning for the full unfolding of the revolution later on.

---

157. Nussbaum (2001) p. 35.
158. Hoover Report (1929) p. xii. The Report appeared a couple of months before the October collapse hailing this particular phenomenon as a feature of the dynamic new economy.
159. Kindleberger (1984) p. 60.

F.   Mergers and the Creation of Oligopolies

Whether a single-purpose mania develops or not, other types of problem are likely to follow from excess investment flowing into the core industries. If there is a time and a place in the evolution of capitalism when 'free competition' actually develops, it is during the installation period. Many, truly many, enter the fray; only a few are destined to become the giants of each of the new industries. But, as late-Frenzy is reached, not only overinvestment but also other perverse mechanisms begin to operate.

The velocity of technical change, typical of the early phases of technological revolutions ends up creating the problem of premature obsolescence. Since the mid-1990s, for instance, the speed of increase in computer power, in new generations of software or cellular phones and in dot.com companies on the Internet, hardly allowed users the time for learning or for amortizing investment. But no producer could afford to stay behind in the innovation race.

Wells in 1889 described a very similar situation in relation to steamships since the mid-1870s:

> The numerous and expansive steamer constructions of 1870–73, being unable to compete with the constructions of the next two years, were nearly all displaced in 1875–76, and sold for half, or less than half, of their original cost. And within another decade these same improved steamers of 1875–76 have, in turn, been discarded and sold at small prices, as unfit for the service of lines having an established trade, and replaced with vessels fitted with triple-expansion engines and saving nearly fifty per cent in the consumption of fuel. And now 'quadruple-expansion' engines are beginning to be introduced and their tendency to supplant the 'triple expansion' is unmistakable.[160]

With accelerated technical change, price competition can be excessive. Given that each paradigm provides the potential for a quantum jump in productivity through successive innovative improvements, lower and lower prices become a possibility and are typically brandished as weapons in the competition for market power. Yet, as Schumpeter would hold, perhaps as a provocation to more orthodox economists, too much price competition ends up thwarting innovation and hurting profits.[161]

So, movements towards oligopoly or cartel-type agreements are likely to take place as some of the firms involved become strong enough. This was the case in the USA in the 1880s and early 1890s, when falling prices were making competition deadly. The resulting wave of cartel-type collusion led to the Sherman Antitrust Act of 1890, which turned the wave into a full merger move-

---

160.   Wells (1889:1893) p. 30.
161.   Schumpeter (1942) Ch. 8.

ment.[162] Financial power can also be wielded to take over the competition, as happened from the end of the nineteenth century and has again been happening since the late 1990s, with aggressive takeovers and 'mega-mergers' marking the trend towards global oligopolistic alliances.

These acquisitions or fusions are greatly facilitated by the enormous amounts of money pursuing investment opportunities that are siphoned into the system towards late-Frenzy. In an article in *Fortune* magazine, Geoffrey Colvin gathered evidence of overpaying for some of the mergers and acquisitions and suggested that this was probably due to having excess money.[163]

This aggregation process is another one of the changes brought about by each technological revolution and its enabling infrastructure. As a consequence, the typical size of the largest firms in each paradigm can be greater than that in the previous one and the 'shape' is also likely to be different. In the third surge, vertical integration from raw materials to final client in a core product became the 'ideal' form of the most powerful firms of the period. In the fourth surge, horizontal integration was more typical, so that final product manufacturers widened their range of similar products, rather than integrate backwards into raw materials. In the present fifth surge, transcontinental networks encompassing the whole range of segments both horizontally and vertically – or 'diagonally' as Auliana Poon[164] suggested – in several related markets for goods and/or services are emerging as the strongest organizations. So these absorption or merger trends can simply be one of the means through which the optimum size and typical structure are reached each time. This would put further emphasis on the crucial role of available finance to feed the process.

G.   Ethical Softening and Opacity

Frenzy is the true 'gilded age', the golden shine on the base metal heart. Love of money flourishes more than at any other phase and the ways of acquiring it in limitless quantities recognize no boundaries. Individual interest is glorified; social interest scorned. Being rich is being 'good'; anything else is failure. The ethics of success at any price are the only valid norms. That is the attitude driving the ample diffusion of the doubtfully legitimate financial practices developing in the gambling context of the frenzy phase. That permissive atmosphere generates an opacity that is highly convenient for corruption and for the flourishing of outright illegal activities.[165]

---

162. For a discussion of the merger question in this period, see Chandler (1977) Ch. 10.
163. Colvin (1999).
164. Poon (1992).
165. Strange (1998) Ch. 7 'Finance and crime'.

In Britain, in the installation period of the second surge, government officials took commissions for helping get railway 'rights.' The Japan of the 1980s
was riddled with tax evasion and corruption, unfortunately facilitated by a
general relaxing of state regulation and supervision of financial practices.[166]
The vast money-laundering networks for the trafficking in drugs in the 1990s
are similar to those of 'bootleggers' in the USA in the 1920s or those of weapons dealers and of corruption money in various similar periods. All this ends
up generating the easy movement of masses of 'shady' money across the financial system and adding to the glut of idle funds.

Mafia type and other corrupt activities probably exist at all times and in
many places. Yet, when the established institutional system is breaking down
and losing legitimacy, while the power of financial capital is at its highest to
escape the control of weakened governments, there is a climate of ethical soft-
ening. So social resistance to these activities is less organized and the obstacles to constrain them are less effective. The dangers of such an unregulated
system were powerfully revealed when discovering the ease with which ter-
rorists used financial channels to protect their movements of funds.

The other sort of illegal activity that tends to flourish at these frenzied times
involves the participants in the financial world itself. The sight of easy wealth
quickly made with someone else's money is too strong a temptation for both
big and small financial agents. This is then a time for swindlers. The infamous
Charles Ponzi, whose name has become the label for pyramid-type swindles,[167]
was able to mount his real estate fraud in Florida in the euphoric atmosphere
of the mid-1920s. The 1980s and 1990s have also produced a large crop of
such crimes.[168] It is the conditions that make it more likely, because so much
temptation brings forth the 'talent'. As Gibbons put it in the nineteenth century: 'there is perhaps no record of a bank fraud extant of which the perpetra-
tor was not honest yesterday'.[169]

But even among the legal activities there are some practices that certainly
fall in the area of illegitimacy. For example, from the 1970s onward and with
greater intensity in the 1990s, many financial 'innovations' can be classified
as taking advantage of legal loopholes to evade regulation, such as seeking to
hold funds that are not classified as deposits to reduce the reserve ratios or the
many new ways of earning commissions for performing financial intermediation 'off-the-record'.[170]

---

166. See Chancellor (1999) Ch. 9 and Reading (1992:1993) Ch. 7.
167. Minsky (1982) uses the term as a category for any sort of highly risky credit, including
      those which became so because of external conditions.
168. A sample of notorious frauds 1980–95 is given in Kindleberger (1978:1996 revised edn)
      pp. 78–9.
169. Gibbons (1959) quoted by Kindleberger (1978) p. 80.
170. Strange (1998)

If the revelations after the gigantic Enron bankruptcy in 2001 are proven true, it could turn into the emblematic case of opacity and connivance in the frenzy phase of the fifth surge.[171]

As George Soros says, when arguing for government regulation: 'Financial markets are not immoral, they are amoral'.[172]

H. Increasing Tensions between the Money and Real Economies

So the frenzy phase is one of increasing tension between the inflated money economy gone wild and the restructuring real economy. For those pursuing the accumulation of wealth, the higher profits possible in the financial sphere discourage direct engagement in productive activities, except those related to the newest and most dynamic technologies, and attract even more money towards finance. This increases the disparity between the mass of money vying for high returns in the financial system and the actual aggregate rhythm of wealth creation in the production and trade of goods and services. The resulting inflation of asset prices generates unwarranted capital gains completely divorced from the profits and dividends of the real economy represented in them.

Figure 10.1 shows how stock market values broke further and further away from the growth of the economy towards the end of the installation period of the current great surge. The figure plots the Dow Jones index and the gross domestic product of the United States, current and constant, all indexed to a comparable base. Constant GDP represents the real growth of the economy; the gap between current and constant represents the general level of inflation. Since the Dow Jones is quoted at current prices, the widening gap between the Dow and nominal GDP can thus be seen as a rough proxy for differential inflation between the stock market and the economy. It could also be understood as a measure of the increasing relative attraction of financial investment as opposed to direct investment in production.

To have an idea of the size of the paper wealth mountain that can grow in the frenzy phase, one can look at the amount invested in derivatives, which can be seen as a form of risk insurance covering speculators against misjudgments regarding movements of interest or exchange rates or any other investment on future obligations or receipts. As early as 1995, the volume of the 'derivative economy' was estimated by Palma, using IMF data, to have al-

---

171. *The Financial Times* (2002) pp. 18–19, published a collection of articles proposing major reforms in accountancy and other related practices in order to regain investor confidence. The title of the whole report was 'After Enron'.
172. Soros (2000) p. 157.

Figure 10.1   The diverging growth of the New York Stock Market and US GDP, 1971–99

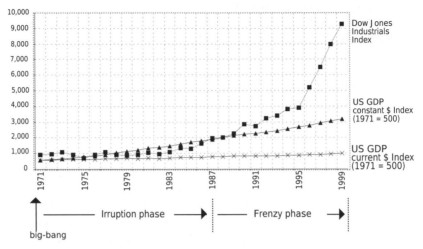

Source: Data from US Department of Commerce, recalculated and organized in phases by the author.

ready reached a notional value of US$64 trillion. This is almost equivalent to the combined value of all bonds, equity and bank assets in the G17 (G7 plus all the smaller European countries), which in the same year was around US$68 trillion.[173]

The tension between financial and production capital can thus become very high. Structural coherence needs to be re-established by some means and these can often be violent and painful. It could occur through a truly great crash, as in 1929, or through what seemed to be a series of partial collapses letting off steam, as at the end of the nineteenth century. The full history of the readjustment of relative paper and real values at the beginning of the twenty-first century will only be appropriately judged with hindsight.

The stress also comes, among other things, from the much greater productivity of the industries and activities associated with the technological revolution in relation to traditional ones. This difference produces such rapid and constant changes in their relative values that, as discussed in Chapter 6, there is a coexistence of 'two moneys', one for the new economy and another for the old, rather than the assumed single and universal measure of 'standard units' of value. If you could in the 1960s buy five cars for the price of one computer and in the 1990s twenty computers for the price of one car, it is difficult to gauge the relative worth of goods. This general uncertainty makes the infla-

---

173. Palma (2000).

tion in stock values all the more credible. The stock market price of Yahoo, which is a virtual company with hardly any physical assets, was greater at the end of the 1990s than that of the whole of Eastman Kodak. Time will tell how much of that difference reflected real value.

Furthermore, since the irruption phase in the 1970s and 1980s several countries experienced periods of hyperinflation, while the volatility in exchange rates required stringent controls, even in relatively homogeneous environments such as the European Union.

Meanwhile, the fortunate participants in the gilded groups, regions and countries, experiencing the booming atmosphere, become ever more convinced of the appearance of a 'new economy' promising unending bliss. From the other side of the fence, this buoyant arrogance looks like scorn.

Such growing differences among products, industries, sectors, groups, regions and nations are the very nature of paradigm shifts. They generate disorder, confusion, perverse inflationary or deflationary trends, which contribute to the general tensions and instabilities characteristic of these periods of structural transition. Re-establishing coherence in relative prices is another requirement for the recovery.

But the basic condition for ushering in a period of synergy, convergence and prosperity, at least in the developed countries and in those that have entered the paradigm and are in a catching-up process, is *adaptive regulation*, especially regarding the behavior of financial capital.[174] This was clear to George Soros, a well-known major actor in the financial scene of the present surge. To him, it is impossible for national institutions, however effective they might be at their level, to properly regulate a global economy. [175]

---

174. This is the core point of Susan Strange's *Mad Money* (1998).
175. The need for global regulation is advocated by Soros in his book *The Crisis of Global Capitalism* (1998) where he presents 'market fundamentalism' as a threat to capitalism, the possible source of a serious crash and a danger to the 'open society'. In his later book he emphasizes this need even further by incorporating it as a subtitle: *Reforming Global Capitalism* (Soros 2000).

11. The Turning Point: Rethinking, Regulation and Changeover

The recessions that follow Frenzy – and the crashes that usually usher them in – are both the consequence of an untenable set-up. By the time the collapse occurs, the conditions are there for the deployment period to begin, but the system has been operating under fundamental structural tensions that, once the breakdown finally occurs, can only be overcome through institutional recomposition.

When the installation period ends, about mid-way into the unfolding of each technological revolution, its paradigm has triumphed and is ripe for widespread diffusion. By then, the main dynamic products have been identified and the dominant designs determined, their industries are structured and well connected with one another, the infrastructure is basically in place and the consumption patterns are pretty much defined. The 'common sense' of the paradigm has diffused enough – and proven its power sufficiently – to be basically installed in people's minds as the new best practice. The potential for production and productivity growth is considerable. What is needed for its realization is a new space for the unhindered expansion of markets, favoring economies of scale and fostering a wave of new investment.

All is poised for the dynamic expansion of the real economy and for the propagation of the paradigm across all industries, weaving a coherent production network. This build-up task would be better performed under the control of production capital, given that its interests and decision-making criteria are more appropriate for the job. In addition, profit expectations – gone wild and unrealistic during Frenzy – have to be brought back in line with a longer-term view.

This essentially means that adequate regulation of financial capital has to be established and an institutional framework favoring the real economy over the paper economy needs to be put in place. Yet financial capital will resist with force. It has been at the helm for many years of successful growth. Its criteria have been 'proven' effective. It appears that personal talent and genius for wealth creation – plus the lack of restrictive rules – were the source of the achievements. Therefore, financial capital is only likely to accept regulation after much of the rapidly made gains have evaporated in the collapse and when the recession has shown the practical impossibility of reviving the casino. There is also growing pressure against financiers from the victims of the many illegal or semi-fraudulent practices that are usually revealed after the fall and the bankruptcies.

As with many processes in capitalism, it is by taking a successful behavior to its extreme that it turns into failure. And it is because of this failure that the appropriate behaviors, practices and norms will be devised, accepted and adopted. As usual, also, there is no mechanical guarantee that the crash will happen in any particular way. Nor can predictions be made about the length or depth of the recession, or about the type of solution applied. All that depends on a multitude of political and other factors that are specific in each case.

A. The Fundamental Causes of the After-Frenzy Recession

The crash of 1929 was of much greater absolute magnitude than the canal or the railway panic of previous centuries, but they were all of a similar structural nature. Each case is unique due to a very wide range of factors, from the political and cultural to the purely accidental. Yet, whether they are called 'mania' or 'new economy', the bubbles at the end of Frenzy share one fundamental characteristic: they are structurally unsustainable. Though they seem to involve the whole economy of the core country or countries in unstoppable prosperity, they are simply a big delusion, a self-reinforced fantasy.

There are three structural tensions that make it impossible to keep the frenzy process going for an indefinite time. There are tensions between real and paper wealth, between the profile of existing demand and that of potential supply in the core products of the revolution, and between the socially excluded and those reaping the benefits of the bubble.

The first structural problem is that the speed at which capital gains are being 'created' by the collective faith of the paper investors can simply not be matched by the speed at which the economy can produce real wealth, in spite of the continued dynamism of the revolutionary industries. Among many others, there was an article in *Fortune Investor*, in February 1999, titled 'Stocks May Be Surging Toward an Earnings Chasm', which states that 'barring a miracle, there's no way corporate earnings can increase fast enough to keep giving investors the huge returns they've gotten used to'.[176] Two years later an article in *Le Monde* announced that, thanks to the crisis, firms had been finally freed from the impossible dogma of 15 per cent return on equity.[177] Similar pressure on producers had been put in previous frenzies, because the con-

---

176. Tully (1999).
177. *Le Monde* (2001).

ditions for attracting investors are set by the capital gains capacity of the high fliers in the mania.

The other two structural tensions stem from the same basic cause: the whole frenzy phenomenon is, at bottom, a huge process of income redistribution in favor of those directly or indirectly involved in the casino, which funds the massive process of creative destruction in the economy. That regressive distribution generates a double vicious cycle: one is economic, expressed in the market; the other is social, expressed in political terms. Both get worse as the bubble increases.

The economic vicious cycle sets in as the reversal of the virtuous cycle that created the casino prosperity. The concentration of income in the prosperous fringe of the population works wonderfully for providing a high investment rate, accompanied by a high dynamic demand for the early products of the revolution and many others that complement the new lifestyle. But this very success brings many of those tested products to the point where continued profitability requires even greater economies of scale and even faster expansion of markets. Mergers are only a band-aid solution. The growing imbalance appearing between the profile of potential profitable production and the existing profile of demand gets worse and worse.

Debates about the macroeconomic balance between supply and demand are generally restricted to the question of relative volumes. Rarely is there reference to the qualitative balance between the *profile* of what is produced and the profile of demand in terms of income distribution. Business people, by contrast, understand this very clearly. If you want to sell basic foods, your potential market grows with the number of low-income families; if you sell luxury cars, or even palm-top computers, you look to the upper end of the spectrum. So the rhythm of potential growth is modulated by the qualitative dynamics of effective demand. Therefore, even if the quantity of money out there equals the value of production, if it is not in the right hands, it will not guarantee that markets will clear.

Naturally, firms will always try to adapt the direction of innovation and their product mix to the profile of demand, but the consumption capacity of any group has limits, which will impose restrictions in scale of production that translate into obstacles to productivity growth. Thus concentration of income can lead to premature market saturation.

In the case of the present turning point of the fifth surge, if innovations were made to profitably bring down the price of basic computers by half, market volume might not even double. Most people who cannot buy a computer at $1000, cannot buy one at $500 either. However, if a wave of investment were to take a good number of developing countries out of crisis, world trade and markets would grow so fast that prices would naturally go down (through economies of scale) and present sales numbers would look dwarfed.

Historically, there have been many types of solutions to the premature saturation problem, from export markets, through government spending for wars or other purposes, to income distribution within the country or across the world. The effectiveness and durability of each solution depends on many factors, among them on the specific nature of the constrained production potential. In the first surge, after the British had absorbed as much in cotton garments as their market allowed, the whole world was flooded with them and even the slaves in the American plantations wore them.[178] In the third surge, which was based on a heavy engineering revolution, the markets expanded worldwide, for big capital equipment and infrastructures. In the fourth surge, Hitler expanded markets for mass production through a war economy, while the Western democracies did it later through a mixture of income redistribution and government spending.

Nevertheless, the choice is not without a price, given the other vicious cycle resulting from regressive income distribution. This other process of worsening tensions is a social and political one, generated by the impoverishing impact on the excluded. As the gap between the rich and the poor widens beyond a critical point, anger and violence erupt and make it more and more difficult for the rich to maintain the game and for politicians to retain power, if they ignore the social demands.

The blindness of the elites is rooted in biased visibility. Frenzy does bring prosperity to quite a few, not just to those engaged in the financial sphere. The roaring twenties and the brilliant nineties were felt by many as the best period they had ever known or imagined possible. In this atmosphere, the privileged cannot see or prefer not to see the other side of the fence. Yet their ostentation of wealth is usually highly visible to the poor, the excluded and the dispossessed. So, Frenzy is a period that can be described in very different terms, depending on the point of view of the observer. It is 'the best of times' for many; it is 'the worst of times' for many more.

In the earlier surges, these opposing situations and differing views occurred in the *national* space; in the current surge they are also – and especially – occurring in the *global* space.

The ratio of the average GNP per capita (1987 prices) of the richest countries with a fifth of the world's population, to the GNP per capita of the poorest countries with a fifth of the world's population, grew from 30 to 1 in 1960 to 60 to 1 in 1990, and 74 to 1 at present [1999]. The OECD projects that the gap will grow even larger ... More than 80 developing and transition countries have per capita incomes lower than ten or more years ago. Twenty have per capita incomes lower than in 1960.[179]

---

178. In 1805 Britain was still consuming twice as much as she was exporting. By 1814, the domestic market took only 43 per cent of a greatly expanded output. Hobsbawm (1962) p. 53.
179. Jolly (1999) p. 5.

Writing just after the Asian crisis of 1997 and the Russian 'meltdown', George Soros warned that 'there comes a point when distress at the periphery cannot be good for the center'. He further added that 'the pain at the periphery has become so intense that individual countries have begun to opt out of the global system, or simply fall by the wayside'.[180]

When the economic structural tensions that make the bubble unsustainable come to a head, the outcome is written on the wall: some form of breakdown followed by a serious recession. What cannot be predicted is the specific manner in which society will overcome these tensions.

B.   The Collapse of the Bubble

The implosion of the NASDAQ bubble in April 2000 was a deathblow to Internet mania, but its consequences were bound to stretch much further. It's like taking the plug out of the tub: the water cannot be brought back in. Although it was several months before the rest of the US stock market began to slowly slide down, recession was clearly threatening the US economy by January 2001. This weakening of the core economy soon spread out worsening the 10-year long Japanese stagnation, that had followed the bursting of the early bubble in that country, and weakening the recovery of many of the export-led economies in Asia. The impact in Europe was delayed, but then accelerated by the consequences of the terrorist acts of September 11th, 2001.

For entrepreneurs, venture capitalists and investors riding the eternally rising wave of capital gains in NASDAQ, the shock was severe. No explanation could be satisfying. A year later a venture capitalist in Silicon Valley said to *The Financial Times* that 2001 had been like a 'nuclear winter'.[181] Yet, just looking at the behavior of the index, as shown in Figure 11.1, should have been enough to warn of impending disaster.

Chris Freeman was one of many economists arguing the inevitable outcome in his paper on 'A Hard Landing for the "New Economy"',[182] though he was one of the very few connecting the likely collapse with technical and institutional change issues. *The Economist*, as it did in the 1840s,[183] ran several articles from the late 1990s predicting the inevitable fall;[184] Alan Greenspan, Chairman of the Federal Reserve Board, popularized the expression 'irratio-

---

180. Soros (1998) p. xiv.
181. Abraham and Daniels (2001).
182. Freeman (2001a).
183. *The Economist,* 25 October 1845, cited by Chancellor (1999) p. 136.
184. *The Economist* (1998). See for example, 'Will Internet shares join tulip bulbs and the South Sea Company on the list of great financial bubbles?'.

Figure 11.1 The rise and fall of the NASDAQ bubble, 1971–2001

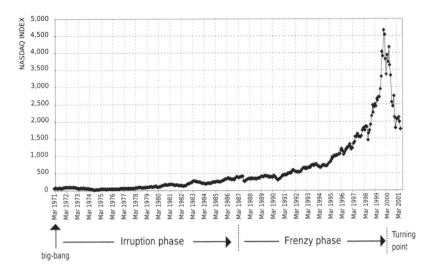

Source: U.S. Department of Commerce. Phase indications by the author.

nal exuberance,' of which Professor Shiller claims authorship.[185] Nevertheless, as happened in early 1929 with Paul M. Warburg, the banker, who warned about the 'orgy of unrestrained speculation' and Roger Babson, the statistician, who foresaw 'a terrific' crash, with a fall of 60 to 80 points in the Dow (20 to 30 per cent at the time), all warnings went unheeded and were forcefully rejected.[186] Then and now the feast continued unabated. It is precisely because participants refuse to recognize the delusion that bubbles can be inflated.

The investment firms – or the independent promoters, in the earlier surges, like George Hudson in the second[187] – take the center stage and all the temporary glory. Their growth, towards the end of the bubble, seems to outpace even the stars of the boom. From 1927 to 1929, the stocks offered by investment trusts, trading, and other financial firms themselves, went from less than 2 per cent of the new capital issues in the New York Stock Exchange in 1926 to over 37 per cent in 1929.[188] In the USA in 1999, venture capital (VC) firms alone were able to attract between $36.5 and $48.3 billion (depending on the definition),[189] which was between 4 and 5 dollars per $1000 of total US GDP.

---

185. Shiller (2000).
186. Quoted by Galbraith (1990:1993) pp. 6–7.
187. Bailey (1995).
188. Schumpeter (1939) p. 878.
189. Mowrey (2000). This article appeared in what was considered the number one journal in

By 2001 many of those VC firms with previously fantastic profits were filing for bankruptcy protection. In October 2001 some of the major financial firms were going through 'rationalization' processes. The executive president of Merrill Lynch declared to the *Wall Street Journal* that it clearly seemed that their firm, and the industry in general, were significantly oversized. So they were planning cuts and even closures in their offices all over the world, to bring the firm down to a size that made sense in relation to the profit-making opportunities existing in the market.[190]

C.   The Party's Over: Crashes as the Door to Regulation

Until the collapse of the bubble, the agents of financial capital live through a period when they follow a strictly financial logic, setting their own lax rules and being highly successful with them. So, the 'yuppies' of each casino economy in the frenzy phase are impervious to calls for regulation. As Galbraith remarked, they all wish to think that it is not the facilitating circumstances of the period that are making it possible for them to become rich but 'their own superior insight and intuition'.[191]

Falling down from such high pedestals may bring them back to reason. When tensions from decoupling and polarization explode in collapses or panics or crashes they are more likely to accept new rules and regulations and some of them may no longer be there to oppose them.

Edwin F. Gay, writing in early 1929 in the Introductory chapter to the so-called 'Hoover Report', subtly broke ranks from the exuberant optimism of the book and reviewed the 'four previous periods of efflorescence in the USA', noticing that they all ended in major panics and crashes, which in their wake 'gave impulse to banking and monetary reforms'.[192]

Crashes serve as catharsis and as calls to orderly behavior, but not if there is an automatic parachute for irresponsible investors. Without some significant bankruptcies and failures (not bailed out!) it is highly improbable that financial capital will ever accept and abide by the necessary regulation.

This raises the question of when and for how long should 'lenders of last resort' intervene. Should they ever let the rope break? The game is not an easy

---

the Internet world in the USA. Born in 1998, at the height of Frenzy, it reached more than 300 pages, setting a record of 7,558 advertising pages in 2000. In August 2001 it had closed as a paper journal; a month later it was sold in a bankruptcy auction for half a million dollars plus assumed subscription liabilities (Web issues of *The Industry Standard*, August 26 and September 24).

190. *Wall Street Journal Americas* (2001) Spanish edition.
191. Galbraith (1990:1993) p. 5.
192. Gay (1929).

one, of course, and the stakes can be huge. In 1998, *Newsweek's* Wall Street editor, Allan Sloan, scandalized about the orchestration by the Federal Reserve Board of the $3.65 billion bail-out of Long-Term Capital, the biggest hedge fund in the USA, reports that:

> Alan Greenspan argued ... that the Fed didn't dare let Long-Term Capital go out of business because its failure could have triggered worldwide havoc. Markets are already nervous about the seemingly endless series of financial collapses ... [though, Sloan adds] the IMF has thrown billions into the pot, with little success so far ...[193]

So, once the destabilizing forces have got loose, the risks of not rescuing are huge. Could the risks of rescuing be equally high or even higher the more time goes by?

Historical experience seems to show that big crashes teach big lessons, though both Galbraith and Kindleberger observe that such lessons are short-lived. Nevertheless, many of the new rules born out of such panics do remain both in the law and as 'common sense'. After 1929, the general consensus on the need to avoid the many excesses visible after the fall, made it possible to establish a Keynesian framework, which lasted and was fairly effective until the early 1970s. And yet, at the time, it took more than a decade and a devastating world war for that framework to be accepted and its regulation applied.

Thus, the crashes at the end of the installation period can create the conditions for the state to regulate, turning the tables in favor of production capital and leading to a period of more harmonious growth. When they do have this effect, the recession is certainly a high price to pay, but it is typical of the contradictory nature of capitalism.

D.   The Model and the Historical Record

Has the installation period always led to Frenzy? Has it always ended with a crash? The case of the third surge shows how specific historical conditions can significantly deviate from the basic model, but still be explained by the relationship between technological opportunities and the behavior of production and financial capital.

What happens, for instance, if installation is not intense? What happens if, as in the case of Britain in the third surge, the established industrial structure does not modernize enough and if the love affair of financial capital with the new technologies is only mild? British financial capital, after having learned in the maturity phase of the second surge how extraordinarily profitable for-

---

193.   Sloan (1998).

eign investment could be, did not concentrate on intensely developing the technological revolution at home. Or rather, it concentrated on those specific elements of the revolution that were connected with the previous surge, such as railways, steam engines and telegraph, and served to multiply their power in the empire. Modern steel production was put at the service of worldwide railways and telegraph and especially powerful steamships with vastly improved engines. Copper and gold mines, agriculture and meat production were developed in all continents, enriching the shipping, trading and insurance businesses and keeping financial capital busy and profitable. Frenzies and bubbles took place abroad and that is where the crashes happened. The biggest of them all, in Argentina in 1890, almost brought down the whole system.

Baring, the pre-eminent British financial firm responsible for the bulk of the loans in the Argentinian bubble, was fully bailed out by the Bank of England with the help of other European countries. This action was judged by Ellis T. Powell, a contemporary enthusiast of the growing coordinating role of the financial market, as 'the salvation of England from another crisis which, if it had been suffered to develop, would have left its mark on financial history for the next fifty years'.[194]

Faced with setbacks abroad, British financial capital recoiled for a while, staging what was called the 'home boom' that by no means can be defined as a typical frenzy phase. Nevertheless, the international casino economy in Lombard Street did come to a halt. For five years after the Baring episode 'the Stock Exchange lay fallow, with business and credit worn to a shadow'.[195]

While British finance was making its grand tour of the globe, the shares of British industries, including crucial ones such as chemistry and electricity, were still traded in the local banks.[196] In the meantime Germany and the USA were developing giant concerns with the decided support of the most powerful financial firms. These countries had been forging ahead ever since their unification, the USA after the Civil War and Germany after the Franco-Prussian War. The first benefitted from idle British capital, during the maturity phase of the second surge; the second from the enormous indemnity from France. Both experienced an early boom, with a frenzy character, and an early crash in 1873. Both went through a serious and prolonged recession and then resumed growth in earnest. As suggested before, the processes of forging ahead do not necessarily follow the regular sequence. The state played an important role to help the drive to industrial power in very different ways, but in both cases it included tariff protection.

There were big financial panics in the USA in 1884 and 1893, but they were not typical after-frenzy crashes. If anything, the 1884 crash was closer to the

---

194. Powell (1915:1966) p. 522.
195. Landell (1912) quoted in Powell (1915:1966) p. 529.
196. Kindleberger (1984:1985) p. 205.

model. In fact, in the pre-1893 years, though the economy was growing quite fast, the stock market was traversing a period of low volume and not very intense activity.[197] The true madness in the US stock market happened during Synergy, between the 'rich man's panic' of 1903 and the crash of 1907. So the strong drive to forge ahead led to a sort of frenzied synergy.

Financial capital in the USA, at the end of the nineteenth century, rather than hand control over to production capital took full possession of it and exercised direct management of the merged production giants. Judging by Sobel's account, J.P. Morgan, the great financier, had almost as much power over the national economy as the President of the United States. By 1900, 'the Morgan-directed banking fraternity was dedicated to maintaining order and liquidity, carrying out functions which in other countries were assigned for central banks'.[198]

It is not within the scope of this book to analyze in depth any historical case. The brief overview of the specific developments occurring in the three core countries of the third surge was meant more as an example of the care required in the use of the model, both to formulate questions and to propose explanations.

There is no mechanical sequence to be found, without looking at the actual behavior of financial and production capital and to the specific manner and rhythm in which the technological revolution is being installed and where. In the end, all the techno-economic phenomena will be very much conditioned by the institutional and political context of the specific moment in the countries involved. And this is particularly important in cases of falling behind and forging ahead. What is significant, in terms of the value of the model, is that there are causal chains and identifying features that can help the analysis and the interpretation not only of the regularities but also of some of the deviations from the basic pattern.

E.   Politics and the Question of Handing over Power to Production Capital

The period of deployment, or the second half of each surge, will consist mainly of the expansion of the paradigm across the production structure, of the intense use of the infrastructure and the growth of production to attain economies of scale, all within the innovation trajectories of the technological revolution being deployed. Hence, it will be a time of constant investment in production capacity and constant widening of employment and markets. That is why

---

197.   Sobel (1965) p. 129.
198.   Sobel (1965) p. 159.

real 'golden ages', in the sense of shared prosperity, are more likely to happen when production capital, rather than financial capital, is at the helm.

It is production capital that is mainly interested in further pursuing each technological trajectory, in order to profit fully from the investment already made, from the learning and experience acquired, from the externalities available, including the education of consumers and suppliers, and from the innovative paths well mastered. Since market saturation is one of the main limits encountered in deploying the growth potential of a technological revolution, ensuring consistent extension of markets is the way to facilitate the pursuit of those goals. Consequently, it is progressive distribution and worldwide advances in development that can best guarantee a continued expansion of demand.

Finance capital, by contrast, is mobile and does not accumulate equipment or technological experience, so it is less capable of guiding economic decisions at these times. Given the choice, it would prefer a short-lived capital gains investment, like some of the dot.coms of the 1990s bubble, rather than setting up more long-term, dividend-producing, capacity. In the early times of the technological revolution, finance follows the judgment of the new entrepreneurs. By the time Frenzy arrives, the entrepreneurs are being led by the criteria of the financiers. These might not know much about the technology but they certainly know a lot about which ventures will make money faster. In the 1930s, Keynes expressed concern about the increasing control of the ownership of capital investment 'by persons who do not manage and have no special knowledge of the circumstances, either actual or prospective, of the business in question'.[199] In the late 1990s, Peter Drucker sharply voiced a similar idea in an interview with *Fortune*: 'Securities analysts believe that companies make money. Companies make shoes!'.[200]

It is not easy to hand over control. During the frenzy phase financial capital becomes much more powerful and production capital learns to live by its rules and to submit to its criteria. Turning the tables requires not only a serious weakening of financial capital through the collapse of the paper wealth mountain it had constructed, but also the intervention of political forces.

By the end of the installation period, polarization has usually reached morally unacceptable extremes and has probably stirred the anger of the excluded. These are the sorts of forces that can put pressure on the political world towards the necessary structural adjustments, favoring the real economy of production and restraining some of the more damaging financial practices. The outcome of such power struggles is, of course, unpredictable.

---

199.   Keynes (1936) p. 153 of the 1961 edition.
200.   Schlender (1998) p. 170.

F.   The Long Depression of the 1930s in the United States

Most of the big crashes after the big manias led to depressions of around two years or less. This is congruent with the hypotheses being presented here. Each of those big bubbles in the frenzy phase is riding on an enormous potential for real growth and widespread prosperity. Once the distortion is eliminated, a healthy economy should be able to emerge. So a question that needs to be answered is why the Great Depression in the USA, after 1929, lasted so long.

As suggested above, crashes at the end of Frenzy serve as the clang of awakening to the need for recoupling the various broken links: between paper values and real values, between the new modernized economy and the old one and, especially, between the regulatory and institutional framework and the new dynamics of the economic world. Only the first is achieved by the crash, the other two are conscious – or intuitive – social processes, facilitated by the lessons of the crash and the recession.

Regarding recovery in the 1930s, one cannot look at the USA only. In Germany, with Hitler's rise to power, the institutional framework was reoriented to facilitate the development of mass production (and later of mass destruction and genocide). The war economy that began after 1933 in Germany could be seen as a synergy phase of a sort. Fortunately, the Nazis failed to conquer Europe and lost the war; otherwise, National Socialist Germany might have been the center of a longer-lasting fascist world. At that same time, the Soviet economy too was developing very fast with another mode of growth that was also capable of intensively deploying mass production. This wide range of options for the deployment of that particular paradigm – including the Keynesian democracies that will have the USA as their core – is an indication of how much is at stake and how much is decided about the future of each country and of the world at the turning point of each surge.

Growth also resumed in the mid-1930s in England, France and other countries in Europe. But these countries had not gone through a Frenzy as intense as that of the United States, hence they did not have such a monumental collapse to come out from; but, neither did they benefit from the advantages of the frenzy phase: that is, they did not have a fully installed industrial base for deploying mass production, nor had they developed a vast road network accompanied by electric utilities, nor had the paradigm diffused as deeply as in the USA for the establishment of a mass-consumption mode of growth. So, neither alone nor together could those countries pull the world onto a synergy period and their recoveries were fragile.[201]

---

201.   An additional point to make is that the nature of the particular paradigm can favor certain comparative advantages. For the deployment of the 'homogenizing' consumption patterns of mass production, large size and population were an advantage. The USA and the Soviet Union had them (and so would have been the case of a Nazi empire in Europe).

In the meantime, Roosevelt's New Deal, which tried to apply many of the right recipes for successful synergy, was being systematically opposed for fear of Socialism. Resistance came, not only from the financial world, which was going to be regulated, but also from production capital, which had the most to gain from it. In the ideological confrontations that characterized the world of the 1930s, state intervention in the economy could not yet be fully accepted in the USA. In 1933 the 'conservatives predicted that FTC [Federal Trade Commission] supervision was only the first step in the eventual communist takeover of the United States'.[202] It took the experience of collaboration in the military–industrial complex, during the Second World War, to understand that capitalists could coexist in a mutually beneficial relationship with a strong state that assumed an active coordinating and balancing role in the economy.

In a sense, it could be said that the direct US participation in the war was already the beginning of Deployment. Manufacturing equipment for the increasingly motorized war, fully utilized and expanded the potential of the installed mass-production paradigm, which had been built up during Frenzy – and, much more gradually, in the difficult 1930s. Further still, in terms of the socio-institutional framework, the many elements that were experimented with then, in terms of the role of the state and of international cooperation, could somehow be considered a 'dress rehearsal' for shaping the post-war Synergy, including the acceptance of US world leadership.

Thus, at the crossroads of the turning point in the surge, the outcome is very much determined by politics, ideologies and relative power. Therefore the length of the recession or depression does not depend on economic factors only, not even on economic policies and measures narrowly understood. Nor is the decoupling that leads to the crash a purely economic phenomenon.

It is because a proper regulatory framework is not in place that financial capital can create havoc. It is because financial capital does not let regulation hinder it that the adequate framework is neither designed nor established earlier. And after recession sets in, whichever political groups have or seize the opportunity to represent the collective interests of society will have the power to deeply shape the future.

---

202. Sobel (1965) p. 299.

12. Synergy: Supporting the Expansion of the Paradigm across the Productive Structure

Whatever time it takes to set up the framework to overcome the recession, the beginning of Deployment is usually characterized by synergistic growth, extension of markets and increasing employment.

The atmosphere is likely to be quite different from that which prevailed during the casino economy, because real growth in production becomes the basic source of wealth. The confident optimism of company expansion replaces the arrogant self-complacency of cunning speculation. It is perhaps the only period when aggregate statistics are consistent for safe extrapolation and the *ceteris paribus* assumptions of much economic theory become plausible. Growth is generally seen as firmly rooted in real production and the relative values of money across the various sectors of the economy stabilize and seem understandable to most people. In that context, rules are accepted as ultimately beneficial for all.

Regarding the relationship between financial and production capital, it has often been mentioned above that the synergy phases in two major historical cases, the third and fourth surges, were quite different in the United States. In both there was a return to the primacy of the *real* economy, in the sense that the direct control of production, infrastructure and services became the main driver of the accumulation of wealth, rather than the indirect hands-off ownership of securities, rent-producing assets or financial instruments. But, in the 'Progressive Era' the financiers or their direct agents sat on the boards of railways and industries and took the main decisions. In the Post War Golden Age, they could be in the board as stakeholders with some influence, but professional managers, representing – even embodying – production capital, applied their growth criteria to the development of the corporations. As Chandler would define them, the situation in the synergy phase of the third surge could be termed 'financial capitalism' and, in that of the fourth, 'managerial capitalism'. [203] Both counted on technical and professional persons to perform managerial functions, but the criteria they followed were different.

---

203. Chandler (1977) pp. 9–10.

Yet synergy is essentially about recoupling for expansion. As in any marriage, the question of which of the partners is in control is resolved depending
on the relative power of each. It will also depend on the specific circumstances,
the nature of the triumphant paradigm and the unique political scene of the
time. The markets of the third surge, for instance, were driven by heavy engineering while those of the fourth included centrally the mass production of
consumer goods. In the third surge capitalism reigned supreme, in the fourth,
there was competition with Soviet Socialism, turned during Synergy into a
permanent Cold War.

For those and other reasons, even more than the Victorian Synergy of the
second surge in Britain, the post-Second World War synergy phase in the USA
has been the clearest historical case of production capital being in control.
This was so much so that, for a while, the stock market was hardly present as
a dynamic force. In Sobel's words: 'Wall Street completely failed to reflect the
nation's economic exuberance [in 1947]; stock prices did not rise with the
rapidly increasing profits of listed corporations'.[204] This situation continued to
basically hold throughout the synergy phase. In 1962, a government report on
the nature of private capital investment, stated that:

> Capital requirements were financed chiefly from internal sources during the post-
> war period ... [when only] ... one fourth of total requirements [was financed] by
> borrowing from banks and other institution lenders and by selling securities in the
> capital markets... As compared with the 1920s, corporate financing in recent years
> featured a higher reliance on internally generated funds, a modest rise in the impor-
> tance of long-term borrowing, and a sharp reduction in stock flotations.[205]

That behavior not only differs from the frenzy phase of the 1920s but also
from the previous synergy phase in the USA, when that country was still in the
process of forging ahead.

A.   An Adequate Framework for Fruitful Recoupling

Perhaps because it comes after the collapse of an unregulated world, Synergy
is a time of orderly and ordered behavior. If regulation of the economic world
was put in place during the turning point recession, it is generally accepted; if
it was not, it is consistently sought by social and political forces.

Though they are more likely to originate in governments or world institutions, some of the new rules in the area of finance are self-imposed, precisely
to avoid the need for government supervision. They usually involve a new

---

204.   Sobel (1965) p. 321.
205.   Joint Economic Committee, US 87th Congress, 1st Session (1962) pp. 32, 40–41.

framework for banking and monetary practices. Next to them rules of the game are established to condition business, labor relations and so on, as well as regulatory innovations on the international level. But each set of regulations is unique because it needs to match the specific characteristics of the paradigm it is accommodating.

The suspension of convertibility of the pound, which seemed merely a war expedient, in practice favored – and protected! – the full propagation of the first technological revolution which was unfolding mainly, if not only, in Britain. From the second surge onwards, growing legislation to facilitate joint-stock banks and companies with limited liability helped, in one country after another and at different rhythms, the conversion of early family capitalism to modern corporate capitalism.

Accountancy and disclosure legislation is usually enacted to avoid the specific abuses revealed during the previous Frenzy. After the crash of 1929, in order to overcome some of the more harmful practices then revealed, strict disclosure rules were established for the safety of investors, together with the separation of savings from investment banks. For the safe deployment of the present fifth surge, after the Enron revelations, there were calls for regulation to separate consultancy from auditing and for new accounting rules that would make it difficult for off-balance sheet operations to be used to deceive investors.[206] But even the normal accountancy procedures unveil their loopholes in times of Frenzy. David Wessel in the *Wall Street Journal* remarked that 'what makes the Enron scandal so serious ... [is that] it highlights that the bookkeeping that is "generally accepted" these days is too often meaningless, if not false'.[207]

Not all regulation is written down, but good practices guaranteeing stable growth are generally supported. In Britain, the Bank Act of 1844 clearly separated money issue from credit, which was crucial, but did not enable the role of lender of last resort. After the railway panic of 1847, suspension of the Act was seen as necessary, and continued to be the 'accepted practice' in emergencies.[208]

Some rules help strengthen firms; others reinforce market growth and social cohesion. The admission of private joint-stock banks to the London Clearing House fostered the development of networks of branch banks to take advantage of the railway. In 1842 and 1844, laws were enacted improving conditions of work in mines and factories. In 1846 came the crucial decision finally to repeal the Corn Laws, and fully establish free trade. All this had happened

---

206. *The Financial Times* (2002a).
207. Wessel (2002).
208. Kindleberger (1978:1996) p. 149.

in the last years of the installation period and opened the way for the Victorian Synergy to follow.[209]

At that time in Britain, however, wealth was still mainly in the hands of aristocrats and merchants. The stock market was in its infancy and financial capital was only beginning to acquire functional autonomy. Thus it could be said that the triumph of production capital over finance capital in the second great surge took the form of a triumph of industrial capital over the wealthy landowning and commercial classes.[210]

The flourishing of the *belle époque* Synergy, in the 1890s and 1900s, was marked by the development of worldwide financial and commercial networks. This was made possible by international telegraph and rapid transport. It had been made easier since the 1880s by the universal Gold Standard, with London and the British Central Bank serving as centers of the system. International recognition of patents was formally established after the 1883 Paris Convention for the Protection of Industrial Property, universal standards and norms were agreed and institutionalized to facilitate worldwide compatibility of parts and products and so on.

In that same phase, another set of institutional innovations addressed the issue of governance on the national level. The large-scale social security experiment conducted by Bismarck in Germany, when forging ahead since 1883, was followed in the *belle époque* Synergy by similar laws being adopted by one European nation after another. According to Geoffrey Bruun, 'this wave of labor legislation, so rapid and universal in the Western world, made the 1890s a significant period in social history. Obviously, the spirit of the times was changing. Hours of work, salaries, health, social security, protection, the risk of invalidity and old age pensions stopped being a personal issue' and became more and more a responsibility taken up by the state.[211]

For the full development of the Age of the Automobile, a wide range of institutions was set up. Many of them were to put order in international finance, investment and trade: The International Monetary Fund (IMF), the World Bank, the Bank of International Settlements (BIS), the Marshall Plan and supervisory agencies, the reserve role assigned to the US dollar in the Bretton Woods accords, the General Agreement on Tariffs and Trade (GATT) and others. Many more were to establish an orderly framework at the national level: Keynesian policies, separate regulatory bodies for banks, securities, insurance, savings (to avoid the mixed financial services that allowed risking people's savings in

---

209. On the crucial importance of this for the deployment of the paradigm, see Lloyd-Jones and Lewis (1998).
210. The irony is that these gradually turned to financial investment and, by 1900, it is claimed that most of industry was in the hands of the old aristocracy. Lieven (1993), pp. 119–22.
211. Bruun (1959:1990) p. 169 (note: the 1990 edition consulted is a Spanish translation).

the casino of the 1920s) and so on,[212] plus protective agencies such as the Federal Deposit Insurance Corporation (FDIC) and the Securities and Exchange Commission (SEC) in the United States, to restore public confidence and oversee bank and stock exchange behavior, plus the Banking Act of 1935 'to make the Federal Reserve System an instrument of national economic management'.[213]

Social innovations were equally plentiful. They went from such fundamental aspects as the welfare system, including income safety nets, health and education, to accessory elements such as the provision of reliable national statistics to help business planning in a mass-production world.

Many, but certainly not all, of the necessary institutional changes are made during the period of installation or during the 'time of reckoning', just before the prosperity of the deployment period begins. All along, there continue to be strong feedback loops that signal further required improvements, which are implemented after synergistic growth is underway. Schumpeter, always preferring the market and the economy to have the upper hand, remarked that institutional innovation of this sort was usually the codification of already accepted practice,[214] which is probably partly true.

B. Enabling Institutional Innovations

To help bring about this new prosperity, however, innovations geared to smooth operation in the context of the new paradigm will also be necessary in money, banking and financial practices. As with all innovations, the date of introduction is less significant than the time of intense diffusion. Already the whole installation period of each great surge brings forth multiple innovations in the field of finance. Some are temporary or doubtfully legitimate and are destined to disappear or become very marginal (for the time being). Others, especially those connected with accommodating the investment, production, trade and consumption processes of the new technologies will probably generalize and expand. The propagation of the paradigm to further and further branches of the economy in the deployment period is likely to require those very instruments, together with others tailored to the emerging business practices. These might include innovations in types of money, banking services and forms of credit or finance, which create the facilitating conditions for the full adoption

---

212. Susan Strange, when reviewing the regulatory systems of this period, notes that although the American, French, Japanese, British and German systems exhibit significant differences, they all share what she calls the 'Chinese walls' separation between the various types of banking and financial services. Strange (1998) Ch. 8.
213. Strange (1998) p. 143.
214. Schumpeter (1939) Vol. 1, p. 307.

of the new paradigm across the whole range of the economy in each country and in the world. They would be closely coupled with those measures of public policy (national and international) that establish the rules of the game and the institutional framework for banking and finance. Once Bretton Woods makes the US dollar into 'gold equivalent' at the end of the Second World War, for instance, international finance adapts and generates the corresponding practices.

The required innovations also involve the internal working of the financial system, the types of instruments and conditions that facilitate the specific types of credit required for the incorporation of the new paradigm.

Synergy of the first surge saw the multiplication of country banks to help industrialists make local payments, to move money between the country and London, especially that of traders, and to facilitate collection of government revenue.[215]

To usher in the Victorian boom, checks became means of payment; joint stock which had been developed for large projects became more common; vendor shares, debentures, preference shares and other instruments made the incipient capital markets flexible and adaptable. In France the *Credit Mobilier* experiment was established for industrial loans.

The *belle époque* prosperity was supported by generalized limited liability, legislation facilitating the formation of giant corporations, self-regulation of stock markets and so on. While Britain specialized in arrangements for financing great engineering projects all over the world, as well as perfecting their expertise in short-term credit and insurance to finance international trade, in Germany, medium-size, medium-term loans were developed to finance purchasers and exporters of the new small electric capital goods.

The post-Second World War golden age was facilitated as much by the Bretton Woods agreements as by the development of ample personal banking services, widespread consumer and home buying credit (both made less risky by unemployment insurance); urban development financial schemes, specialized banking and other arrangements for the smooth functioning of the fast growing real estate and insurance sectors; government loans; and so on.

It is clear that the burgeoning knowledge economy will require a very wide range of new instruments and even the overturning of some 'eternal truths' about the tangible nature of assets.

---

215.   Kindleberger (1984) p. 79.

C. A Shared and Embedded Paradigm: Flourishing Synergy and Convergent Expansion

What makes the Synergy prosperity an era of good feeling is its tendency to encompass greater and greater parts of the economy and larger and larger parts of society in the benefits of growth.[216] After a period of acute polarization on several fronts, when prosperity was extremely lopsided, the system searches for coherence through the widespread application of the now established paradigm, as the logic of both production and consumption. Depending on the type of institutional framework established, it could be a time when the capitalist promise of achieving the common good through individual pursuit appears credible. The Victorian prosperity and the *belle époque* in some countries in Europe, incorporated wide sections of the middle classes; the post-Second World War period incorporated the working classes.

Technology and production are the instruments of such promise; they are the engines that pull the economy and successive social strata forward. Cities are embellished, infrastructure is brought to every corner of the country and made available to an increasing number of people, together with education, which in this phase is often reformed and widened, both in duration and in coverage of the population. The 'modern' style of living established by the rich during Installation spreads or trickles down further and further in a simplified and less expensive version, thanks to economies of scale. And all this is done in collaboration with financial capital, which flourishes in its role as intermediary in a style which is certainly less exuberant and adventurous than in the casino economy, but highly profitable in a more stable way.

Together with the expansion of the infrastructure comes a flurry of what could be called *'induced branches,'* which are investment opportunities created by the particular features of the paradigm in question. They include construction, transport and trade accompanying the particular nature of the expansion, as well as other activities that complete the new production and consumption spectrum. In the fourth surge, these included the flourishing of a service economy; in the case of the current surge, they will probably involve many activities related to intermediation in the information world and to production in the knowledge economy.

So the range of sectors that support growth and need financing in this phase encompasses:

- the core industries of the paradigm, which are still growing, advancing and expanding;

---

216. Tylecote (1985 and 1992) was the first to discuss the importance of income distribution as a determining element of the possibility of a 'long-wave' prosperity.

- the infrastructure, increasing its coverage and services;
- the whole of the old economy being modernized and rejuvenated; and
- a group of new branches of industry and services that are supplementary to the others and complete the fabric of the economy within the logic of that paradigm.

It is certainly enough to keep most of financial capital busy at home (and to make it withdraw from the now less attractive periphery), though this is likely to be different in the present fifth surge, which has involved globalization from the beginning.

Growth during Synergy, in the first phase of the full deployment period, takes place in the midst of increasing externalities. One of the effects of the bubble economy is to have invested enough in infrastructure to last for quite a while and to provide a basic coverage to enable massive use at decreasing costs. During the whole of the installation period, the diffusion of the techno-logical revolution was wide and deep enough to have allowed the paradigm to become fully visible. Consequently, when Deployment arrives, growth takes place provided with a set of widely shared principles for most effective and profitable practice as well as an implicit understanding of the various techno-logical trajectories to exploit.

As discussed in Part I, the paradigm gradually becomes territorially and socially embedded in terms of the availability of the physical and technical infrastructure, the technically trained personnel, distribution and supplier net-works, consumer habits, norms and regulations and cultural adaptation. This context leads to a situation of high agreement between financial capital and most production capital about what is a worthwhile and promising investment. These conditions lead in turn to mutually beneficial collaboration and to in-creasing and stable interrelations between banks or financial firms and their production clients.

D.   The Changing Role of Technology

By the end of Frenzy, the potential of the technological revolution has been understood, the technological paradigms (in the restricted Dosi sense) in terms of innovation trajectories, have been clearly defined, the competition between options regarding the main products and processes has led to what Brian Arthur has termed the 'locking-in'[217] of the winning dominant designs. By that time too, the main industries of the revolution are reaching their basic structures in terms of leadership, forms of competition, relative size of firm and production

---

217.   Arthur (1988).

facilities and other defining features. This means that if the installation period can be seen as a gigantic experimental stage for testing the various avenues of the new paradigm and establishing the basic constellation, the deployment period could be described as the build-out of that constellation and the extension of the chosen avenues.

Consequently, technological innovation could be said to move from an intense period of exploration, led by financial capital and its goals, to a period of consolidation and expansion of markets, following the criteria of production capital. What this means will depend on the specific socio-institutional framework established and on the type of product.

One of the avenues for innovation is facilitating widespread adoption by making the products truly user friendly and mutually supported. It is what Brian Arthur has called 'arrangements-for-use':

> What's needed for the revolution to fully blossom are the thousand and one small details – sub-technologies, arrangements, architectures – to fall into place that adapt us to the new technologies and them to us. This takes time. And more than anything it defines the buildout period not as a period that merely exploits the earlier innovations, but as one that creates the arrangements that bring the new technologies into full use.[218]

An avenue somewhat related to that one is to pursue wider and larger markets. The concentration of income in the frenzy phase is likely to also have concentrated innovation on the luxury end of the market spectrum. Conditions for improvement of income distribution in the deployment period could guide innovations toward cost reductions in the more basic versions to expand markets as fast as incomes allow. In this case, innovations are 'creamed' at the upper end of the market and become 'cash cows' at the lower end.

Process innovations become a focus of attention as soon as achieving market volume becomes one of the main determinants of profits.[219] Speed, reliability, quality and cost reductions receive special attention and can lead to major advances along the paradigm trajectories. In the case of the fifth surge, increasing attention to the environment, which can be considered part of the socio-institutional framework with or without enforceable regulation, is likely to signal directions for both product and process innovations.

There are two areas, though, where cost reduction innovations are crucial for the growth of the whole economy: the core inputs and the infrastructure. If these are cheaper and better, more and more producers will use them to modernize their products and processes and to increase their own markets. A virtuous cycle ensues, as this growth in demand will in turn facilitate further gains in productivity in the inputs and the infrastructure themselves.

---

218. Arthur (2002).
219. Abernathy and Utterback (1975).

In the third surge ever-cheaper steel and ever-cheaper rail and sea transport accelerated the development of transcontinental markets from the 1890s. In the fourth, the cheapening of oil-based fuels, electricity and road transport gave positive support to the very high growth rates of national mass markets. It is likely that in the fifth, this growth-enhancing role will be played by the ever-lower cost and ever-wider use of microelectronics and telecommunications.

The specific manner in which innovation is financed during this period can also change. In the fourth surge the R&D laboratory became a feature of most large corporations and state-funded laboratories, either independent or in universities, became common. One of the features of the current surge is the importance of innovations as creators of value and the ease with which changes can be introduced in production, due to flexible equipment and organizations. This will certainly define much more dynamic arrangements for promoting and financing technical change.

E.   The Passage to Maturity: Tensions and Dispersion Again

As the maturity of the paradigm is approached, gradually the spectrum of opportunities for new investment becomes narrower, the product life cycles of later products – even of later technology systems – become shorter, investment in increasing productivity is less and less effective, new profit opportunities are harder to come by and so on.

This loss of momentum could manifest itself in a sort of mid-life crisis as, for example, the crash of 1857 in Britain and the 1960 recession in the United States.

Maturity brings merger time again, but not to escape price competition, as during Frenzy, but to amass market share in search of economies of scale to boost falling profits, due to stalling productivity and market saturation. The many other profit-enhancing practices of financial capital in this phase were amply discussed in Chapter 8.

Thus arrives Maturity, the late phase of the deployment period, with its superficial brilliance and its political turmoil. The workers organize and demand, sometimes very actively, the benefits that had been promised and not delivered.[220] The young, the artists and the discontented also denounce and romantically rebel. Meanwhile, as the period wears on, investment opportunities will dwindle while idle capital grows and grows. Soon, for both production and financial capital, it will be emigration time again – often together – in search of new outlets abroad, or outside the established paradigm, in unusual

---

220. For a discussion of these periods of labor unrest and their relation to long-wave patterns, see Freeman and Louçã (2001) pp. 355–63.

innovations. Thus the great surge spreads out into the periphery fueled by the willingness of financial capital while, at the core, the next technological revolution is about to irrupt and challenge the established production structure.

Nevertheless the successes of the early phase of the deployment period have strengthened the confidence of the defenders of the establishment. For them, by the maturity phase, complacency has arrived, progress seems guaranteed and the great virtues of the system can be proclaimed with certainty.

In spite of the recurring ups and downs in the economic and social performance of capitalism, there seems to be an underlying faith in the eventual arrival of a period without cycles and without social problems as a result of the operation of the system. This mixture of ideas and convictions with yearnings and desires resurfaces with great strength during two particular phases of the surge: Frenzy and Synergy. In the first, it is the growth of the financial bubble and the incredible profits achieved that create the delusion of a new economy, which is all the more credible the more money arrives at the believer's bank. In the second, it is the steady growth and the gradual diffusion of well-being for a relatively long period that create the illusion of an ever-improving society. The first mirage will be broken by the bursting of the bubble; the second by the growing social discontent followed by the economic decline of the established production structure.

Another surge is about to emerge; another turbulent period of installation, with increasing control of financial capital, will spread the next paradigm, until it reaches a critical mass at the next turning point.

13. The Changing Nature of Financial and Institutional Innovations

So far it has been proposed that the irruption of technological revolutions every 40 to 60 years unleashes a process of transformation that affects every aspect of society. For approximately the first half of the surge, financial capital drives the diffusion process, forcefully pushing the revolution forward. During the second half, it is usually production capital that conducts the growth process propagating the paradigm across the economy. Throughout the successive phases of diffusion, deep and widespread transformations must occur, which demand adequate innovations not only in the production sphere – in products, processes and modes of organization – but also in finance and institutions. These innovations condition the extent to which a technological revolution will deliver its potential and the distribution of its economic and social benefits. In turn, it is the characteristics of the specific revolution that will determine the nature of the problems to solve by the innovations in both those spheres and, through the principles of the paradigm, the manner in which to solve them.

A. Financial Innovations from Phase to Phase

The process of switching from a production-led economy in the deployment period to a finance-led economy in the installation period (and vice versa), profoundly affects the direction and intensity of innovation in the financial sphere itself. In fact, as has been discussed throughout Part II, in each of the phases the behavior of finance capital is strongly influenced by the changing quantity and quality of opportunities for augmenting paper wealth. Sometimes the paper values represent real wealth; at others they may be just a perverse form of redistribution. Generally there is a changing mix of both. The same variety will appear in relation to the nature of innovations.

Table 13.1 proposes a typology of financial innovations, classifying them according to their main purposes and ranking them from the most useful for the 'real' economy to the least useful. The top ones provide the life-blood for entrepreneurship and production; the lowest ones take blood out of the economy through manipulating paper wealth.

Table 13.1   A tentative typology of financial innovations

Type and purpose of financial innovations

A Instruments
to provide
capital for
new products
or services

For radical innovations (bank loans, venture capital and others)
To enable large investments and/or spread risks (joint stocks, bank
syndicates and so on)
To accommodate the financial requirements of new infrastructures
(for both construction and operation)
To facilitate investment or trade in novel goods or services

B Instruments
to help
growth or
expansion

For incremental innovations or production expansion (like bonds)
To facilitate government funding in different circumstances (war,
colonial conquest, infrastructural investment, welfare spending)
For moving (or creating) production capacity abroad

C Moderniza-
tion of the
financial
services
themselves

Incorporation of new technologies (communications, transport, security, printing and so on)
Development of better forms of organization and service to clients
(from telegraph transfers, through personal checking accounts and
high street banking to automatic tellers and E-banking)
Introduction of new financial instruments or methods (from checks
to virtual money, local, national and international services and various types of loans and mortgages)

D Profit-taking
and spreading
investment
and risk

Instruments to attract small investors (various forms of mutual funds,
certificates of deposit, bonds, IPOs, 'junk bonds')
New instruments to encourage and facilitate big risk taking (derivatives, hedge funds and similar)

E Instruments
to refinance
obligations or
mobilize
assets

To reschedule debts or restructure existing obligations (re-engineer-
ing, Brady Bonds, swaps and others)
To buy active production assets (acquisitions, incorporations, mergers, takeovers, junk bonds)
To acquire and mobilize 'rent'-type assets (real estate, valuables,
futures and similar)

F Questionable
innovations

Discovering and taking advantage of legal loopholes (fiscal havens,
off-the-record deals and so on)
Discovering and taking advantage of incomplete information: 'making money from money' (foreign exchange arbitrage, leads and lags
and similar)
Making money without money (from pyramid schemes to insider
trading and outright swindles)

Type A and B innovations are those related to the basic role of finance as an intermediary in relation to production investment, either to initiate activities (A), or for growth, expansion and extension (B). Type C innovations improve the performance of the financial world itself – from banks to investment firms – as a service production activity. Type D innovations, could be seen as a form of marketing for financial services: they make it easier – and apparently less risky – for possible clients, large and small, to engage in investment activities. They also facilitate the profit taking of the original creditors, in cases of venture capital, or of the successive investors in bull markets capturing capital gains. Type E innovations refer to the role of financial services as vehicles for mobilizing existing assets or obligations from hand to hand, that is, as channels for change of ownership. Finally, type F innovations are the various manipulative practices – mainly legal, though often illegitimate – in which financial agents can participate, most of which tend to be socially undesirable but not easily curtailed.

In the USA, in the early 1910s, it became common for banks to set up investment affiliates to be able to buy stock forbidden to them by law, given its high risk for depositors' money. 'Although not illegal in the strict sense of the word, this practice circumvented the spirit of the law, and was called by one writer "a masterpiece of legal humor"'.[221]

Although innovations of all types can occur in all phases, the frequency of each type can change significantly. Each phase has characteristics that will bring forth certain types of financial innovation as shown in Table 13.2.

The irruption phase, just after the big-bang, presents the maximum intensity and variety of innovations. In the first place, it will provide a crop of type A innovations, involving venture capital in whatever form is adequate for the particular revolution, as well as forms of funding trade in the new products. At the same time, new ways of financing development in the periphery (type B) are likely to accompany the last period of diffusion of the old industries and some incursions into the new. That is also a time when type C innovations will abound. The financial world is keen to incorporate technological advances in communications, security, printing and so on as well as organizational changes that will allow higher productivity and wider coverage for their services.

In the 1860s and 1870s, the 'ticker tape' (1867) and the telephone (1878) were capable of providing a quantum jump in speed of information and decision making. Wall Street took them up immediately, but the London Exchange delayed their introduction by around five years (in 1872 and 1882 respectively). R.C. Michie explains that whereas the New York Stock Exchange was owned by its members and they were all interested in fast access to information from wherever they were, the owners of the London Exchange were a

---

221. Reported by Sobel (1965) p. 183.

small group of a much larger membership. For them, facilitating access to outsiders reduced the value of the institution and the income they derived from it.[222] So, as with every other aspect being discussed, the institutional setting will influence both the speed and the manner in which innovations are adopted.

Yet, the irruption phase is also a time when the revolution is still only a minor part of the economy, while the bulk of the industries of the old paradigm are mature and offer few good investment opportunities, so idle money piles up and fosters innovations of types D, E and F. So Irruption witnesses the maximum variety and intensity in financial innovation.

Table 13.2   *The shifting behavior of financial capital from phase to phase of each surge*

Phase	Prevalent types of innovation						Prevalent characteristics of finance during the phase
	A	B	C	D	E	F	
Irruption	☐	☐	☐	☐	☐	☐	Maximum intensity of real financial innovation
Frenzy				☐	☐	☐	Escape control, attract funds, speculate, inflate assets
Synergy	☐	☐	☐				Adaptive innovations to accompany growth
Maturity		☐			☐	☐	Accompany outspreading, escape control and manipulate

In fact, the whole of the installation period is one of intense experimentation and innovation not only in technology but also in financial practices. The intense connection with the technological revolution from the very early phase builds up a reservoir of appropriate financial innovations capable of dealing with the various peculiar aspects of each paradigm for the whole duration of the surge. Ironically, the many distortions that intensify in the frenzy phase will serve to indicate the type of regulation necessary to avoid them. And this applies not only to the various institutions and instruments of the financial world, but also to the accountancy practices and disclosure rules of the production companies in which the investment is made.

It should be noted that Table 13.2 refers to the prevalent direction of *innovation*, that is, to the phase in which certain types of financial instruments or practices tend to be profusely 'invented', introduced and imitated. The application of those practices can last a long time and can often define the normal way of operation in later periods. The most appropriate of the practices developed during the early phases of the revolution will often generalize in the

---

222.   Michie (1987) pp. 250–51.

deployment period, when the new paradigm becomes the 'common sense' for investment and operation across all the sectors of the economy.

When Frenzy arrives, type A practices will still be very strongly helping to spread the new technologies. However, the limit to the absorptive capacity of the still incipient technologies and ways of production generates a profitability gap. The resulting urge to mimic the high profitability levels of the new industries attracts increasing numbers of hopeful investors (and of doubtfully profitable companies) into what becomes the casino economy, moving the pendulum towards type D, E and F innovations. As the bubble builds up, there is a search for new (or renewed) ways of making money out of moving assets from hand to hand or out of manipulating money, generating asset inflation and increasing the real or apparent wealth of the participating investors, without augmenting the wealth of society.

The most notable shift in innovative behavior in finance occurs after the burst of the bubble, between Frenzy and the 'golden age' of early Deployment. In the synergy phase, type A, B and C innovations will tend to prevail, in the form of adaptive innovations to accompany the full deployment of the paradigm. These innovations support a 'back to basics' trend, towards safe price/earnings ratios and towards making money by participating in the real profits made by the productive activities that are being financed.

By Maturity, in contrast, decreasing opportunities are being chased by more and more idle money coming from the 'cash cows' of the well-established industries. Thus creativity in finance moves toward type E innovations for concentration of ownership and power, as well as toward new foreign investment practices of type B. These can be relatively sound investments or very unsound ways of stuffing the peripheries with loans, like geese, and building unpayable sovereign debts, likely to default in the next installation period. When in 1837, Mississippi, Louisiana, Maryland, Pennsylvania, Indiana and Michigan repudiated their debts, 'anger was expressed that foreign banks and investors should now, in hard times, ask for payment of debts so foolishly granted and incurred.'[223]

Other innovations in this phase imaginatively search doubtful means of propping up profits. These are likely to be of the F type, trying, for instance, to increase opacity to stockholders or to fiscal authorities. In the 1960s in the USA, the importance of profit squeezing through accountancy practices and legal loopholes became so large that there were frequent complaints about the supremacy of financial managers over those of production and marketing. In the years before the First World War, in the USA, 'Wall Street was under constant scrutiny from one government agency or another' and so were banks and insurance firms. The uncovering of the so-called 'Money Trust' by the Glass

---

223. Galbraith (1990:1993) p. 62.

group made the need for regulation clear. Among the consequences was the Glass–Owen Act, creating a timid forerunner of the Federal Reserve System, as another attempt to create a sort of central bank in the United States.[224]

Many of those manipulative practices will overflow into the irruption phase, after the next big-bang, as parts of the rationalization and the survival tactics of the existing production structure that continues battling for profits and markets behind the astounding economic success of the technological revolution.

B.   Financial Innovations from Paradigm to Paradigm

As financial innovations change in nature and purpose, following the life cycle of each revolution, they are deeply molded by the nature of the specific techno-economic paradigm being deployed. This involves not just the adaptation of financial instruments and services to the specific changes in the production sphere, but also the application of the paradigm as a generic technology and as new organizational and operational principles in the financial firms themselves.

The local banks of the first industrial revolution could handle savings and loans and even some international trade operations, but would not have been able to engineer the gathering of the huge sums involved in the building of the railways of the second – much less of the third – surge. These required a new manner of attracting and handling finance, which was found through joint-stock companies and limited liability. The enormous financial empires of the *belle époque* could easily manage the financing of major engineering works all over the world and support great industrial concerns, with thousands of workers and major transactions, such as US Steel and General Electric in the USA or Siemens and AEG in Germany. Those financial giants probably would have found it difficult to even envisage the task of providing the myriad of small consumer credit arrangements necessary for furthering the markets of the fourth surge.

In fact, one of the major transformations in the economy brought by the mass-production revolution was the conversion of daily living into an activity supported by the equivalent of 'home capital goods'. People's salaries became more than the source of subsistence, in terms of food, health and shelter. They became the form of purchasing, by installments, a whole range of durable goods, from the automobile, the refrigerator and the washing machine to home entertainment equipment such as radio, records, TV and tape plus, obviously, the house to put them in. The expression 'capital goods' is used here not only to refer to their extended terms of payment and the financial processes needed

---

224. Sobel (1965) pp. 200–201. But even that ended up under the control of financial capital: 'Not until the New Deal would the system gain real independence from Wall Street'. (Ibid.)

to support them, but also to the prolonged productive use of the services provided. Nevertheless, none of the production activities that took place in the home went to the market. Something analogous can be said about the other major product of the mass-production revolution: weapons and military equipment. Financing government investment, for equipping the sophisticated weaponry of the Cold War, as well as the many public services (utilities, transport, education, health or others, depending on the country), can be said to have become a *new* activity, given its significantly greater volume, compared with the previous surges and its much more varied and complex quality. So, the fourth surge led to a new economy that had government as a fundamental economic actor, while it opened to consumers forms of financing previously reserved for 'capital goods'. This facilitated massive demand and, through it, fueled the industries that served as the engines of growth.

In the late 1920s in the USA, Edwin A. Seligman, a professor at Columbia University, was already signaling the deep transformations that would follow from the diffusion of these accessible forms of credit. In the preface to his book *The Economics of Instalment* [sic] *Selling: A Study in Consumers' Credit, with Special References to the Automobile*, he states:

> I am convinced that an entirely new chapter is here opening up both in theory and business life. After more than a century devoted to the elaboration and the technique of banking and commercial credit, designed to fit the industrial revolution, we now stand at the brink of another revolution in economic science and economic life, scarcely inferior to its predecessors.[225]

The current revolution presents what might be an even greater challenge for the financial world. To begin with, knowledge, experience and information have become capital goods. This time, it is not the way of purchasing that defines them as such, but the fact that – although intangible – they can create new value, which can also be intangible. A growing portion of the economy, in terms of investment and trade, will be related to intangibles and will require appropriate instruments as well as conceptual creativity. How can knowledge capital be measured? Can it serve as collateral? What is the value of a product that is infinitely reproducible at almost zero cost? All those questions need to be solved in practice for the system to flow. In addition, on the lower extreme of the spectrum, the fast-growing number of cottage industries, be they artisan or high-tech, is posing further challenges to the banking system. These involve not only adequate financial instruments for investment and operation of micro firms, but also the need for new schemes for equalizing the irregular incomes that may be typical of an increasing proportion of self-employed per-

---

225. Seligman (1927) p. v.

sons in the population. At the upper extreme, globalized operations in production, trade and finance are all profoundly shaped by the potential of the information and telecommunications revolution as well as by its flexible networks paradigm. Globalization already involves an unprecedented scale of transactions in terms of volume and frequency, but especially a quantum jump in complexity. Suffice it to mention the difficulty implied in dealing with multiple moneys and changing exchange rates, both for daily operations and for calculating asset values. The power of data processing and the virtual and instantaneous nature of transactions have been rapidly transforming financial instruments and ways of functioning, while security problems have grown to serious proportions. There is surely much more to come.

C.   Institutional Innovations: From Old to New Economy

Appropriate financial innovations need to be supported and regulated by adequate institutional innovations attuned to the same paradigm. Without their corresponding legal frameworks, neither local banks nor joint-stock companies would have been safe and reliable for participation to occur. Without welfare and unemployment insurance schemes, masses of consumer durable goods would have had to be returned due to consumer default with each economic downturn. Without recognized labor unions, salaries would not have been enough to serve as solvent demand much beyond food and basics. Without a massive tax system, government demand would not have been forthcoming. Without a legal compartmentalization of the various financial roles, from savings and loans to investment, the functioning of the economy of the fourth surge could have been unstable. Information technology has probably made such compartments impractical, but other forms of regulation can probably make financial 'super-markets' safe for users. It now seems improbable for the world economy to reach a path of stable growth without a protective network of global, national and local regulation. An adequate set of institutions is needed to complement, shape and guide the transformations that take place in the economic sphere. Yet, it cannot be a blissful return to what worked in the previous paradigm; it must be the complex design of what will work with the new one. Globalization is not just a much more active international economy; it is a fundamentally different set-up.

Each technological revolution does then indeed lead to a 'new economy'. However, it is not, as was widely believed at the end of the 1990s (as at the end of the 1920s), one without cycles and with eternal bull markets in the stock exchange. What is indeed true is that technology is behind the transformations. But this is not, as often held, an unprecedented phenomenon. Equivalent leaps in productivity and similar new product explosions have occurred with each surge. That is what makes development a pulsating process.

The new economy that emerges with each technological revolution consists of radical changes in the patterns of investment, production, trade and consumption. These new patterns and the distinct categories of goods and services involved lead to new market behaviors and require appropriate forms of dealing with them. The different nature of the new products and technologies does change certain aspects of the functioning of the economy for that particular surge, but it does not overcome its capitalist nature or its basically cyclical character.

In the current information revolution, several authors have developed interpretations of the new economy based on the strong contrast between tangible and intangible goods, between 'atoms and bits'.[226] Some claim that this new economy is different enough to require a new *economics*[227] for its study and management. This may very well be so and is wholly within the logic of the present model. For the previous paradigm, John Maynard Keynes developed a new economics, providing both a different understanding and a whole new set of policy tools. Although the debate still rages,[228] these policies, where applied, pretty much achieved their purpose of tempering the business cycle and supporting smooth growth, full employment and consistent investment, for the duration of the deployment period of the fourth great surge.

That set of policies and that vision of economics lost effectiveness when the economy of the mass-production revolution, for which it was designed, became exhausted at the end of the 1960s. Once productivity stopped growing and investment opportunities dwindled, the whole basis of the model broke down and *stagflation*, that unusual combination of inflation with unemployment, rendered its main policy tools impotent. This made it easier for finance capital to make a systematic assault on state intervention and regulation and for the monetarists to move to pre-eminence in the economics profession.[229] Soon, the successful flourishing of the microelectronics revolution and the wave of real competition that characterizes the early installation period, facilitated the unearthing of the *laissez-faire* philosophies and the neo-classical theories in economics, championed by the Thatchers and the Reagans. The process of creative destruction taking place in the economy was accompanied by the demolition of the old edifice of state intervention and regulation, which had stopped being effective in that specific form. In the frenzy phase, the reign of market fundamentalism was supreme, to the benefit of the new technological entrepreneurs and especially of the violently growing financial capital, but to

---

226. See, for example, Negroponte (1995).
227. See, for example, Soete (2000).
228. While Milton Friedman and Anna Schwartz (1963:1971) held it never could work, there are Keynesians, such as Dow (1998), who hold that the policies were never properly applied.
229. See Hodgson (2001) and Chang's (1997) discussion on 'The Economics and Politics of Regulation'.

the detriment of those left out at the other extreme of the polarized global economy, particularly the bulk of the developing world.

The recession that follows the collapse of the bubble once again creates conditions for the emergence of a new economics and of new policies. As discussed above in relation to financial innovations, these policy tools will have to closely conform to the characteristics of the current technological revolution and its paradigm. The nature of the new economics and of the tools it provides for government action – and for designing its scope – will have enormous bearing on the direction given to the potential of this technological revolution.

PART III

The Recurring Sequence,
Its Causes and Implications

14. The Sequence and its Driving Forces

The narrative in the preceding chapters went far into proposing a historical structure based on recurrence. It was approached from a systemic interdisciplinary point of view including technology and institutions, which can be roughly ranged within evolutionary economics. The type of model constructed is grounded on the idea that it is possible to find dynamic regularities and recurrent sequences of change in the workings of the capitalist system. This in itself already raises very fundamental issues, related to worldviews, that cannot be approached without revising some of the basic premises. It is not the intention of this book to enter such discussions. An in-depth treatment of those questions can be found in Freeman and Louçã's *As Time Goes By*.[230]

The object of this concluding part is to summarize the model and to invite a debate about its implications. This chapter brings together the model in its main elements and discusses the driving forces involved. Chapter 15 explores some of the questions raised by this interpretation and looks into its consequences for theory and policy.

A.   A Summary of the Sequence and its Elements

According to the model presented here, when a *technological revolution* irrupts in the scene, it does not just add some dynamic new industries to the previous production structure. Through the configuration of a *techno-economic paradigm*, it provides the means for modernizing all the existing industries and activities. The process of diffusion of both the revolution and its paradigm across the economy constitutes a *great surge of development*.

Each surge has two distinct periods. The first two or three decades are the period of *installation*, during which the critical mass of the industries and infrastructures of the revolution are put in place against the resistance of the established paradigm and driven increasingly by the criteria and the turbulent dynamics of financial capital. At about mid-surge there is a *turning point* when the tensions that had built up are surmounted, creating the conditions for the period of *deployment*. During this period, which also lasts two or three decades,

---

230.   Freeman and Louçã (2001) Part One.

the transformation potential of the revolution spreads across the economy, yielding its full development benefits. Growth in this period is driven mainly by the longer-term criteria of production capital, with an institutional framework that tends to pursue a better balance between private and collective interests.

Each period in turn goes through two different phases, defining the changing character of the assimilation process, so that the recurring sequence is made up of four phases lasting around a decade each: *Irruption*, *Frenzy* – turning point – *Synergy* and *Maturity*.

Given the modernizing power of the revolution and its techno-economic paradigm, each surge ends up raising the whole productive structure to a higher plateau of average productivity, while weaving a different fabric of interrelations among the branches of the economy. This evolution by long leaps would be the manner in which progress takes place in capitalism.

Figure 14.1 Development by surges: the elements of the model and their recurring changes

Elements of the model	Previous Surge (A)	
SURGES: Diffusion of successive technological revolutions and paradigms (A), (B), ... (N)	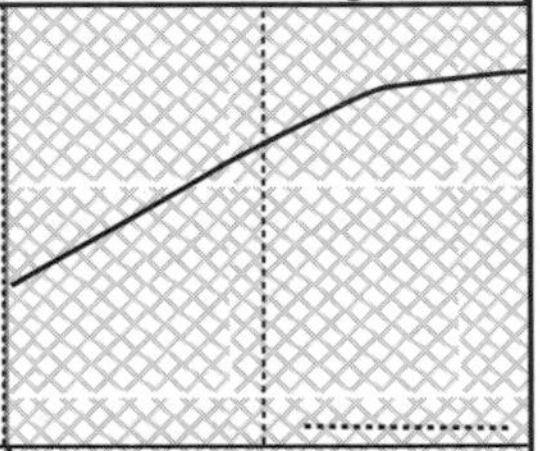	
Phase	Synergy	Maturity
PERIOD	DEPLOYMENT PERIOD A	
TECHNOLOGICAL REVOLUTION (TR)	Full bloom and maturity of revolution A Gestation of revolution B	
TECHNO-ECONOMIC PARADIGM (TEP)	Full reign and deployment of paradigm A	
FINANCIAL CAPITAL (FK)	Financial and production capital recoupled	Idle finance looking for opportunities
PRODUCTION CAPITAL (PK)	Production rules	Mature production looking for markets
SOCIO-INSTITUTIONAL FRAMEWORK (SIF)	Socio-Institutional framework adapted to and shaping paradigm A	
GROWTH	Converging growth of most industries* using paradigm A	

Note: * Refers to all production activities, including services, infrastructure and so on.

However, such massive economic transformations involve complex processes of social assimilation. They encompass radical changes in the patterns of production, organization, management, communication, transportation and consumption, leading ultimately to a different 'way of life'. Thus each surge requires massive amounts of effort, investment and learning, both individually and socially. That is probably why the whole process takes around half a century to unfold, involving more than one generation.

The *socio-institutional framework* adapts to each paradigm and, in turn, shapes the preferred direction in which the technological potential will be deployed and how its fruits will be distributed. But, this deep adaptation eventually becomes an obstacle for the introduction and diffusion of the next technological revolution. A society that had established countless routines and

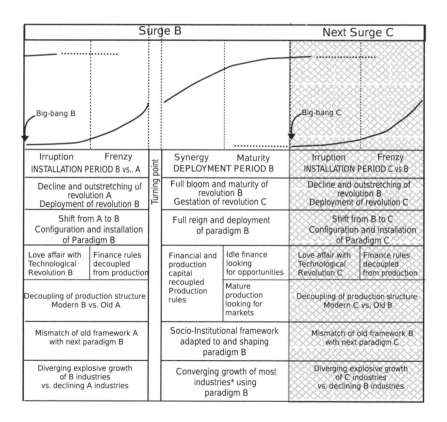

habits, norms and regulations, to fit the conditions of the previous revolution, does not find it easy to assimilate the new one. So, a process of *institutional creative destruction* will take place, with the simultaneous dismantling of the old framework and the gradual installation of the new. Nevertheless, some of the most significant institutional changes are only induced, after about half a surge, by the mounting social and economic pressures.

In the economy, the interrelations between financial and production capital determine the rhythm and the direction of growth. *Production capital* ensures the full deployment and the widest spread of each technological revolution. *Financial capital* enables the succession of surges. When production capital at the end of a surge becomes conservative, due to having so much investment and experience tied to it, financial capital will break loose and end up either helping the initial *big-bang* of the next revolution or following it up by backing the new entrepreneurs in spreading it. When financial capital, during the period of installation of the new paradigm, takes the economy on a frenzied ride up a paper-wealth bubble, the new and modernized production capital will be ready to take over and lead a more orderly growth process, in the 'golden age' that sees the full deployment of that revolution.

This changeover is aided by the institutions of governance and constitutes the *turning point* of the surge. It usually occurs after the bursting of the bubble and in the midst of the recession that follows. Changes in the rules of the game are necessary to curb the damaging short-term practices of financial capital, and induce it to cater to the more long-term interests of production capital. Some form of response is also required to the intense social pressures that come from the polarized income distribution characteristic of the frenzy phase. This response will modify the dynamics of the market profile, in terms of possible spending patterns, and will eventually influence the direction and rhythm in which potential supply will develop from the synergy phase onwards.

Figure 14.1 presents a condensed version of all the elements of the model, locating a particular surge (B) between the end of the previous one (A) and the beginning of the next (C). In it, the repeated pattern of emergence, replacement and deployment of technological revolutions and techno-economic paradigms can be identified, as well as the regularities in the changing behavior of financial and production capital and of the socio-institutional framework, along the four phases.

As has been the case throughout the previous narrative, the figure concentrates on the dynamics of the core societies and does not cover the whole life cycle of each surge. To do this, it would have to include both the gestation period, before the big-bang, and the redeployment period, after the next big-bang, when the mature industries of that surge outstretch and struggle for profitable survival by 'rationalization', by reaching for markets in the periphery and/or by spreading production to locations with comparative advantages. There is only an allusion to this by the graphic prolongation of the curves of each surge.

Thus the figure does not properly deal with the surge as it spreads across the world, as was briefly discussed in Chapter 5. From that wider perspective, the long surges span a whole century, with each successive one covering a larger portion of the globe. A similar table constructed from the point of view of the peripheral countries would be very different indeed, with a significant displacement of the phases. Further still, the table for the closer peripheries would also differ from that of the further ones (understanding 'distance' as economic and not merely geographic).

B.   The Forces Behind the Sequence

The summary above suggests that there are three features in the functioning of the capitalist system driving development by surges and determining the recurrent sequence that characterizes them:

- technical change occurs by clusters of innovations forming successive and distinct technological revolutions that modernize the whole productive structure;
- financial and production capital are interrelated but functionally separate agents, each pursuing profits with different criteria and behaviors; and
- the socio-institutional framework has much greater inertia and resistance to change than the techno-economic sphere, which is spurred by competitive pressures.

Each of these features refers to how change takes place in one of the spheres that co-evolve in the process of development: technology, the economy and social institutions. It is the manner in which these changing spheres interact and influence each other that generates the sequence (see Figure 14.2)

Technology is the fuel of the capitalist engine. That technical change should evolve by revolutions has only little to do with scientific and technological reasons. It is the mode of absorption and assimilation of *innovations* in the economic and social spheres that requires technical change to occur in coherent and interrelated constellations. Once a technological revolution irrupts and begins to propagate, its techno-economic paradigm emerges and guides the trajectories of further technical change. Thus, the bulk of technological development will be internally compatible and easy to introduce, thanks to interrelations and increasing externalities. Yet there will always be plenty of developments outside those trajectories, due to the relative autonomy of science and technology. That is why, when the potential of one revolution is spent, there is a pool of radical innovations capable of coming together to form the

Figure14.2   The dynamics of the system: three spheres of change in constant reciprocal action

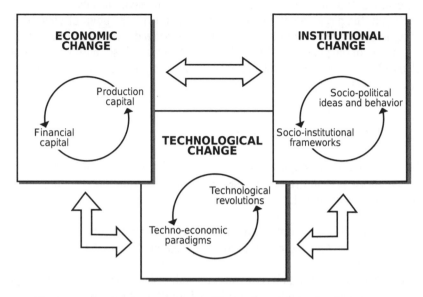

next. Hence, a certain degree of scientific and academic freedom is an essential component of the dynamics of the system.

The economic sphere is the scene of the growth process, where production and financial capital interact. More than merely interdependent, these two functional forms of the profit motive are indispensable to each other: real production supports paper wealth; borrowed money supports innovation and real investment. But it is not a simple, tranquil relationship, but rather a very turbulent one. The tensions and distensions of financial and production capital, their couplings and recouplings, will determine the rhythm and the direction of economic growth in each phase. And, at the two hinges of the surge, from Installation to Deployment and vice versa, when power struggles between them come to a head, the two other spheres will intervene. Technology will provide the big-bang leading to the next installation period, to be steered by financial capital. At the turning point, when the system stalls in recession, the state and other institutional, social and economic actors will establish the regulations and other changes in the framework, to help launch the deployment period based on the solid expansion of production capital.

The institutional sphere is the seat of politics, ideology and of the general mental maps of society in each period. It is also the network of norms, laws, regulations, supervisory entities and the whole structure responsible for social governance. Being the embodiment of society, it includes in a certain sense the other two spheres. The people involved in the changes that occur in technology and the economy spread the common sense of each new techno-economic paradigm to their other spaces of activity. It is like the propagation of a virus, from person to person, weakening the old mental maps and introducing the new. Thus, during each surge, there is increasing coherence and isomorphism between the structure and way of functioning of firms, and that of all sorts of organizations, from schools to hospitals, to political parties and government departments. This is the source of both the inertia at the end of a surge and the capacity to design appropriate new institutions and regulations at the turning point. The inertia in Maturity is rooted in the two or three decades of success of the deployment period that have strengthened the logic of the prevailing paradigm in minds and institutions. The capacity to change is stimulated by the opposite feelings. During the installation period, a sense of impotence and frustration accumulates and a growing incongruence is experienced between the new and the old paradigm. So, though institutional change is subject to greater inertia than economic change, it responds to social and political pressures and has the internal resources to move in the appropriate direction.

The three spheres interact in such a way that each time there is inertia in one, the processes of change brimming in another eventually exercise enough pressure to unleash the necessary modifications in the first. Yet inertia is not always negative. As suggested before, it can and does play a salutary role by erecting barriers to inopportune change, allowing the full spread of the benefits of each of the revolutions. So, as in most processes of advance, development in the capitalist system occurs through combining the forces of conservation with the forces of transformation.

C.   The Difficult Balance Between Private and Social Interest

The model proposed takes into account the fundamental structure of the capitalist system, which is in constant tension, managing the balance between private and social interests. The profit motive acts as the basic engine of private interest, moving both finance and production capital. The social interests, incarnate in government and the various organizations of civil society, are constantly trying to shape the conditions of growth and the distribution of its toils and of its fruits.

The actual social benefits, in each particular phase, will depend on the extent to which there is a positive or negative sum game between individual and collective interests and on whether the social and political forces leaning to one or the other side are capable of recognizing these – rationally or intuitively – and act effectively to attain their aims.

As Keynes remarked in the 1920s:

The world is *not* so governed from above that private and social interest always coincide. It is *not* so managed from below that in practice they coincide. It is *not* a correct deduction from the Principles of economics that enlightened self-interest generally *is* enlightened; more often individuals seeking separately to promote their ends are too ignorant or too weak to attain even these.[231]

These differences in – real and perceived – individual and social interests are particularly acute at the end of the installation period. The collapse of the bubble and the ensuing recession – even depression – can be very painful for both the rich and the poor; the former can see a good part of their wealth evaporate, the latter are likely to sink even deeper in their misery. Yet, this brutal way in which the system forces the recoupling is merely the direct consequence of the extreme internal tensions created by the bubble itself. That is why, at such times, the role of the state and of the various social forces becomes indispensable for shaping the direction in which society will move for the following two or three decades.

Yet, when maturity sets in and the next revolution is ready to emerge, it seems that only the uncontrollable drive of financial capital has the conditions to push the icebreaker across the frozen seas, intensifying the process of economic and institutional creative destruction.

It could be that it is in the nature of capitalism to advance by going to extremes in pendular movements: from the installation periods, characterized by the unhindered unleashing of private profit seeking, to the deployment periods, when those forces are moderated and ordered for more widespread social benefits.

The historian Edwin F. Gay, founding Dean of the Harvard Business School, is reported to have arrived at such a vision of capitalism, through studying the history of the United States. According to Cruikshank, the historian of the Business School:

> [E.F. Gay] developed a dynamic vision of economic history [as] a record of swings of the pendulum between periods when social controls dominated and periods dominated by the actions of aggressive individuals. The former periods were static, characterized by security and stability. The latter periods ushered in by the introduction of new tools, weapons or other forces, were controlled by the powerful individuals who introduced these forces. These dynamic periods ... were crucial to economic development ... The role of the economic historian, as Gay perceived it, was to study and comprehend these cycles and to suggest ways of restraining their excesses.[232]

---

231. Keynes (1926) (original emphases).
232. Cruikshank (1987).

15. The Implications for Theory and Policy

A. The Power and the Dangers of an Interpretation Based on Recurrence

When reading the accounts of the 1870s and 1880s written by those who lived through them,[233] one is inevitably struck by the similarities between the evolution of compound engines and ships and that of chips and computers, between the process of generation of a world economy through transcontinental transport and telegraph and the present process of globalization through telecommunications and the Internet. By making the relevant distinctions between that context and this one, the power of those technologies and of these, the worldviews of that time and our own, we can learn to distinguish the common and the unique in all such processes. The same happens when reading the glowing accounts of economic success in the 1920s[234] and the similar writings about the 'new economy' in the 1990s. If one is willing to accept *recurrence* as a frame of reference and the uniqueness of each period as the object of study, then the power of this sort of interpretation comes forth very strongly.

In the author's own experience, not being a historian or a finance economist, the historical record became a laboratory for testing the hypotheses of the model.[235] In essence, the job was one of conducting genuine experiments in regularity. After identifying a phenomenon that could be part of the recurrent sequence, it was possible to 'test' for its appearance again and again in each similar historical phase, following the preliminary model. In this manner, by successive approximations, the various elements of the process could be either dismissed or modified or tentatively confirmed. In some instances, there were strong differences, such as the absence of a crash in Britain in the 1890s or the prominence of finance in the 'Progressive Era' in the United States or the extraordinary length of the 1930s depression in that same country. Those cases forced the author to delve further and, in the end, served to reshape and enrich the hypotheses. A model built on the basis of four and a half cases requires bold stylization and open-minded testing. Naturally, the job is far from

---

233. See, for example, Wells (1889:1893).
234. See the Introductory Summary of the so-called Hoover Report. Hoover (1929) pp. i–xxi.
235. That is the point made by Gustav Schmoller, the main exponent of the German Historical School in Economics, about the use of history. Schmoller (1893) pp. 261–269.

complete and further research is likely to help modify and strengthen these tentative results. For the moment it is for the reader to judge the usefulness of the general framework.

Obviously, any dogmatic or rigid application of the model will defeat its purpose. Its main value is serving as a tool to help organize the richness of real life but not to hammer facts into tight boxes.

With the particular proposal being made here, there is great danger of wanting to find exact dates for the end or beginning of a phase or period, when in fact most of the processes involved are overlapping and do not allow such precision. The dating used in this book is basically a working approximation to help transmit the ideas. The peril is further compounded when analyzing different countries because of the uneven spread of each revolution and the sequential displacement of phases as propagation advances from one country to another.

There is also the risk of exceeding the limits of determinism beyond what could be considered reasonable in a real historical setting. Though technology takes pride of place in the explanation, it is as much determined by social and institutional factors and by the economy and finance as it, in turn, influences them. As Chris Freeman has shown, the relative autonomy of science, technology, politics, economics and culture has to be taken into account in any attempt at explaining the processes of development as they actually occur.[236] In particular, even though wars and civil wars are certainly related to the processes that have been discussed, they have their own dynamics. The Napoleonic Wars and both the First and Second World Wars obviously dominated some phases of economic development and accounted for many of their specific features. The same may unhappily be true of the present conflicts, which Mary Kaldor has called *new wars*.[237] So, even though the explanatory hypotheses presented here involve unavoidable simplification, the full complexity of the feedback loops has to be kept constantly in mind when using the model for analyzing specific historical cases.

An additional difficulty is the interdisciplinary nature of the model. Looking at it from the standpoint of any one of the many disciplines, into which the social sciences have come to divide social reality, will diminish the value of the framework and move away from its intention.

Finally there is the question of the level of abstraction. The proposed model refers to long-term dynamics and cannot explain individual events. Obviously to analyze particular financial crises one is better advised to use Minsky's or Kindleberger's models.[238] What this framework can be used for is to enrich the

---

236.   Freeman (1995) pp. 11–19 and Freeman and Louçã (2001) pp. 123–35.
237.   Kaldor (1999).
238.   Minsky (1975 and 1982), Kindleberger (1978).

understanding by providing the wider context within which a particular panic occurs. The same can be said about individual radical innovations or the intro-duction of any single regulatory institution. This is a bird's-eye view where the bulk of phenomena are roughly ordered in terms of the general gist of the times.

The justification for an exercise that claims to give order to the historical record at the expense of its infinite complexity and richness is its heuristic value. Having a structure with which to ask questions and against which to assess regularity and to fully value uniqueness is all that one can expect. It can be no more than a very blunt and fuzzy instrument and its power depends on an intelligent and flexible use.

B.   Changing Times; Changing Views

If what is proposed here reasonably approaches the way the system works, then one could expect to find traces of these changes in the history of eco-nomic thought. To begin with, it can throw light on the recurring and varying interest in certain economic topics. Kindleberger's later editions of *Manias, Panics and Crashes* open with the following paragraph:

> There is hardly a more conventional subject in economic literature than financial crises. If few books on the subject appeared during the several decades after World War II, following the spate of the 1930s, it was because the industry of producing them is anticyclical in character, and recessions from 1945 to 1973 were few, far between and exceptionally mild. More recently, with the worldwide recession of 1974–75 and the nervous financial tension of the 1980s, the industry has picked up. When it first appeared in 1978, this work thus reflected a revived interest in an old theme, a theme that became increasingly salient in the decades that followed.[239]

The model may also serve to explain the changing intensity of certain de-bates and the ebb and flow of certain views. For instance, if the relationship between financial and production capital really goes through some stages of clear collaboration and others of tense decoupling, the heated debates about the link between the real and the money economy would be temporarily 'won' by one side or the other. Such changes of view were observed by Pigou when he remarked how money was alternately viewed as a mere wrapper of produc-tion or as a powerful 'evil genius,' following the changes from Deployment to ruthless Installation and to Deployment again, around the two great wars of the twentieth century.[240]

---

239.   Kindleberger (1978:1996) p. 1.
240.   Pigou (1949) pp.18–19. Quoted in Part I, Ch. 1, p. 6 of this book.

Though Greenspan's early warnings against 'irrational exuberance' were correct, his later claim about the arrival of a 'new economy', understood as non-cyclical growth, came just as the euphoria was about to give way to the NASDAQ collapse. This echoed the assertions of Irving Fisher, the brilliant economist, who had the misfortune of declaring in mid-1929 that 'stock prices had reached what looked like a permanently high plateau'.[241]

The *Methodenstreit* between the historical school and the neo-classicals, which in practice expelled the state, Society and the historical context from economic theory, occurred in the period of installation of the third surge, which in the periodization proposed here is parallel to the installation period of the fifth, when the monetarists defeated the Keynesians.[242]

With a longer time frame, in Heilbroner's classic about the 'worldly philosophers',[243] where he locates each of the great economic thinkers in the context of his times, we get a glimpse at the possible experiential source of some of their interpretations. If David Ricardo had not been a successful stockbroker living in the midst of the maturing first surge, he might not have realized the threat to industrial profits coming from the protective Corn Laws and the rising cost of land, so he might not have come up with a theory of rents. If Veblen had not lived through the 'savage world' of the 1880s and 1890s he might not have developed his views about the negative role of financial capital in contrast with that of the engineers. If Keynes had not experienced both the turbulence of the 1920s and the 'sick world' of the 1930s he might not have searched for an explanation for depression and a recipe for getting out of it.

Capitalism, as an object of study, evolves through successive and distinct surges of growth, which in turn evolve through different phases, some chaotic, others more synergistic, none everlasting. So asking when and where a theory was developed, and especially when and where it gained acceptance, may turn out to be a very relevant question.[244] Furthermore, the expectation of a change in the tide – from one 'orthodoxy' to another – can be firmly rooted in an understanding of the nature of capitalist society and its functioning.

If the specific nature of 'what is going on' has some influence upon the way economists and others interpret the world, this may underpin the transient fortunes of different theories at different times. The extremely long period of installation since the 1970s, characterized by increasingly globalized free competition, nurtured the idea that markets were all that counted and that the state was incompetent and its influence undesirable in the economic sphere. After the collapse of the NASDAQ bubble, and the onset of uncertainty and reces-

---

241.   Cited by Galbraith (1990) p. 80.
242.   See Hodgson's (2001) *How Economics Forgot History*.
243.   Heilbroner (1953).
244.   As reported by Toporowski (2000), this point was made in methodological terms by Chick (1992) and by Kregel (1995).

sion, this view began to change. Already the unbearable situation in a great number of 'economies in transition' and developing countries – or rather 'undeveloping' countries[245] – was leading to a questioning of this temporary dogma. As time moves on and free competition is replaced by global oligopolies, as has occurred in past surges and has been happening in many sectors, more widespread doubts are likely to arise. Gradually, with or without a truly deep depression, it is quite probable that institutions and regulation will again be deemed necessary. Perhaps then those economists and other social scientists that propound the importance of combining state and market may once more find a good place under the sun.

C.   Changing Times, Changing Policies

The ultimate test of usefulness of a model such as the one presented here is in relation to policy making, be it in business, in social organizations or in government.

Although no strong claims are made with regards to its predictive ability, the model does suggest that the near future is often not an extrapolation of the near past and that, through a reasonable approximation to the stage of the sequence we are in, the direction of the next change can be roughly gleaned. So, this framework may give some guidance and criteria for action in times of significant change. It is at those times that help is needed in asking the proper questions both of the present and of the longer-term past in order to construct a better future. As Eric Hobsbawm has remarked, it is the power to recognize the turning points that will help economists, politicians and businessmen to prepare for the next war, not for the last.[246]

This is no small task. If we look back into recent history we can have a measure of the amount of audacity required to visualize the future, even a decade or two ahead. How easy do we think it may have been for people in the depression of the 1930s to conceive the possibility of effective policies for full employment and for the control of business cycles? How many would have believed in the early 1940s, when empire building was still on the agenda, that most developing countries would soon gain independence? Or, in the mid-1920s, how realistic would proposals have seemed for strict regulation of financial capital and for the official recognition of labor unions? How many in the 1960s could have envisaged the collapse of Bretton Woods, stagflation, deregulation and the decline of the welfare state? Yet, with hindsight it is pos-

---

245.   For a particularly tragic example of this process see the case of Mongolia in Reinert (2001).
246.   Hobsbawm (1997) p. 162.

sible to locate all those events in an understandable sequence in relation to the two great surges involved.

Therefore, the main practical implication of the proposed model is to take advantage of what the past can teach us in order to see policy as responding to a moving target. At each turn, the range for creativity in terms of viable responses would be shaped by the nature of each successive technological revolution and its paradigm, as well as by the character of each phase of its unfolding. Whether the actual responses are timely or delayed, adequate or inadequate, will depend on a multitude of cultural, political, economic and other factors, including the specific conditions of the national and world economy and the previous decisions of the more influential actors.

The design of appropriate policies at each turn requires identifying the direction of change by understanding the paradigm and identifying the phase of the surge. Neither task is simple and both the willingness to understand and the goals pursued when responding are politically conditioned.

At the same time, political ideas in terms of their policy translations are not immune to paradigm changes. In political terms, the periods of installation are times of cleavage inside political and ideological groupings. Whatever specific forms they had taken in the previous surge, whatever their location in the rough distinction between the individualistic and the socially responsible positions, an internal divide begins to cross each group (see Figure 15.1).

Figure 15.1 Paradigm shift and political cleavage

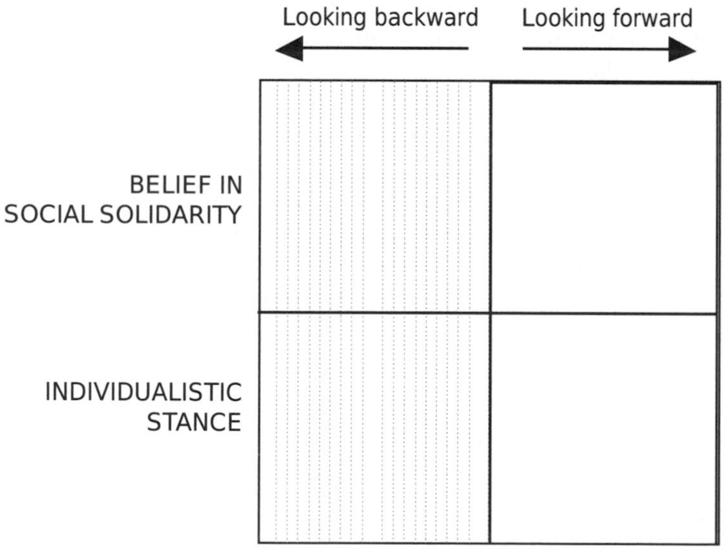

Source: Perez (1998).

The new line is drawn between those who look back with nostalgia, trying to hold on to past practices, and those who embrace the new paradigm and propose new institutions to fit the new conditions. This blurs the previous connection between certain values or goals and the specific means of attaining them. Though the goals may remain unchanged, the adequate and viable means to pursue them change with each paradigm shift. This can lead to temporary confusions, internal confrontations, divisions, revamping of traditional parties, new movements and other forms of realignment, which are likely to redefine the political spectrum for the following few decades.

So, the complexities involved in policy making during these periods of change can lead to emotional and political havoc in what had been apparently stable territories and well-defined ideological frontiers.

Yet if this model is a reasonable approximation to the way the system works then it is wise to try to engage in the design of regulations and institutions so they will be ready and in the arena of debate when the moment comes for them to be accepted. This is particularly relevant in the frenzy phase when the economy appears dominated by the interests of the financial world, which also has the power to impose them, until the resulting economic tensions and political pressures make them untenable or a major crash wipes out the source of confidence. This idea is behind Triffin's position, who when proposing changes to the international monetary system, said: 'My alternatives may not be feasible now but perhaps one day, after the necessary catastrophe, they may be rediscovered and made use of.'[247] Soros also, when proposing the creation of an international credit insurance corporation for guaranteeing loans to developing countries, remarked that it could be an acceptable idea only when creditors and debtors alike were seriously scared.[248]

Proposals can only be effective, however, when bearing in mind that institutional change is much slower and culturally more complex than technological or economic change. Overcoming the inertia of vested interests, long-held prejudices and dogmas, cultural views, practical routines and ingrained habits, especially when they had previously been successful, requires impressive events and powerful political pressures. In addition, during the installation period, attention tends to concentrate on the 'destruction' half of the process of institutional creative destruction. The inefficacy of the old institutions to handle the emerging technological revolution and the drive of financial capital for free-wheeling action come together to dismantle the restraining regulatory framework. The confrontation between the defenders of the old regime and the aggressive new deregulators – strong from riding on the high waves of the

---

247. Reported by Strange (1998) p. 20.
248. Reported by Strange (1998) pp. 189–90.

technological revolution in the midst of a sea of economic troubles – leaves little space for the proposal and acceptance of the required new and modern rules. Indeed, it is difficult to even design the appropriate framework before the paradigm is fully configured. The potential to be fostered begins to be recognized only after considerable diffusion. Similarly, the problems to be overcome can only be identified after having experienced them.

It is then possible to envisage the present model as an early-warning tool, providing criteria to guide policy making. Yet, effectiveness would demand a very profound and subtle understanding of the nature of the system and its driving forces. Could the bubble and its consequences be avoided? Could some institutional agent – or the capitalists themselves – identify the onset of maturity and facilitate the next revolution and its flourishing? Could the decline of the old industries be forestalled by conscious modernization? Could the shift of power at the turning point be engineered without the recession and the social tensions involved? Would all that imply modifying the nature of capitalism? Or, could it be – as Karl Polanyi's notion of the Great Transformation,[249] or Beveridge's version of the Welfare State[250] – a set of reforms for the construction of another stage of more humane capitalism? The answers to those questions do not merely require research but a very deep understanding of the many human and social complexities involved.

In a more modest way, the model can simply serve as a frame of reference for social actors within the system as it now operates. Under those circumstances, those who grasp the sense of the times, correctly interpret the potential and the direction of change and deeply understand the characteristics of the relevant paradigm, are more likely to be able to pursue their goals with viable and realistic proposals.

---

249. Polanyi (1944).
250. See Beveridge (1944:1967).

Epilogue: The World at the Turning Point

In June 2002, as this book is going to press, the world is at the turning point. The decisions being taken at this crossroads will determine how long, how deep and how widespread the current recession will be and whether what lies ahead is a depression, a gilded age or a true golden age.

According to the interpretation presented in this book, the installation period of the current fifth great surge ended with the draining of the NASDAQ bubble, in March 2000. The recession that then began to threaten the US economy, developed through the first months of 2001 and intensified after the destruction of the World Trade Center, set the stage for a profound institutional restructuring.

It is not yet clear whether the stock markets have seen the worst of their troubles or whether the reconnection between paper and real values still awaits a big jolt or two. But the structural problems causing the recession are already there to be solved, and the Information Revolution is awaiting the appropriate conditions to display the second half of its growth and its wealth-generating potential.

If the world economy is to move towards a phase of synergistic growth, a new regulatory framework is needed, along with the global organizations capable of making it effective. This is a time for institutional imagination. Financial regulation is only a small part – though perhaps the most crucial – in the wide range of transformations required. Given the nature of the current paradigm, such changes are needed at several levels of differentiated action: local, regional, national, supranational and, especially, global.

In the equivalent period of the fourth surge, at the beginning of the recession following the crash of 1929, Keynes warned about the need for understanding the nature of the problem in order to be able to confront it. In his essay 'The Grand Slump of 1930', he defined the situation thus:

> The world has been slow to realise that we are living this year in the shadow of one of the greater economic catastrophes of modern history... At this moment the slump is probably a little overdone for psychological reasons. A modest upward reaction, therefore, may be due at any time. *But there cannot be a real recovery, in my judgment, until the idea of lenders and the idea of productive borrowers are brought together again* [added emphasis]... Seldom in modern history has the gap between the two been so wide and so difficult to bridge. Unless we bend our wills and our intelligences, energised by a conviction that this diagnosis is right, to find a solution

along these lines, then, if the diagnosis *is* right, the slump may pass over into a depression, accompanied by a sagging price level, which might last for years, with untold damage to the material wealth and to the social stability of every country alike.[251] (original emphasis)

That is precisely the dilemma facing world leaders today: misjudge the situation and treat it as one more passing recession or rise up to the task of confronting a serious structural problem, starting by understanding its nature.

History, however, tends to play tricks on the beholder by providing events that divert attention from the underlying forces at play. It has been as easy for many to blame the recession on the terrorist attack of September 2001 as it was, in the mid-1970s, to blame stagflation on the OPEC oil price hike. Though both events certainly intensified the phenomena, they didn't *cause* the recessions, which in both cases had clearly begun earlier and were of a structural nature. Explanations based on exogenous shocks (often, in fact, partly symptoms of the same deeper causes) lead to an impotent insistence on applying old economic recipes to new structural problems. Such recipes can only lead to fragile and short-lived successes, vulnerable to relatively minor events.

Financial capital has already done its job of leading the intensive spread of the new paradigm and the installation and testing of the new infrastructure. Sufficient portions of the business community and of consumers have assimilated the new common sense to be able to continue the transformation process. Now is the turn of production capital to take the leadership, expanding production and widening demand, with financial capital in a supporting role.[252] However, this change in the rules of the game may not be easy, because the financial collapse has not been spectacular enough to wipe out excess self-confidence.

Nonetheless, it is through institutional recomposition that the synergy phase can be ushered in. Going from drained bubble to golden age requires overcoming the three structural tensions that have built up and caused the recession.[253] All three demand well directed institutional action.

The tension between the growth of paper values and real wealth creating capacity, which was partly relieved by the collapse, can only be overcome by strict and decisively enforced regulation to restrain the practices of the casino economy. The cluster of revelations about the accountancy scandals in Enron, WorldCom and other major corporations should not be seen as a sudden and unexpected epidemic of dishonesty striking the business community. Rather, they are the consequence of the extreme pressure for unrealistic profit levels

---

251. Keynes (1930:1931:1972) pp. 126 and 133.
252. See pp. 123–4 above.
253. See pp. 115–8 above.

that the world of finance put upon the world of production during the Frenzy bubble. A dip in profits, which is a normal occurrence in the life of any company, meant a catastrophic collapse in value. Hence, during Frenzy, crime paid well.[254] Only such measures as will bring profit expectations down to realistic levels will allow production firms to conduct their business with strategic goals in mind. At this turning point, short-term financial criteria, apart from the risk of stimulating dishonesty, can no longer serve to guide investment and technology decisions directed to the steady expansion of production and markets. As at equivalent moments in the past, regulation is one of the main instruments to achieve that switch.

The second tension – between the potential for production expansion, on the one side, and the profile and rhythm of existing demand on the other – requires policies to willfully activate the markets of the new engines of growth. The premature market saturation in microelectronic chips, computers, software, telecommunications and Internet-based services affects the whole economy. Those are the dynamic sectors that have the potential to induce multiple new business activities around them, as well as to pull all the other industries and the whole world economy forward. Therefore, the choice of which industries are stimulated by government demand will make a huge difference, as will policies that affect the shape of income distribution.

Yet, in the globalized world of the present paradigm, demand is also global. The best promise of massive market expansion would seem to be in the incorporation of more and more countries to global growth, investment, production and consumption. Growth in the larger countries of the developing world, together with China, Russia and the ex-socialist group of Eastern Europe, could serve as a first tier to pull the others forward. It is quite obvious that these potentially huge markets are a very long way from saturation.

Nevertheless, the remaining potential in the markets of the advanced world should not be underestimated. The feeling of intense technological change of the 1990s Frenzy can lead, when followed by recession, to misguided pessimism regarding the future expansion of the Information Revolution and the Knowledge Society. A comparison with the Age of Mass-production can be instructive. At the end of the equivalent frenzy phase, in 1929, there were 23 million registered automobiles in the USA at a time when the adult population was 72 million. That market coverage of 32%, which appeared unsurpassable then, approached real saturation at over 70% by the end of the golden age, around 1970.[255] Similar figures apply to the markets for home electrical appliances and to the construction, coverage and use of the infrastructures of

---

254. See pp. 75-6, 109–11 and 142 above.
255. US Department of Commerce (1975), pp. 10 and 716.

that paradigm: the all-ecompassing networks of roads and electricity. The markets that were attained from the 1940s[256] through the 1960s, including the flourishing of synthetic materials and of innumerable induced activities in commerce and services, around suburban living and electricity, made the market levels of the 1920s Frenzy look relatively small. The parallels with computers and the Internet can readily be made.[257]

Regarding the third tension – the political and social pressures generated by the chasm between the countries that have been getting richer and those trapped in debt and economic crisis – effective action to ease it would be the most decisive contribution to overcoming the market saturation problem in an increasingly globalized economy. Not reversing global polarization, in itself, poses serious threats to the safety and stability of the prosperous countries. These include massive migrations, various forms of violence and the outbreak of serious economic crises, such as that of Argentina, which could affect others in their wake.

Hence, the tasks are complex and wide-ranging: designing an adequate and enforceable regulatory framework; devising ways of effective intervention to reshape the demand profile to extend the Information Revolution; and decisively acting on both sides of the world divide to stimulate a truly global economy, expanding wealth generation across the planet.

No idea is too bold as long as it applies the 'common sense' principles of the new techno-economic paradigm. As at other turning points, imagination has to look forward, not back, and there are no ready-made recipes. Each technological revolution is different, each paradigm is unique, each set of solutions needs to be coherent with the problems to overcome and with the logic of the techno-economic paradigm, its opportunities and its best practice. Each specific mode of growth, constructed for deploying the second half of each revolution, involves a set of ideological values that shapes the manner in which those opportunities are deployed and which of them will be favored.[258]

The present generations are living through a period requiring intense social and institutional creativity. There is a growing sense of urgency that leads to many proposals coming forth, of greater or lesser scope, with greater or lesser ambition, going from alternative economic theories to practical measures and

---

256. See the discussion about institutional inertia prolonging the depression in the 1930s in the USA, pp. 125–6 above.
257. And the similarity extends to the pessimistic forecasts. Landes (1969), p. 484, reports that the economic adviser to the Federation of British Industries predicted in 1944 that the economy would peak out because the latest cluster of innovations, associated with electricity and motor transport, was exhausted.
258. Fascism in the 1930s made choices within the potential of mass production that were different from those made by Keynesian democracies after the war.

policies.[259] There is also ample scope for redirecting business imagination and technological innovation towards the deeper transformation of world society, through developing truly knowledge intensive ways of producing and living.

What lies ahead are many social conflicts and confrontations, negotiations, agreements and compromises leading to fundamental decisions on policies and institutions, at all levels and in many areas. The range of the possible is very wide and history has shown that violence, messianic leaders, economic theories and many other social, political and ideological factors can influence the choice. The forces that will engage in those battles are gathering now. Those present on the arena, with viable proposals, will take part in the shaping of the social and economic history of the next two or three decades. A golden age of worldwide expansion is possible. Making it happen will require thinking big, deciding wisely and acting boldly.

Caracas, June 30, 2002

---

259. Examples of collective efforts at building alternative economic theories are The Other Canon (www.othercanon.org), The Post-Autistic Economic Network (www.paecon.ne) and the PEKEA (Political and Ethical Knowledge on Economic Activities) Research Programme (pekea.free.fr). Among the proposals signaling the direction of change, see Chris Freeman's (2001b) brief and powerful essay 'If I ruled the world,' Richard Jolly's (2002) measures to confront inequality, the Sagasti and Bezanson report on Global Public Goods, Radosevic (1999) and Ostry (1992) on harmonizing global regulation of foreign investment and the reports of the UNU-WIDER Research Programme (http://www.wider.unu) to help overcome world poverty. Ambitious proposals to reform the global financial and trade institutions are George Soros (2002) and Stiglitz (1992:1997 and 2002).

Bibliography

Abraham, Paul and Daniels, Caroline (2001), 'A Desert Wind Blows Over Sand Hill Road', *Financial Times, IT Review*, October 3, p. 1.

Abramovitz, Moses (1986), 'Catching Up, Forging Ahead and Falling Behind', *Journal of Economic History*, Vol. 46, pp. 385–406.

Aglietta, Michel (1976:1979), *A Theory of Capitalist Regulation*, London: New Left Books.

Altshuler, Alan, Anderson, Martin, Jones, Daniel, Roos, Daniel and Womack, James (1984), *The Future of the Automobile*, Cambridge, MA: MIT Press.

Amsden, Alice (1990), *Asia's Next Giant*, New York: Oxford University Press.

Arthur, W. Brian (1988), 'Competing Technologies: An Overview', in Dosi et al. (eds), pp. 590–607.

Arthur, W. Brian (2002), 'Is Technology Over? If History Is a Guide, It Is Not', *Business 2.0*, March, pp. 65–72.

Ayres, Robert U. (1989), *Technological Transformation and Long Waves*, Laxenburg, Austria: IIASA.

Bailey, Brian (1995), *George Hudson: The Rise and Fall of the Railway King*, Gloucestershire: Stroud.

Baran, Paul A. and Sweezy, Paul M. (1966:1968), *Monopoly Capital: An Essay on the American Economic and Social Order*, New York and London: Modern Reader Paperbacks.

Barras, Richard (1986), 'Towards a Theory of Innovation in Services', *Research Policy*, Vol. 15, pp. 161–73.

Barras, Richard. (1990), 'Interactive Innovation in Financial and Business Services: The Vanguard of the Service Revolution', *Research Policy*, Vol. 19, No. 3, pp. 215–39.

Bell, Daniel (1973:1976), *The Coming of Post-Industrial Society*, Harmondsworth, Middlesex: Peregrine/Penguin.

Berghahn, Volker R. (1994), *Imperial Germany, 1871–1914. Economy, Society, Culture and Politics*, Providence, RI and Oxford: Berghahn Books.

Beveridge, Sir William (1944:1967), *Full Employment in a Free Society*, London: George Allen & Unwin (Second impression).

Blair, John M. (1972), *Economic Concentration: Structure, Behavior and Policy*, New York: Harcourt Brace Jovanovich.

Boyer, Robert (1988), 'Technical Change and the Theory of *Régulation*', in Dosi et al., pp. 67–94.

Bruun, Geoffrey (1959:1990), *Nineteenth Century European Civilization 1815–1914*, London: Oxford University Press. Spanish edition, *La Europa del Siglo XIX 1815–1914*, México: Fondo de Cultura Económica.

Cain, Peter J. and Hopkins, Antony G. (1993), *British Imperialism: Innovation and Expansion 1688–1914*, London and New York: Longman.

Carnegie, Andrew (1920), *Autobiography of Andrew Carnegie*, Boston and New York: Houghton Mifflin.

Castells, Manuel, vol. 1 (1996), vol. 2 (1997), vol. 3 (1998), *The Information Age, Economy, Society and Culture*, three volumes, Oxford: Blackwell.

Chancellor, Edward (1999), *Devil Take the Hindmost: A History of Financial Speculation*, New York: Farrar-Straus-Giroux.

Chandler, Alfred D. (1977), *The Visible Hand: The Managerial Revolution in American Business*, Cambridge, MA and London: Harvard University Press.

Chandler, Alfred D. (1990), *Scale and Scope, the Dynamics of Industrial Capitalism*, Cambridge, MA: Harvard University Press.

Chang, Ha-Joong (1994:1996), *The Political Economy of Industrial Policy*, Basingstoke and London: Macmillan Press.

Chang, Ha-Joong (1997), 'The Economics and Politics of Regulation', *Cambridge Journal of Economics*, Vol. 21, No. 6, pp. 703–28.

Chang, Ha-Joon (2002), *Pulling Up the Ladder? Policies and Institutions for Development in Historical Perspective*, London: Anthem.

Chang, Ha Joon, Palma, Gabriel and Whitaker, D.H. (eds) (2001), *Financial Liberalization and the Asian Crisis*, New York: Palgrave.

Chick, Virginia (1992), 'The Evolution of the Banking System and the Theory of Saving, Investment and Interest', in Arestis, P. and Dow, S.C. (eds), *On Money, Method and Keynes, Selected Essays*, London: Macmillan, pp. 193–205.

Colvin, Geoffrey (1999), 'El Año de las Megafusiones', *Fortune Americas*, January 18, pp. 6–9.

Coriat, Benjamin (1978), *L'Atelier et le Chronomètre*, Paris: C. Bourgois.

Crouzet, François (1964), Wars, Blockade and Economic Change in Europe 1792–1815, *Journal of Economic History*, Vol. 24, pp. 567–88.

Cruikshank, Jeffrey L. (1987), *A Delicate Experiment: The Harvard Business School 1908–1945*, Boston, MA: Harvard Business Review Press.

Diebold, John (1952), *Automation: The Advent of the Automatic Factory*, New York: Van Nostrand.

Dore, Ronald (2000), *Stock Market Capitalism: Welfare Capitalism. Japan and Germany Versus the Anglo-Saxons*, Oxford: Oxford University Press.

Dosi, Giovanni (1982), 'Technical Paradigms and Technological Trajectories: A Suggested Interpretation of the Determinants of Technical Change', *Research Policy*, Vol. 2, No. 3, pp. 147–62.

Dosi, Giovanni, Freeman, Christopher, Nelson, Richard, Silverberg, Gerald, and Soete, Luc (eds) (1988), *Technical Change and Economic Theory*, London and New York: Pinter and Columbia University Press.

Dow, J. Christopher R. (1998), *The Major Recessions, 1920–1995*, Oxford: Oxford University Press.

Drechsler, Wolfgang (2000), 'Money as Myth and Reality', in Backhaus, Jürgen G. and Stadermann, Hans-Joachim (eds), *Georg Simmel's Philosophy of Money: A Centenary Appraisal*, Marburg: Metropolis, pp. 33–45.

Dyos, H. James and Aldcroft, Derek H. (1969), *British Transport, An Economic Survey from the Seventeenth Century to the Twentieth*, Harmondsworth, Middlesex, Baltimore, Maryland, Ringwood, Victoria and Markham, Ontario: Penguin Books.

Engels, Friedrich (1845:1920), *The Condition of the Working-Class in England in 1844*, London: Allen.

Ernst, Dieter (2001), 'Responses to the Crisis: Constraints to a Rapid Trade Adjustment in East Asia's Electronics Industry', in Chang, Ha-Joon et al. (eds), *The Asian Crisis*, London: Macmillan.

Evans, Peter (1995), *Embedded Autonomy: States and Industrial Transformation*, Princeton, NJ: Princeton University Press.

Faulkner, Harold U (1951), *The Decline of Laissez Faire, 1897–1917*, New York: Rinehart.

Financial Times (2002a), 'Enron and the Role of the Banks', January 17, Editorial.

Financial Times (2002b), 'After Enron', February 19, pp. 18–19.

Freeman, Christopher (1974), *The Economics of Industrial Innovation*, Harmondsworth, Middlesex: Penguin Books.

Freeman, Christopher (1995), *History, Co-evolution and Economic Growth*, Laxenburg: IIASA Working Paper.

Freeman, Christopher (ed.) (1996), *The Long Wave in the World Economy*, International Library of Critical Writings in Economics, Aldershot: Edward Elgar.

Freeman, Christopher (2001a), 'A Hard Landing For the "New Economy"? Information Technology and the United States National System of Innovation', *Structural Change and Economic Dynamics*, No. 12, pp. 115–39.

Freeman, Christopher (2001b), 'Viewpoint: If I Ruled the World', *Science and Public Policy*, Vol. 28, No. 6, December, pp. 477–9.

Freeman, Christopher, Clark, John and Soete, Luc (1982), *Unemployment and Technical Innovation. A Study of Long Waves and Economic Development*, London: Frances Pinter.

Freeman, Christopher and Louçã, Francisco (2001), *As Time Goes By: From the Industrial Revolution to the Information Revolution*, Oxford: Oxford University Press.

Freeman, Christopher and Perez, Carlota (1988), 'Structural Crises of Adjustment: Business Cycles and Investment Behavior', in Dosi et al. (eds), pp. 38–66.

Freeman, Christopher and Soete, Luc (1997), *The Economics of Industrial Innovation*, 3rd edition, London: Pinter.

Friedman, Milton and Schwartz, Anna (1963:1971), *A Monetary History of the United States*, Princeton, NJ: Princeton University Press.

Galbraith, John Kenneth (1990:1993), *A Short History of Financial Euphoria*, New York: Whittle–Penguin.

Gay, Edwin F. (1929), 'Introduction', in Hoover, pp. 1–12.

Gerschenkron, Alexander (1962), 'The Approach to European Industrialization: A Postscript', in *Economic Backwardness in a Historical Perspective*, Cambridge, MA: Belknap Press, pp. 353–66.

Gomulka, Stanislaw (1990), *The Theory of Technical Change and Economic Growth*, London: Routledge.

Grübler, Arnulf (1990), *The Rise and Fall of Infrastructures, Dynamics of Evolution and Technological Change in Transport*, Heidelberg and New York: Physica-Verlag.

Heilbroner, Robert L. (1953), *The Worldly Philosophers: The Great Economic Thinkers*, New York: Simon & Schuster.

Hilferding, Rudolf (1910:1981), *Das Finanzkapital,* Vienna: Volksbuchhandlung Ignaz Brand &Co. (English translation) Bottomore, T. and Kegan, Paul (eds), *Finance Capital*, London: Routledge.

Hirsch, Seev (1965), 'The United States Electronic Industry in International Trade', *National Institute Economic Review*, No. 34, pp. 92–107.

Hirsch, Seev (1967), *Location of Industry and International Competitiveness*, Oxford: Clarendon Press.

Hobsbawm, Eric J. (1962), *The Age of Revolution*, New York, Ontario and London: Mentor.

Hobsbawm, Eric J. (1975:1996), *The Age of Capital 1848–1875*, New York: Vintage.

Hobsbawm, Eric J. (1997:1998), *On History,* London: Abacus.

Hodgson, Geoffrey M. (2001), *How Economics Forgot History: The Problem of Historical Specificity in Social Science*, London: Routledge.

Hoover, Herbert, Chairman (1929), *Recent Economic Changes in the United States, Report of the Committee on Recent Economic Changes of the President's Conference on Unemployment*, New York, London: McGraw-Hill.

Jevons, William Stanley (1866), *The Coal Question: An Inquiry Concerning the Progress of the Nation, and the Probable Exhaustion of Our Coal Mines*, 2nd edition, revised, London: Macmillan.

Johnson, Chalmers (1982), *MITI and the Japanese Miracle: The Growth of Industrial Policy 1925–1975*, Stanford, CA: Stanford University Press.

Joint Economic Committee, US 87th Congress, 1st Session (1962), *Variability of Private Investment in Plant and Equipment*, Washington, DC, pp. 32, 40–41.

Jolly, Richard (1999), 'Global Inequality', *Wider Angle*, UNU, No. 2, December, pp. 5–6.

Jolly, Richard (2002), 'Global Inequality: How Tom Paine Would Rage', presentation at the Headstrong Society, Lewes, May 10.

Kaldor, Mary (1999), *New and Old Wars: Organized Violence in a Global Era*, London: Polity.

Keynes, John Maynard (1926:1931), 'The End of Laissez Faire', in *Essays in Persuasion*, in Keynes (1972), Vol. IX, pp. 272–94.

Keynes, John Maynard (1930:1931), 'The Grand Slump of 1930', in *Essays in Persuasion*, in Keynes (1972), Vol. IX, pp. 126–49.

Keynes, John Maynard (1936), *The General Theory of Employment, Interest, and Money*, New York, Chicago, Burlingame: Harcourt, Brace & World, Inc.

Keynes, John Maynard (1972), *Collected Writings of J.M. Keynes*, for the Royal Economic Society, London: Macmillan and Cambridge University Press.

Kindleberger, Charles P. (1978:1996), *Manias, Panics and Crashes, A History of Financial Crises*, New York, Chichester, Brisbane, Toronto, Singapore: John Wiley & Sons, Inc.

Kindleberger, Charles P. (1984:1985), *A Financial History of Western Europe*, London, Boston, Sydney: George Allen & Unwin.

Kindleberger, Charles and Laffargue, Jean-Pierre (eds) (1982), *Financial Crises. Theory, History and Policy*, London, New York, New Rochelle, Melbourne, Sydney: Cambridge University Press.

Kleinknecht, Alfred, Mandel, Ernest and Wallerstein, Immanuel (eds) (1992), *New Findings in Long Wave Research*, New York: St. Martin's Press.

Kondratiev, Nikolai (1925:1979), 'The Long Waves in Economic Life', *Review of Economic Statistics*, Vol. 17 (1935), pp. 105–15 (original Russian version 1925 published in German in 1926). Reproduced in *Review*, Vol. 2, No. 4, Spring 1979, pp. 519–62.

Kregel, Jan (1995), 'Neoclassical Price Theory, Institutions and the Evolution of Securities Market Organization', *Economic Journal*, Vol. 105, No. 429, March, pp. 459–70.

Kuhn, Thomas (1962:1970), *The Structure of Scientific Revolutions* (2nd edition, enlarged), Chicago: University of Chicago Press.

Kuznets, Simon (1940), 'Schumpeter's Business Cycles', *American Economic Review*, Vol. 30, pp. 257–71.

Kuznets, Simon (1953), *Economic Change*, New York: W.W. Norton.

Kuznets, Simon (1971:1973), 'Modern Economic Growth: Findings and Reflections', in *Population, Capital and Growth, Selected Essays*, New York: W.W. Norton.

Landes, David S. (1969), *The Unbound Prometheus, Technological Change and Industrial Development in Western Europe from 1750 to the Present*, London: Cambridge University Press.

Latham, A. John H. (1981), *The Depression and the Developing World 1914–1939*, London: Croom-Helm; Totowa, NJ: Barnes & Noble.

Laybourn, Keith (1991), *British Trade Unionism c.1770–1990*, Stroud, Gloucestershire and Wolfeboro Falls, NH: Alan Sutton.

Le Monde (2001), 'Grâce à la Crise, les Entreprises se Libèrent du Dogme des 15 per cent de Rentabilité', December 20, Paris.

Lieven, Dominic (1993), *The Aristocracy in Europe, 1815–1914*, New York: Columbia University Press.

List, Frederick (1841), *The National System of Political Economy*, English edition 1904, London: Longman.

Lloyd-Jones, Roger and Lewis, M.J. (1998), *British Industrial Capitalism since the Industrial Revolution*, London: University College London Press.

Louçã, Francisco and Reijnders, J. (eds) (1999), *The Foundations of Long Wave Theory*, International Library of Critical Writings in Economics, Cheltenham, UK, Northampton, MA, USA: Edward Elgar.

Mackay, James (1997), *Sounds out of Silence: A Life of Alexander Graham Bell*, Edinburgh: Mainstream Publishing Co.

Mandel, Ernest (1975), *Late Capitalism*, London: New Left Books.

Mandel, Michael J. (1997), 'The New Business Cycle', *Business Week*, Latin American edition, March 31, pp. 38–54.

Marichal, Carlos (1988), *Historia de la Deuda Externa de América Latina*, Buenos Aires: Alianza Editorial.

Marx, Karl and Engels, Friedrich (1847), *The Communist Manifesto*.

McKinnon, Ronald and Pill, Huw (1997), 'Credible Economic Liberalizations and Over Borrowing', *American Economic Review*, Vol. 87, No. 2, May.

Meadows, Donella H., Meadows, Dennis and Randers, Jorgen (1972), *The Limits to Growth*, New York: Universe Books.

Mensch, Gerhard (1979), *Stalemate in Technology*, Cambridge, MA: Ballinger.

Michie, Ranald C. (1987), *The London and New York Stock Exchanges 1850–1914*, London: Allen & Unwin.

Minsky, Hyman (1975), *John Maynard Keynes*, New York: Columbia University Press.

Minsky, Hyman (1982), 'The Financial-Instability Hypothesis: Capitalist Processes and the Behavior of the Economy', in Kindleberger and Laffargue (eds), pp. 13–39.

Minsky, Hyman (1986), *Stabilizing an Unstable Economy*, New Haven and London: Yale University Press.

Mowrey, Mark A. (2000), 'Web Companies Find 1999 Venture Capital Windfall', *The Industry Standard*, February 7.

Negroponte, Nicholas (1995), *Being Digital*, New York: Alfred A. Knopf.

Nelson, Richard and Winter, Sidney G. (1977), 'In Search of a Useful Theory of Innovation', *Research Policy*, Vol. 6, No.1, pp. 36–76.

Nussbaum, Bruce (2001), 'A Shock to the Equity Culture', *Business Week*, October 8, pp. 34–5.

Ominami, Carlos (ed.) (1986), *La Tercera Revolución Industrial, Impactos*

Internacionales del Actual Viraje Tecnológico, Buenos Aires: Grupo Editor Latinoamericano.

Ostry, Sylvia (1992), 'The Domestic Domain: the New International Policy Arena', *Transnational Corporations*, Vol. 1, No. 1, February, pp. 7–26.

Palma, Gabriel (1978), 'Growth and Structure of Chilean Manufacturing Industry from 1830 to 1935: Origins and Development of a Process of Industrialisation in an Export Economy', D. Phil. thesis, Oxford University. Forthcoming, Oxford University Press.

Palma, Gabriel (2001), 'Three Routes to Financial Crises: The Need for Capital Controls', CEPA Working Paper 2000–17, November 2000, www.newschool.edu/cepa/papers, forthcoming (2002) in Eatwell, J. and Taylor, L. (eds), *International Capital Markets and the Future of Economic Policy*, Oxford: Oxford University Press.

Palma, Gabriel and Marcel, Mario (1989), 'Kaldor on the Discreet Charm of the Chilean Bourgeoisie', *Cambridge Journal of Economics*, April, pp. 245–72.

Perez, Carlota (1983), 'Structural Change and the Assimilation of New Technologies in the Economic and Social Systems', *Futures*, Vol. 15, No. 5, pp. 357–75.

Perez, Carlota (1985), 'Microelectronics, Long Waves and World Structural Change: New Perspectives for Developing Countries', *World Development*, Vol. 13, No. 3, pp. 441–63.

Perez, Carlota (1986), 'Las Nuevas Tecnologías: Una Visión De Conjunto', in Ominami (ed.), pp. 44–89 (also in *Estudios Internacionales*, Vol. 19, No. 76, October–December, Santiago de Chile, pp. 420–59).

Perez, Carlota (1998), 'Desafíos Sociales y Políticos del Cambio de Paradigma Tecnológico', in *Venezuela Desafíos y Propuestas*, Caracas: Universidad Católica Andrés Bello, pp. 63–109.

Perez, Carlota (2001), 'Cambio Tecnológico y Oportunidades de Desarrollo como Blanco Móvil', *Revista de la CEPAL*, No. 75, December (English version 'Technical Change and Opportunities for Development as a moving Target' in *ECLAC Review*, No. 75, forthcoming).

Perez, Carlota and Soete, Luc (1988), 'Catching Up in Technology: Entry Barriers and Windows of Opportunity', in Dosi et al. (eds), pp. 458–79.

Pigou, Arthur Cecil (1949), *The Veil of Money*, London: Macmillan.

Polanyi, Karl (1944), *The Great Transformation*, New York: Rinehart.

Poon, Auliana (1992), *Tourism, Technology and Competitive Strategies*, Wallingford: C.A.B. International.

Powell, Ellis T. (1915:1966), *The Evolution of the Money Market 1385–1915: An Historical and Analytical Study of the Rise and Development of Finance as a Centralised, Co-ordinated Force*, London: Frank Cass and Co. Ltd.

Radosevic, Slavo (1999), *International Technology Transfer and 'Catch Up' in Economic Development*, Cheltenham: Edward Elgar.

Reading, Brian (1992:1993), *Japan: The Coming Collapse*, London: Orion Books.

Reinert, Erik S. (2000), 'Karl Bücher and the Geographical Dimensions of Techno-Economic Change', in Backhaus, Jürgen (ed.), *Karl Bücher: Theory–History–Anthropology–Non-Market Economies*, Marburg: Metropolis Verlag.

Reinert, Erik S. (2001), 'The Deindustrialization of Mongolia', in Reinert (ed.), *Evolutionary Economics and Income Equality*, Cheltenham, UK and Northampton, MA, USA: Edward Elgar.

Reinert, Erik S. and Daastøl, Arno (1997), 'Exploring the Genesis of Economic Innovations: The Religious Gestalt-Switch and the Duty to Invent as Preconditions for Economic Growth', *European Journal of Law and Economics*, Vol. 4, No. 2/3, June, pp. 233–83.

Roberts, Dan (2001), 'Glorious Hopes on a Trillion Dollar Scrap Heap', *Financial Times*, September 6, p. 12.

Rosenberg, Nathan and Frischtak, Claudio (1984), 'Technological Innovation and Long Waves', *Cambridge Journal of Economics*, Vol. 8, pp. 7–24.

Sagasti, Francisco and Bezanson, Keith (2001), *Financing and Providing Global Public Goods: Expectations and Prospects*, Stockholm: Ministry for Foreign Affairs (Fritzes Kundservice, S-106 47)

Shin, Jang-Sup (1992), 'Catching-up and Technological Progress in Late Industrialising Countries', PhD Thesis, Cambridge, England.

Schlender, Brent (1998), 'Peter Drucker Takes the Long View: An Interview', *Fortune*, September 28, pp. 162–71.

Schmoller, Gustav (1893:1898), 'Die Volkswirtschaft, die Volkswirtschaftslehre und ihre Methode', in Schmoller, *Über einige Grundfragen der Socialpolitik und der Volkswirtschaftslehre*, Berlin: Duncker & Humblot, pp. 213–314.

Schumpeter, Joseph A. (1939:1982), *Business Cycles,* 2 vols, Philadelphia: Porcupine Press.

Schumpeter, Joseph, A. (1942:1975), *Capitalism, Socialism and Democracy*, New York, Hagerstown, San Francisco, London: Harper & Row.

Seligman, Edwin (1927), *The Economics of Instalment* [sic] *Selling: A study of Consumers' Credit with Special References to the Automobile*, New York: Harper.

Shaikh, Anwar (1992), 'The Falling Rate of Profit as the Cause of Long Waves: Theory and Empirical Evidence', in Kleinknecht et al. (eds), pp. 174–95.

Shiller, Robert (2000), *Irrational Exuberance*, Princeton, NJ: Princeton University Press.

Sloan, Allan (1998), 'The Big Hedge-Fund Bailout Helps Some Fat Cats, but Makes Our Case for Free Global Markets Look Awfully Thin', *Newsweek*, October 12.

Sobel, Robert (1965), *The Big Board: A History of the New York Stock Market*, New York: Free Press, London: Collier/Macmillan.

Soete, Luc (1985), 'International Diffusion of Technology, Industrial Development and Technological Leapfrogging', *World Development*, Vol. 13, No. 3, March, pp. 409–22.

Soete, Luc (2000), 'Towards the Digital Economy: Scenarios for Business,' *Telematics and Informatics*, No. 17, pp. 199–212.

Sombart, Werner (1913), *Krieg und Kapitalismus*, München & Leipzig: Duncker & Humblot.

Soros, George (1998), *The Crisis of Global Capitalism: Open Society Endangered*, London: Little, Brown & Company.

Soros, George (2000), *Open Society: Reforming Global Capitalism*, New York: Public Affairs.

Stankiewicz, Rikard (2000), 'The Concept of Design Space', in Ziman (ed.), pp. 234–48.

Stiglitz, Joseph E. (1992:1997), *An Agenda for Development for the Twenty-First Century*, Keynote Address, Annual Bank Conference on Development Economics, 30 April–1 May 1992, Washington DC: World Bank.

Stiglitz, Joseph E. (2002), *Globalization and its discontents*, New York: W.W. Norton.

Strange, Susan (1986), *Casino Capitalism*, Oxford: Blackwell.

Strange, Susan (1998), *Mad Money*, Manchester: Manchester University Press.

The Economist (1998), 'Will Internet Shares Join Tulip Bulbs and the South Sea Company on the List of Great Financial Bubbles?', December 19.

Toffler, Alvin (1980), *The Third Wave*, New York: Random House.

Toporowski, Jan (1993), *The Economics of Financial Markets and the 1987 Crash*, Aldershot: Edward Elgar.

Toporowski, Jan (2000), *The End of Finance: Capital Market Inflation, Financial Derivatives and Pension Fund Capitalism*, London: Routledge.

Trebilcock, Clive (1981), *The Industrialisation of the Continental Powers, 1780–1914*, London: Longman

Tully, Shawn (1999), 'Stocks May Be Surging Toward an Earnings Chasm', *Fortune Investor*, Vol. 139, No. 2, February 1.

Twain, Mark and Warner, Charles Dudley (1873), *The Gilded Age: A Tale of Today*, Hartford, CT: The American Publishing Co.

Tylecote, Andrew (1985), 'Inequality in the Long Wave: Trend and Cycle in Core and Periphery', *European Association of Development Institutes Bulletin*, No. 1, pp. 1–23.

Tylecote, Andrew (1992), *The Long Wave in the World Economy: The Current Crisis in Historical Perspective*, London and New York: Routledge.

US Departament of Commerce (1975), *Historical Statistics of the United States, Colonial Times to 1970*, Washington, DC: Bureau of the Census.

Utterback, James M. and Abernathy, William J. (1975), 'A Dynamic Model of Process and Product Innovation', *Omega*, Vol. 3, No. 6, pp. 639–56.

Van Duijn, Jacob J. (1983), *The Long Wave in Economic Life*, London, Boston, Sydney: George Allen & Unwin.

Veblen, Thorstein (1899), *The Theory of the Leisure Class: An Economic Study of Institutions* (Versión castellana Herrero, Vicente, traductor, Teoría de la Clase Ociosa, Fondo de Cultura Económica, México, 1944).

Veblen, Thorstein (1904:1975), *The Theory of Business Enterprise*, New York: Augustus Kelley.

Vernon, Raymond (1966), 'International Investment and International Trade in the Product Cycle', *Quarterly Journal of Economics*, No. 80, pp. 190–207.

Von Tunzelmann, G. Nick (1997), 'Innovation and Industrialization: A Long-term Comparison', *Technological Forecasting and Social Change*, No. 56, pp. 1–23.

Wade, Robert (1998), 'The Asian Debt-and-Development Crisis of 1997–?: Causes and Consequences', *World Development*, Vol. 26, No. 8, pp. 1535–53.

Wade, Robert (2001), 'From "Miracle" to "Cronyism"', in Chang et al. (eds) (2001), pp. 63–81.

Wade, Robert (1990), *Governing the Market: Economic Theory and the Role of Government in East Asian Industrialization*, Princeton, NJ: Princeton University Press.

Walker, William (1986), 'Information Technology and Energy Supply', *Energy Policy*, Vol. 14, No. 6, December.

Wall Street Journal Americas (2001), Spanish edition in *El Nacional*, Caracas, October 17, p. F–4.

Wells, David A. (1889:1893), *Recent Economic Changes, and Their Effect on the Production and Distribution of Wealth and the Well-Being of Society*, New York: D. Appleton & Company.

Wells, Louis T. Jr. (ed.) (1972), *The Product Life Cycle and International Trade*, Cambridge, Mass: Harvard University Press.

Wessel, David (2002), 'When Standards Are Unacceptable', *The Wall Street Journal*, February 7.

Wiebe, Robert (1967), *The Search for Order, 1877–1920*, New York: Hill and Wang.

Wolf, Julius (1912), *Die Volkswirtschaft der Gegenwart und Zukunft* (A. Deichertsche Verlags-buchandlung).

Womack, James P., Jones, Daniel T. and Roos, Daniel (1990), *The Machine that Changed the World*, New York: Rawson Associates.

Ziman, John (ed.) (2000), *Technological Innovation as an Evolutionary Process*, Cambridge: Cambridge University Press.

Index

Abramovitz, Moses, 59
Accountancy standards. *See* Regulatory
  frameworks
Africa, 65, 105
Argentina, 66, 104, 105, 122, 169
Arkwright, Richard, 11, 37
Arthur, W. Brian
  locking-in of dominant design, 134
  arrangements for use, 135
Asia, 11, 14, 18, 66, 104, 105, 118
Asset inflation phenomenon, 4, 43, 51,
  77, 98, 102, 142

Bailing out, 104, 120–21, 122
Baran, Paul, 85
Belgium, 97, 103
Best-practice. *See* Techno-economic
  paradigms
Beveridge, Sir William, 166
Bifurcation. *See* Decoupling-recoupling
Big-bang events
  see also Irruption phase;
    Technological revolutions
  definition/description, 11
  dates, 3, 11–12, 57
  conditions, 56
  financial capital
    attracted by, 38–9
    helping, 47, 154, 168
  gestation of revolution before, 63, 65
  identification with hindsight, 90
  initiating technological revolutions,
    3–4, 11–12
  irruption phase following, 49
  model, role in 12
  opportunity explosion, 90
  paradigm configuration after, 29
  turbulence following, 26, 41, 43
Bismarck, Otto von, 130
Brazil, 66, 93
Bretton Woods, 12, 52, 163
Britain, 49, 59, 85

banks, 94, 96
core country, 11, 14, 18, 47, 57, 78, 87
corruption, 110
crises, 88, 98
financial capital
  third surge, 122, 132
  industry funding, 58, 94, 122, 130
first surge, 65, 91–2, 107, 117, 129
foreign investment, 83–5, 104
gold standard, 58
irruption phase, 49
oligopolies, 82
third surge with Maturity features, 58
trade unions, 45–6
triple core in third surge, 10, 12, 63–4
Victorian Synergy, 53, 128
Bubbles
  see also Crises; Frenzy phase
  asset inflation, 4, 43, 51, 98, 102
  delusion, 43, 137
  Frenzy characteristic, 36, 52, 115
  Internet, xvii, 7, 79, 106, 120
  Japanese early, 103, 118
  manias, 28, 51, 106–7, 118
  NASDAQ, 118–19, 162
  new infrastructural investment, 41,
    106–7, 134
  paper versus real values, 76, 112
  real estate manias, 101, 106
  recurring sequence, 5
  regulation rejected, 51–2, 120
  structural tensions, 115, 118, 158
  technology as object of speculation,
    79
  warnings unheeded, 118–19
Business Week, 40, 107

Capital gains
  bubbles, 75, 101, 115, 118
  disparity paper-real values, 76, 111
  financial capital, 71, 124, 140
  pressure on production capital, 115–6

Capitalism
  bad face, 4, 50
  basic regularities, 5–6, 115, 151
  best face, 5, 54, 133
  changing nature, 7, 23, 62, 121, 129,
    157, 158, 162, 166
  cyclical, 146, 162
  diffusion across world, 20, 59, 63,
    65, 83, 154–5
  expanding by surges, 20, 59, 145
  faith in, 137
  features causing sequence, 155–7
  'free competition', 108
  Gay, Edwin F., 158
  Keynes, John Maynard, 157–8
  modes of growth, 24–5
  pendular swings of, 52, 158
  private and social interest, 52, 157–8
  progress, 152, 20
  recurring sequence, 3–4, 151–4, 162
  role of financial and production
    capital, 72, 158
  Schumpeter, Joseph, 22–3
  successful behavior taken to
    extremes, 115
  technology as fuel, 155
  three spheres of change, 155
  unfulfilled promises, 55
Carnegie, Andrew, 4, 11, 32, 92
Casino capitalism, 99
Casino economy, 3, 75–6, 103, 105, 116,
  120, 122, 142
Castells, Manuel, 19, 25
Catching up, 21, 31, 90–91, 103
  Asian Tigers, 104
  European countries, 103
  Germany, 85
  governmental funding, 93
  idle money helping, 85, 103–5
  internal, between industries, 44
  Soviet Union, 103
  USA, 93, 103
  windows of opportunity, 21, 66, 103–5
Centrifugal trends. *See* Decoupling-
  recoupling; Social polarization
Clusters
  of new entrepreneurs, 27, 34
  regional irruption, 10
  technological revolutions, 6, 8, 155
Common sense
  externality, 27, 42

principles, generalized, 4, 17, 19, 26,
  42, 44, 114, 168
techno-economic paradigms as, 7,
  15, 16, 26,
Competition
  dominant design, 134
  fierce 'free', 5, 51, 105
  globalized, 38, 162–3
  leading to oligopolies, 5, 51, 76
  mergers and oligopolies, 55, 82,
    108–9, 136
  new versus old industries, 40, 61
  price lowering excessive, 108
  truly free, 108, 146, 162–3
Consumer credit, 42, 94, 143–4, 145
Core countries
  see also Peripheral countries
  Britain falling behind, 121–3
  Britain, 11, 14, 18, 47, 57, 78, 87
  Maturity, 31, 90
  paradigm first deployed in, 10
  triple core in third surge, 10, 12, 63–4
  USA, 11, 14, 18, 57, 78, 87, 127–8
Core industries
  capital hungry in third surge, 92
  engines of growth, 44–5
  expanding in Synergy, 133
  mergers and oligopolies, 55, 82,
    108–9, 136
  rejuvenated, 94–5
  technological revolution, 13–14
  test beds for next revolution, 95
Corn laws, 52, 55, 162
Corruption, 51, 109, 110, 142–3, 168
Crashes. *See* Bubbles; Crises
Creative destruction, 22
  financial capital, 43, 75, 116, 158
  discontinuous leaps, 59
  institutional, 146, 154, 165
  Schumpeter, Joseph A., 22–3, 37
  Social impact, 41
  Sombart, Werner, 22
Crises
  see also Bubbles; Frenzy phase
  Argentina, 1890, crisis, 104, 122
  Asia 1997, 104, 105
  catching up countries, 88
  catharsis, 119
  causes of recession after, 115–16
  currency, 88
  dates of major, 78

Frenzy ending with, 52, 76
frequency changing with phases, 79
frenzy phase, 105
forging ahead untypical, 122
installation period, 43, 167
Kindleberger model, 79
lessons learned, 121
manner unpredictable, 115
mid-period, 79, 98, 136
mismatch, cause of crash, xviii
model and real history, 121, 159
model, inclusion in, 77, 106
paper values readjusted, 112, 115
recession following, 3, 114–18
recoupling need for, 125
recurrence of major, 77, 79
recurring interest in, 161
regulation, pressure and acceptance
    after, 5, 120–21, 125, 129
technology related, xviii, 118, 165
turning point after collapse, 47
simultaneity of major, 63
USA, 88, 104–5
Cycles,
    economic, 23, 146
    life of technological revolutions, 29–
        32, 63
    loan fever and default, 86
    short in mature paradigms, 54, 81, 85
    overlap, 9, 154–5
    Schumpeter, 23
    vicious/virtuous, 42, 116, 117, 135
Chandler, Alfred, 16, 17, 44, 45, 109,
    127
Chang, Ha Joon, 93, 104

Debt crisis 7, 77
    frenzy phase, 102, 105
    1930s, 88
    Latin American, recurrent, 86–8
    Marichal Carlos, 86–7, 103
    sovereign debt in Maturity, 86
    Third World 1980s, 86, 102
    unpayable debts, 103
    USA, 1837 and 1873, 86, 103, 142
Decoupling-recoupling
    see also Social polarization
    deployment period, 74
    economy and institutions, xviii, 41, 99
    financial and production capital, 50,

54, 75, 76, 99
    frenzy phase, 75
    high technology and traditional
        economy, 40
    paper and real value, 50, 76
    recessions forcing recoupling, 158
    synergy phase, 128
    technological revolution assimilation
        process, 26
    within the economy, 39–41, 61, 99
Defaults. *See* Debt crises
Deflation. *See* Money and value
Deployment period
    see also Synergy phase; Maturity
        phase
    definition/description, 36, 135, 151–2
    adequate financial innovations, 128–
        32, 142–5
    dates, 78
    engines of growth, new, 44–5
    era of 'good feeling', 26
    institutional framework enabling, 17,
        128–32
    lagged across world, 10
    mode of growth appropriate, 26
    paradigm triumphant 44
    production capital leading, 53–4,
        154
    recoupling
        economy and institutions, 43–4
        financial and production capital,
        76
        within the economy, 44, 61
    reforms continuing, 53
    single money economy, 62
    social shaping of paradigm, 22, 42–
        3, 53, 77, 153–4
    structural tensions overcome, 47
    two phases, 47–8, 74
Depressions. *See* Recessions and
    depressions
Developing countries. *See* Peripheral
    countries
Development
    by surges, 20, 59
    pulsating process, 145
    uneven propagation, 60–67
Diffusion of paradigms. *See* Propagation
    of techno-economic paradigms
Disaccumulation, 20

Dosi, Giovanni
    paradigm as Kuhnian analogy, 8
    paradigm in restricted sense, 134

Economic development
    uneven, 6, 20, 59, 60–7
Economic theories
    phases of surges influencing, 161–3
    shaped by economic changes, 146–7
    state, role of, 162–3, 166
Edison, Thomas Alva, 29, 32, 92
Employment
    full in synergy phase, 54
    irruption phase unemployment, 49, 90
    labor unrest in maturity phase, 45, 55
    rising in deployment period, 44
    stagflation, 146
Engels, Friedrich, 4, 25, 50
Evolutionary economics, 151
Exclusion-inclusion mechanism
    causing revolutions, 16, 28, 32, 88–9
    conservatism of, 34–5
    Rosenberg and Frischtak condition,
        32
    war expenditure excepted, 28–9
Externalities
    see also Infrastructures
    consumer credit in fourth surge, 94
    cost reduction helping growth, 135–6
    economic, social and legal, 41–2
    exclusion-inclusion mechanism, 16,
        28, 88–9
    increasing in synergy phase, 134
    installed during Frenzy, 53, 114
    over adaptation, 88
    unavailable during irruption phase, 98
Financial and production capital
    see also Financial capital; Production
        capital
    changing relationship with phases,
        73–7, 152–3
    decision criteria distinguished, 71–3,
        124, 155
    different functions and behaviors,
        71–3, 121, 124, 154
    financial and managerial capitalism,
        127
    functional separation, xvii, 6, 33, 155
    profit motive as basic engine, 157
    shifts of power
        between propagation periods, 75,

        114, 121, 123–4, 138, 151–2, 154,
        156, 168
    influence on economic theories,
        161–3
Financial capital
    see also Production capital; Financial
        and production capital
    bail outs, 104, 121, 122
    behavior
        basic, 72–3
        shifting over phases, 74, 141,
            152–3
    Britain and France, similar foreign
        investment bias, 58
    creative destruction, role in, 75
    criteria, 71–3, 124
    definition, 71
    financial crises, recurrent, 77–9
    frenzy phase behavior, 99–113
        decoupling, 75
        economy controlled, 50, 75, 98,
            124
        excess self-confidence, 51, 168
        illegitimate-illegal practices, 101,
            106, 109–11, 142
        money whirlpool, 107
        over-funding the revolutionary
            industries, 51, 105–7
        profit delusion, 76, 115, 119, 137
    Hilferding's notion, 72
    industry, not funded, 92, 122
    innovative behavior changing
        over phases, 138–43
        with paradigms, 143–5
        typology, 139
    institutionalization, 92, 130
    investment shifting to new, 21, 107
    irruption phase behavior, 90–8
    maturity phase behavior, 81–9
        bad loans, 85–8
        export during, 83
        future debt build-up, 86, 142
        idle money in, 49, 77
        peripheral sector investment, 49,
            55, 77, 83–4
        questionable practices, 88
        risk in new technologies, 33, 88
    mobility, 72, 124
    new paradigm, establishing, 47, 168
    new technologies
        new requirements met, 92, 93–4

pioneer in adopting, 96
risk capital innovations, 91
venture capital, 3, 92, 118, 140
periphery, loans to, 87, 142
production capital
decoupling-recoupling, 75, 81,
98, 102, 111, 114, 127–31
different from, 72–3, 124, 155
shifts of power, 75, 114, 121,
123–4, 138, 151–2, 154, 156,
168
profit expectations
excess, 3, 43, 51, 75, 77, 97–8,
106, 116
normal in synergy, 114, 113, 142
pressure on production capital,
75–6, 99, 115–6, 168–9
speculative innovations, 100, 139, 140
surges, enabling succession of, xviii,
154
synergy phase behavior, 76, 127–36
intermediary role, 76, 142
investment opportunities, 133–4
technological advance, role in, 73,
75, 107
technological revolutions, enabling,
xvii, 33–5, 73, 88–9
turning point behavior
regulation, attitude towards, 114–
15, 120–21
crashes and pressure for
regulation, 120
reluctant changeover to
production capital, 123–4, 168–9
windows of opportunity, 93
Financial crises. *See* Crises
Financial innovation
character changing with phases, 75,
138–43
irruption phase, risk, 73
paradigms shaping, 143–5
Financial Times, 106, 111, 118, 129
Ford, Henry, 3, 11, 32
Fordism, 17
Foreign investment
catching-up, role in, 104
changing with phases, 84–5
Forging ahead
during Irruption, 90–1
Japan, 58, 66, 103, 104
protectionism, 51

self-propelled, 85
sequence, not followed, 58, 59, 122–3
windows of opportunity, 21, 103, 104
USA and Germany, 12, 58, 63, 122
France, 58, 88, 97, 98, 103, 107, 122, 132
Freeman, Christopher
dating of technological revolutions,
10
disaggregate versus aggregate trends,
61
dynamic regularities, premises for,
151
institutional recomposition, 169
labor unrest recurring, 55, 136
long waves, 60, 63
relative autonomy of social spheres,
160
technological revolution, life cycle,
63
technology and financial collapses,
118
Frenzy phase
See also Bubbles; Crises; Installation
period.
definition/description, 47–8, 50–2,
74–6, 99–113, 152–3
asset inflation, 4, 43, 51, 77, 98, 102,
104
catching up opportunities, 103
competition fierce, 51, 76, 108–9
casino economy, 75, 116, 120, 142
corruption, 109–11, 141, 168
crashes at end of, 114
dates, 58, 78
decoupling from production, 75
diffusion acceleration, 36, 75
financial capital in control, 4, 50, 75,
98, 124
financial innovations, 100–01, 141–2
gilded age, 109
idle capital, 84, 100
infrastructure installed, 4, 51, 53,
125
Japan, early bubble in, 58
mergers and oligopolies towards end
of, 108–9
model and historical record, 58, 77–
8, 121–3
money whirlpool, 4, 75, 101–2, 107
new common sense established, 4
'new economy', xvii, 75, 100, 113,

115, 137, 159, 162
over-investment, 51, 106–7
paper and real economy tensions, 76,
     111–13, 168–9
paradigm established, 47, 168
policy, influence on, 146–7, 165
profit delusion, 76, 115, 119, 137
propagation of technological
     revolution, 43, 75, 105–7
prosperity biased, 99, 117, 135
redistribution of income, regressive,
     116, 138
regulation
     needed after, 129, 141, 142–3
     rejected, 120
social tensions, 52, 100, 117, 154,
     170
stagnation in old economy, 100, 102
structural causes of recession
     following, 115–16
structural tensions built up during,
     43, 115–18, 168–70
technological experimentation, 51,
     75, 134
tension between financial and
     production capital, 111

Galbraith, John Kenneth
     debt repudiation by US states in
          1830s, 142
     British lending to US states in 1800s,
          86
     financiers, excess self-confidence,
          51, 120
     learning from crashes, 121
     reinvention of financial instruments,
          100–01, 103
Gay, Edwin F., 120, 158
Germany
     catching-up, 85, 93
     corruption, 110
     financial capital, 92, 132
     foreign investment, 83, 104
     forging ahead, 11–12, 58, 103, 122
     Hitler, 41
     institutional innovation, 130
     miracle, 66
     protectionism, 51, 85
     triple core in third surge, 10, 63–4
     Synergy in 1930s, 125
Gestation of technological revolution,

10, 63, 65, 79, 81–9, 88–9
Gilded age. *See* Golden age
Globalized economy
     current surge feature, 66–7, 134
     financial innovations adapted to,
          145
     global oligopolies, 163
     outflow of funds from periphery,
          107
     rich-poor divide global, 5, 117–18
Golden age
     see also Synergy phase
     description, 5, 53
     gilded age, 51, 53, 76, 109
     good feeling, 5, 26, 44, 53, 133
     growth rates in, 26
     production capital at the helm, 124,
          154
     social choice, 43, 53, 76, 167, 171
     synergy phase as, 53
     two or three decades after big-bang,
          24
     Maturity troubles, 46, 54, 55
Government action
     see also State, role of
     catching up support, 93
     changing with phases, 163
     changing with paradigms, 145–7,
          163–6
     Chile in second surge, 102
     economic theories, 162–3, 166
     protectionism, 51, 93, 130
Great surges of development
     see also Propagation of techno-
          economic paradigms
     definition /description, 7, 20
     dates parallel periods, 57
     driving forces, 151–8
     financial and production capital
          changing roles, 71–7
     financial capital, 74
     global reach increasing with each, 155
     long waves, 23
     mid-life crises, 136
     model based on, 23
     overlaps and gaps, 56
     periods and phases, 36–7, 47–59,
          151–2
     policy influenced by phases, 146–7
     productivity rising with each, 8, 20,
          152

six phase model, 63, 65, 154–5
Greenspan, Alan, 118–9, 162
Grübler, Arnulf, 85, 86

Heilbroner, Robert L., 162
Hilferding, Rudolf, 72
Hitler, Adolf, 41, 117, 125
Hobsbawm, Eric, 46, 58, 65, 117, 163
Hoover Report, 107, 120, 159

Idle money
    decreasing investment opportunities,
        49, 77, 81–2, 85–8
    different from Maturity, 83–4, 100
    innovation helped by, 75, 88–9
    leading to debt crises, 85–8
    real estate bubbles, 101
    speculation, 100
    venture and risk capital, 33
Income polarization *See* Social
    polarization
Induced branches, 133, 169–70
Industrial Revolution, 11, 14, 18, 37, 91–
    2
Industry *See* Core industries; New and
    old industries
Inflation and deflation. *See* money and
    value
Information revolution, xvii, 11, 14, 18,
    24, 144–5, 146, 167, 169
Infrastructures
    see also Externalities
    cost reduction virtuous cycle, 135–6
    frenzy phase 53, 114
        installation of, 53, 114
        over-funding, 105–7
    new for each technological
        revolution, 13–15
Innovations
    acceleration perverse in frenzy
        phase, 108
    clusters, 155
    diminishing returns, 75
    epochal, 9
    equipment and whole industries
        made obsolescent, 97–8
    exclusion-inclusion by paradigm, 28
    exhaustion of established paradigm
        as stimulus for radical, 34
    financial, 100, 138–45
    financing, changing with surges, 136

institutional for new economy, 145–7
natural trajectories, 29
outsiders, crucial role in radical, 33
possible, profitable and socially
    acceptable, 33
potentially revolutionary in minor
    uses, 32
radical pioneers on their own, 91–2
radical, 29, 32
regulatory, 128–30
relative autonomy of science and
    technology, 155
Schumpeter and cycles, 23
synergy phase, 134–6
technological, for financial services,
    96, 100, 139
technology as fuel of capitalist
    engine, 155
three spheres of change in socio-
    economic system, 156
Installation period
    see also; Frenzy phase; Irruption
        phase;
    definition/description, 36–7, 47–8,
        135, 151
    catching up, 66, 103–5
    coexistence of two moneys, 61
    coexistence of two paradigms, 43
    dates, 56–8, 78
    decoupling/recoupling
        institutions and economy, xviii,
            41–3, 99
        new and old paradigm, 12, 43
        paper and real economy, 111–13,
            115
        within economy, 39–41, 61
    default recurring, 86–7, 102–03
    Deployment, different from, 44
    financial and production capital, 74
    inflation/deflation, 61–2
    institutional changes during, 131
    labor unrest, 55, 70
    laissez faire, 146
    mid-point crisis, 98
    'modernity' established, 133
    paradigm ready for diffusion, 114,
        134
    political cleavage, 164–5
    social exploration of paradigm, 105,
        135, 141
    structural tensions growing, 52, 157–8

triple core in third surge, 63–4
US Gilded Age, 51
USA and Germany, forging ahead, 58
Institutional adjustment *See* Institutional
 recomposition
Institutional change
 adapted to paradigm changes, 145–7
 inertia, positive function, 157
 three spheres in reciprocal action, 156
Institutional recomposition
 see also Socio-institutional
  frameworks
 continuing in deployment period, 53
 financial and production capital, 124,
  154
 lessons of historical parallels, 163–4,
  169–70
 premature market saturation,
  overcoming, 117, 169–70
 resistance to reform as cause of
  crisis, 25, 125–6
 turning point as crossroads for, 43,
  52, 167
 wide range of the possible, 7, 17, 24,
  42, 53
Institutions. *See* Socio-Institutional
 Frameworks
Intel, 3, 11
Internet,
 mania bubble, 7, 28, 51, 79, 106,
  118, 120
 infrastructure fifth surge, 14
 technology system, 15
 new paradigm, 15, 42, 94, 159
 over-investment, 108
Investment. *See* Financial Capital;
 Production Capital; Stock
 Markets
Irrational exuberance, 3, 106, 118, 162
Irruption phase
 see also Big-Bang events;
  Installation period
 definition/ description, 47, 48, 49–
  50, 73–5, 90–98, 153
 aggregate measures deceptive, 90
 coexistence of two paradigms, 90
 crises less likely, 79
 dates, 11, 56–7, 78
 decoupling between new and old, 39,
  49–50, 90
 development in periphery, 90–91, 140

divergence in politics, 50
 financial capital, 90–98
 financial innovations, intense, 91–3,
  140–41
 investment in technological
  revolution, 84, 91–3
 new technology for finance, 96, 140
 overlaps of successive revolutions,
  89, 90
 opportunity explosion, 90, 92
 productivity expectations rising, 97
 profit expectations, 97–8
 redeployment of old industries to
  periphery, 154–5
 rejuvenation of mature technologies,
  66
 risk and venture capital, 91–3, 140
 unemployment, 49
Italy, 66, 97

Japan
 early Frenzy in fifth surge, 58, 101
 forging ahead, 104, 103
 organizational innovation, 66, 39, 95
 recession, 118
Jevons, William Stanley, 54

Keynes, John Maynard
 countercyclical policies, 25
 historical context, influence of, 162
 investment, concern over control of,
  124
 Keynesian policies, 121, 130, 146
 private and social interest, 157–8
 slump, dangers of, 167
Kindleberger, Charles P.
 country banks in first Synergy, 132
 developing countries, lending to, 86,
  88
 financial crises, dates, 78
 financial crises, model, 79
 historical context, influence of, 161
 illegal financial activities, 101, 107,
  110
 learning from crashes, 121
Kondratiev barrier, 85
Kondratiev, Nikolai, 23, 60, 62, 63
Korea, 66, 93, 104
Kuhn, Thomas, 17, 28, 31
 Kuhnian notion of paradigm, 8, 9
Kuznets, Simon, 9–10, 27, 30

Labor unrest
  see also Social unrest; Social
    polarization
  Installation and Maturity compared,
    55
  in maturity phase, 45–6
  strike waves, 55, 136
Latin America, 86–8, 102, 103
List, Friedrich, 85
Long waves
  see also Great surges of development
  growth statistics, 23
  different approaches, 60
  Freeman and Louçã, 60
  decrease in profit rates hypothesis, 81
  research program shortcomings, 60
  world synchronicity expected, 62–3
Louçã, Francisco
  dynamic regularities, premises for,
    151
  labor unrest recurring, 55, 136
  long waves, 60, 63

Manias, 106–7
  See also Bubbles; Crises; Frenzy
    phase
Markets
  see also Stock markets
  coherence in relative prices needed,
    113
  consumption expanding in synergy
    phase, 54
  exports as outlets, 22
  interest in widening, 5, 114, 123–4
  premature saturation, 52, 116, 169
  saturation, 54, 55, 75, 94
  structural imbalance, 43, 116,
Mass-production revolution, 7, 11, 14,
    15, 17, 18, 42, 143–4, 145, 169–70
Mature industries
  fixed investment as weight, 31
  migration to peripheries, 49, 55, 77,
    154
  price behavior, 62, 90
  rationalization, 94, 154
  stretching technologies, 31, 39, 88
  stagnation, 49
Mature technologies
  behavior of firms, 31, 81–3
  Grüblers's Kondratiev barrier, 85
  last life cycles short, 54, 81, 85

limits to growth, 54–5
migration to periphery, 64–6, 83
revitalized by new paradigm, 31, 95
Maturity phase
  see also Deployment period;
  definition/description, 30, 47, 48,
    54–6, 74, 77, 81–9, 136–7
  crises likely, 79
  dates, 78, 56–7
  debt build-up, 86
  delusion of eternal progress, 137
  financial capital, 81–9
  financial innovations, 142–3
  four phases of propagation, 151
  golden age twilight, 54
  growth and markets in periphery, 45,
    55, 64, 65,77, 83–5
  idle money, 77, 81–2, 85–8
  institutional inertia, 157
  limits to growth, 77
  loans to weaker creditors, 86
  market control maneuvers, 82
  market saturation, 44, 55, 81
  oligopolies, 62, 82–3, 136
  opportunities narrowing, 136
  overlaps of successive revolutions,
    89, 90
  paradigm exhaustion, 44
  political rebellion versus
    complacency, 55, 137
  social unrest, 45–6, 55
  wars during, 28–9, 82–3
Mensch, Gerhard, 32, 33
Mergers. *See* Competition
Metaparadigm
  techno-economic paradigm as, 8
Migrations
  capital
    idle money, 49
    speculative in Frenzy, 84
    tied to production in Maturity, 49,
      55, 77, 84
  frenzy phase, 5, 50, 84
  people, 5, 50, 170
  maturity phase, 49, 55, 77
  skilled personnel, 93
Minsky, Hyman, xv, xviii, 79, 110, 160
Mismatch. *See* Decoupling-recoupling
Model of development by surges
  see also Capitalism; Great surges of
    development; Financial and

Production capital
  summary, 151–7
  abstraction level, 160–61
  causal mechanisms, xvii, 6, 49, 59, 155–7
  determinism, 53, 160
  early warning tool, 166
  forging ahead modifies, 58–9
  fuzzy due to diffusion lags, 67, 160
  general framework and individual events, 160–61
  heuristic device, 49, 161
  hindsight, 90
  interdisciplinary nature of, 160
  long wave models, difference with, 60
  model and real world, 56
  narrative and historical illustrations, 49
  nature, xv, xix
  policy guidance, 163–6
  politics changing, 164–5
  power and dangers of recurrence interpretation, 159–61
  predictive ability, 163
  private and social interest, 157–8
  progress not linear and cumulative, 20
  recurrence and uniqueness, xvii, 6, 56–9, 121–3, 127–32, 159
  recurring sequence, 5–6, 56–9, 152–4
  sequence not mechanical, 123
  six phase model, 65, 154–5
  strong stylization, 59
  structural imbalances, 43
  technology and finance, xviii
  three spheres interacting, 155–7
  turning point as conceptual device, 52
  use, 6–7, 49, 160, 166
Modernization, 98
  across the economy, 6, 8, 15, 36, 44, 134, 151, 152, 155
  habit breaking, 4
  generic technologies, 39
  new technology for finance, 91, 139–40
  peripheral countries, 65, 66
  political, 50, 165–6
  rejuvenation of industries, 85, 94–5, 99
  replacement and upgrading, 4
  restructuring helped by

  externalities, 51, 135
  superiority forcing, 49
Modes of growth
  see also; Institutional recomposition; Turning point
  description/definition, 25
  Marxian mode of production, 25
  variety in same paradigm, 7, 17, 24, 42, 125
  technological revolution, second half shaped by, 53, 125–6, 167
  turning point, 53, 167
Money and value
  asset inflation, 51, 102
  constant-value measurements difficult, 61–2
  economic theory, changing views, 6, 18–19, 161–2
  hyperinflation, 113
  inflation-deflation, 39, 61–2, 113
  long-term statistics doubtful, 62
  mad money, 99
  notions of value lost, 75, 112–13
  perverse price behavior, 50
  productivities and relative values, 112
  single money in Deployment, 62, 127
  stagflation 1980s, 75, 146
  two moneys, 61, 112
Morgan, J.P., 92, 123

NAFTA, 66
NASDAQ, 106, 119–20
Natural trajectories of innovation, 29
Nelson, Richard
  evolutionary economics, 151
  natural trajectory, 29
New and old economies
  see also New economy
  institutional innovations, 145–7
  latecomer economies, 105
  stagnating sectors during Frenzy, 102
  two productivity levels, two-moneys, 112
New and old industries
  see also Core industries; Mature industries
  chasm during frenzy phase, 99
  installation of paradigms, competition during, 40
  mergers and oligopolies during frenzy phase, 108–9

old industries and infrastructures
redefined, 13
New economics, 146–7
New economy
illusion of, xvii, 7, 100, 113, 115,
137, 159, 162, 145
real change, 4, 43, 75, 112, 144, 145–6
Nietzsche, Friedrich, xv, 22

Oil crisis, xv, 12, 95, 168
Old economies. *See* New and old
economies
Old industries. *See* New and old
industries
Oligopolies. *See* Competition
Opportunity explosion, 90, 92
Organizational change, 9, 16–19
see also Techno-economic
paradigms
activities non-economic, 17–19
financial sector prefiguring, 96
Japanese developments in fifth
surge, 95
networks versus pyramids, 17–19
technological revolutions, involving,
8–9, 15
paradigms, organizational, 17
Over adaptation
conservative force, 30–31, 42
established paradigm, 60–61, 88
Over-investment 51, 106–07

Palma, Gabriel, 102, 103, 112
Panics. *See* Bubbles; Crises
Paper and real economy, xviii, 43, 76,
77, 114, 125, 138
Paradigm shifts, 12, 15, 36
see also Techno-economic
paradigms
in industry, 37–8
political cleavage, 164–5
social creative destruction, 42–3
tensions and instability, 113
windows of opportunity, 21, 103–5
Paradigms. *See* Techno-economic
paradigms
Peripheral countries
see also Core countries;
catching up in installation period,
66–7, 103–05
debt crises, 102

default recurring, 86–8
demand growth potential, 116, 169
growth 'miracles' in irruption phase,
90
idle capital going to, 84
loan fever at Maturity, 86–8
mature technologies, 66, 83, 102–03
outflow of funds from, 107
paradigm diffusion delayed, 62–6,
154–5
Soros, credit insurance for, 165
'undeveloping', 163
USA in 1820-1830s, 104–05
windows of opportunity, 66, 93, 103
Pigou, Arthur, C., 6, 161
Polarization *See* Social polarization
Politics
cleavage in political groups, 164–5
ideological bewilderment, 50
individualism in frenzy phase, 51
influence factor at Turning point,
115, 123–4, 126
legitimacy and governance
questioned, 41
maturity phase, 137
mutual influence with technology, 19
rebels versus complacency in, 55
social expectations frustrated, 5, 55,
136–7
turning point intervention, 124
Premature market saturation, 52, 116, 169
Production capital
see also Financial capital; Financial
and production capital
definition, 71–2
behavior, basic, 72, 152–3
concentration in maturity phase, 82,
94
controlling the economy in
deployment period, 123–4
criteria for expansion, 114, 127, 135,
152
deployment, role in, 154
financial capital
decoupling-recoupling, 75, 81,
98, 102, 111, 114, 127–31
different from, 72–3, 124, 155
shifts of power, 75, 114, 121,
123–4, 138, 151–2, 154, 156, 168
Idle money profits, 77, 94
incumbent conservative, 73

knowledge, activity specific, 72, 73
long terms interests, 154
migrating when mature, 77
new and old, 75, 97–8, 99–100
paper values and real economy, 43,
    111–12, 114, 125, 138
power seeking behavior in Maturity,
    82
pressure from stock markets, 75–6,
    99, 115–16, 168–9
risk taking for rejuvenation, 94
self-financing, 128
stagflation during propagation of
    next paradigm, 75
synergy phase, 76, 127–37
Productivity explosions, xvii, 51
Productivity
    average higher with each surge, 8,
        20, 152
    constriction of growth, 30, 44–5, 55,
        81, 136
    deployment period, normal growth,
        44
    differing levels, 39
    expectations, 97
    growing across the economy, 54
    resistance to change overcome by
        higher, 38
Propagation of techno-economic
    paradigms
    see also Great surges of
        development
    description, 36–46
    acceleration in frenzy phase, 108
    'common sense'
        guiding diffusion, 29
        pioneers developing, 16
    common sense spreading, 16, 157
    consumer learning, 41
    convergence and divergence, 64–5
    cultural change, 156–7
    decoupling and recoupling periods,
        41–6
    deployment periods, 44
    externalities and diffusion loops, 41–
        2
    exclusion-inclusion mechanism, 16,
        28, 42, 88–9
    financial sector leading geographic
        expansion, 96
    four phases of propagation, 47–59

proportion small during Irruption,
    97–8
great surges, diffusion by, 20
innovation during synergy phases,
    134–6
institutional framework enabling, 17,
    42, 131–2
isomorphism, 16
lagged across world, 10, 62–7, 160
last products and industries, 81
periods of installation and
    deployment, 36, 41–6
paradigms as guide for economic
    agents, 9
phases in life cycle, 29–30
polarization, social and economic,
    37–41
productivity, higher levels, 44, 51
recessions as turning points, 36, 43
sectoral and geographic, 61–2
two paradigms during installation, 43
superior technology, inevitable
    triumph, 38

Rationalization. *See* Mature industries
Recessions and depressions
    see also Turning point
    bubble burst followed by, 76
    causes, structural, 115–16, 168–70
    decrease in profit rates hypothesis, 81
    financial capital's time of reckoning,
        76
    Great Depression 1930s, persistence
        of, 125
    institutional change, pressure for, 25
    institutions, role in, 156
    recoupling forced by, 158
    resistance to change prolonging,
        125–6
    structural causes of, 115-16
Recoupling. *See* Decoupling-recoupling
Recurrence
    frame of reference to distinguish
        uniqueness, 159
    testing for, 159
    unique factors hiding, 6
Regulatory frameworks
    acceptance-resistance, 51, 76, 114,
        120, 121, 129
    accountancy and disclosure, 129
    crashes and pressure for, 120

deregulatory pressures, 146
facilitating propagation of
    paradigms, 42
global regulation, call for, 113
information revolution,
    requirements, 24
synergy phase, 128–32
turning point, 114–26
Reinert, Erik, 22, 96, 163
Risk and venture capital, 3, 92, 119–20,
    139–40
diffusion reducing risk perception, 97
irruption phase, 91–3
new entrepreneurs backed, 33, 92,
    139–40
Roosevelt, F.D., 41, 126

Schmoller, Gustav, 159
Schumpeter, Joseph
    aggregate variables, 61
    bandwagon effects, 34
    capitalism, 72
    clustering, 27, 30
    creative destruction, 22, 37
    cycles, 23
    entrepreneurs and financiers xviii,
        33, 71
    government action and market
        mechanisms, 25
    institutional innovation, 131
    market equilibrium, 23
    price competition, excess of, 108
    Schumpeterians, xviii
September 11th, 118, 168
Sobel, Robert, 54
    illegitimate practice, 140
    international investment, 104, 105
    power of financiers, 53, 58, 92, 123,
        126, 143
    State funding, 93
    USA prosperity, 54
    Wall Street subdued in 1947 boom,
        128
Social polarization, 4–5, 37–41
    see also Decoupling-recoupling
    between countries in Installation
        period, 63–4
    global in fifth surge, 107
    opposing visions during Frenzy
        prosperity, 99–100, 113
    political tension, 41, 117, 170

pressure to reverse, 41, 124
rich and poor, 41, 43, 50, 100, 117
technological revolutions leading to,
    39
Social shaping of technological
    revolutions, 22, 42, 53, 77, 153–4
Social unrest
    see also Labor unrest; Social
        polarization
    political forms varied, 41
    recurring problems of governance, 26
Socio institutional frameworks
    see also Institutional recomposition;
        Regulatory frameworks;
    creative destruction, institutional, 154
    inertia, 6, 26, 153–4, 155, 157, 165
    innovations adequate to new
        economy, 145–7
    isomorphism economy-institutions,
        157
    mismatch with economy, xviii, 26,
        43, 99
    paradigm changes in political ideas,
        164
    rhythm of change, 26, 165–6
    surges of development, 152
    wide range possible for each
        revolution, 7, 17, 42, 53
Soete, Luc
    catching up, 21, 31, 90–91, 103
    new Economics, 146
Soros, George, 111, 113, 118, 165, 171
Soviet system
    adequate for mass-production
        paradigm, 7, 17, 42
    catching up, 103
    Cold War, 128
    rejuvenation mechanism lacking, 35,
        66
Spheres of change, 155–7
Stagflation. *See* Money and value
State, role of, 121, 157–8
    see also Government action;
        Institutional recomposition;
        Regulatory frameworks; Socio-
        institutional frameworks
    accepted, 126
    backing catching-up processes, 93,
        104
    collective interest, 52, 130, 157–8
    facilitating technological revolution,

7, 130
markets, 25, 39, 146, 163
theories changing with phases, 146–
    7, 162–3
turning point intervention, 25, 125,
    156, 158
Welfare State, 166
Stock markets
    see also Financial capital; Bubbles;
        Crises
    after crises, 122
    asset inflation, 100, 101–2
    corruption in frenzy phase, 109
    'derivative economy', 111–12
    Dow Jones and US GDP, 112
    fundamentals set aside, 101, 107
    global regulation, call for, 113
    illegal-illegitimate practices, 109–11
    innovations, 138–43
    investment firms in frenzy phase,
        119–20
    paper values divorced from real
        economy, 43, 111–12
    pressure on production capital, 75–6,
        99, 115–16, 168–9
    pyramids and leverage, 100–01
    revival in irruption phase, 50
    risk capital instruments, 91–2, 139–40
    synergy phase, 127
    New York versus London, 58, 140–41
Strange, Susan
    casino capitalism, 99, 165
    corruption and illegality, 109, 110
    innovation in finance, 96, 100
    regulation and finance, 113
Structural adjustment. *See* Institutional
    recomposition
Structural causes of mid-surge
    recession, 52, 115–18, 168–70
Surge. *See* Great surges of development
Sweezy Paul, 85
Synergy phase
    see also Deployment period; Golden
        age
    definition/description, 47, 48, 53–4,
        74, 76, 127–37
    benefits of growth widespread, 133
    capitalism best face, 5, 53, 133
    coherent trends within economy, 62,
        127
    cost reduction virtuous cycle, 135–6

crises likelihood of, 79
dates, 78
economies of scale, 53
employment, full, 54
externalities, 134
financial capital backs production
    capital, 76, 128–31
golden age, 5, 43, 46, 53, 76, 154
growth during, 134
income redistribution, 54
induced activities, 133–4, 169–170
innovations
    financial, 128–32, 142–3
    institutional, 131–3
    technological 134–6
investment concentrated in core, 64
new paradigm generalized, 54
production a time for, 5, 53, 133–6
regulation accepted, 128–31
social choice, 43, 53, 76, 167, 171
technology, role for, 133–6
third surge in USA, 123, 127

Taiwan, 66
Techno-economic paradigms
    see also Propagation of techno-
        economic paradigms
    definition/description, 7, 8–9, 15–16,
        125, 151–3
    articulation in irruption phase, 50
    closure, 35
    coexistence of two, 43, 56, 90
    common sense new, 7, 15, 16, 26
    deep adoption, 32
    different principles for, 18
    economic theories influenced by,
        146–7
    exclusion-inclusion mechanism, 26
    financial innovations shaped, 143–5
    generalized in synergy phase, 54
    generic technologies, 16
    guide for
        economic agents, 9, 17, 27–8, 134
        viable policy, 7
    habit breaking, 7
    life trajectory, 29–30
    limits of, as guidelines to search new
        technologies, 31
    limits showing at maturity, 54
    locking-in of dominant designs, 134
    maturity, 136

modernization, 152
organizational principles, 15, 17, 19
outsiders as radical innovators, 32
overadaptation
    as conservative force, 30–31, 42
    revolutions as result, 61, 31–2
    socio-economic environment, 88
politics and ideologies, influence on,
    164, 165
process innovations, 135
propelling and inhibiting functions,
    19, 42, 153–4
social cost of change, 26
social shaping of, 42, 77
surges of development, 152
Techno-economic split, 48–9
Technological revolutions
    see also Great surges of
        development; Techno-economic
        paradigms
    definition/description, 8, 9–15, 151–3
    articulation, 33–4
    attractor for diffusion, 11
    bifurcation of production structure, 90
    big-bang and financial manias, 3
    clusters of entrepreneurship, 31
    coexistence with previous one, 56, 90
    core industries and infrastructure,
        13–15, 63
    dates, 56–7
    diffusion, xix, 7, 8, 19, 77
    double nature, 8–9, 15, 151
    emergence conditions plus random
        factors, 56
    ending dates not significant, 12
    financial capital
        love affair, 73, 91–3
        role in emergence, 33–5, 88–9
    five historical occurrences, 9–15, 57
    institutional and economic
        facilitators, 41–2, 128–32
    institutional framework enabling, 17
    life cycle, 29–30, 36, 63, 152–3
    limits to potential, 30
    maturity phase setting stage for, 55–6
    mismatch with institutions, xviii, 26,
        43, 99
    new economy, xvii, 4, 112, 145–6,
    opportunity explosion, 90, 92
    phases of propagation, 48, 74
    politics, 19

propagation by surges, 20, 23, 151
recurring financial crises, 78
regulation adapted to, 23–5, 145–7,
    170
social assimilation, prolonged, xvii,
    22–7, 152–3
social shaping of, 22, 42–3, 53, 77,
    153–4
technical change continuous and
    discontinuous, 27, 73
technology systems, successive, 15
turning point at mid-potential, 114,
    123, 167, 169–70
typical structure and size of firm
    changing, 109
The Economist, 118
Third world. *See* Peripheral countries
Toporowski, Jan
    asset inflation, 98, 51, 102
    eras of finance, 99
Turning point
    See also Institutional
        recomposition; Recessions-
        depressions
    definition/description, 36, 47, 52–3,
        76, 114–26, 151, 154
    dates, 57
    depression of 1930s, 125–6
    individual and social interests, 52
    institutional recomposition, 43, 48
    lessons of historical parallels, 163–4,
        169–70
    paradigm ready for deployment, 114
    political factors, 26, 126, 163–6,
        170–71
    politics involved, 126
    premature market saturation, 116–17,
        169–70
    production capital, power to, 123–4,
        154
    recession after bubble collapse, 47,
        114
    recognition of, 163
    regulation acceptance, 5, 52–3, 120–
        21
    social unrest, 52, 117, 124
    structural tensions to overcome, 47,
        52, 115–18, 168–70
    time of indetermination, 53
    wide range of the possible, 24, 53
Tylecote, Andrew, 10, 133

Unemployment. See Employment
USA
    catching-up, 85, 103, 104
    core country, 11, 14, 18, 47, 57, 78,
        87, 127–8
    corruption, 110, 140
    crises, 88, 98, 120, 122, 123
    debt defaults in 19th Century, 102
    decoupling economy, 40
    depression 1930s, prolonged, 125–6
    Dow Jones compared to GDP, 112
    financial capital, 92, 142, 143
    foreign investment, 83–5
    forging ahead, 11–12, 58, 85, 103, 122
    fourth surge, production migrating to
        peripheries, 64
    frenzy phase, 101
    Gilded Age, 51
    high tech versus traditional economy,
        40
    irruption phase, 49
    New Deal, 41, 126
    oligopolies, 82
    post-war golden age, 53, 128
    Progressive Era, 53, 159
    protectionism, 51
    regulation, 130–31, 132, 143

    state supported catching-up, 93
    triple core in third surge, 10, 63–4

Value. *See* Money and value
Veblen, Thorstein, 4, 50, 71, 162

Wars
    cold war and technology, 28–9
    excluded from analytical model, 83,
        160
    forging ahead after, 58, 122
    maturity phase, 82
    Second World War
        dress rehearsal for post-war role
        of state in economy accepted,
        121, 126
        Synergy, 126
    technology and war expenditures,
        82–3
Wells, David A., 38, 61, 94, 95, 97, 108,
    159
Wells, Louis T., Jr., 64
Windows of opportunity, 66, 93, 103
Winter Sydney
    evolutionary economics, 151
    natural trajectory, 29